WHAT YOUR COLLEAGUES ARE SAYING . . .

Figuring Out Fluency—Addition and Subtraction With Fractions and Decimals is a must-read book to ensure students develop computational fluency through brilliant targeted strategies to help students work with fractions and decimals flexibly. The authors provide clear examples, strategies grounded in research and best practice, and student-centered engaging games to help each and every student develop computational fluency while developing their math identity and agency! The clever games can be used both in class with students and shared with families! As a former middle school mathematics teacher and K–5 coach, I can see that this book is a must-have for all mathematics teachers, interventionists, support staff, and coaches.

Georgina Rivera
K–8 School Administrator, Bristol Public Schools
Second Vice President Elect, NCSM
Bristol, CT

It can be extremely difficult not to fall back on rules and procedures when trying to navigate fluency with fractions and decimals. Thankfully, *Figuring Out Fluency* offers a conceptual roadmap that every teacher can turn to as they look to build meaningful fluency in their classroom.

Graham Fletcher
Math Specialist and Consultant
McDonough, GA

These strategies, routines, games, and centers are the perfect companion pieces to the math instruction I provide in my classroom daily. I appreciate the strategy briefs for families so they can support their child at home. Every teacher needs this book!

Andrea Fields
Fourth Grade Teacher
Woodrow Wilson Elementary
Manhattan, KS

This is the resource that the educational world has been wishing and waiting for! This carefully crafted guide tackles mathematical concepts that traditionally leave students confused and teachers frustrated! It will inspire and support educators in their journey to integrate rigorous, high-quality fluency practice.

Allyson Lyman
Elementary Principal
Emporia Public Schools
Emporia, KS

T0354083

This book is a must for all Grade 3–8 teachers who teach fraction and decimal operations. It is chock full of strategies, automaticities, assessments, and activities that are easy to understand and empowering to teach. Students' confidence will soar when they learn how to use these efficient, flexible, and accurate strategies.

Theresa Wills
Assistant Professor, Mathematics Education
George Mason University
Fairfax, VA

This *Figuring Out Fluency* companion is one of those rare finds that provides activities to implement immediately with students while also embedding professional learning for teachers and coaches. I appreciate the intentional design, specific strategies, and observational tools that focus on sense making and application—two critical components of transfer. The examples of how to assess fluency help educators visualize practices that provide valuable information about student strengths while ensuring students maintain a positive mathematical identity.

Catherine Castillo
Coordinator of Elementary Numeracy
Springfield Public Schools
Springfield, MO

The explicit strategy instruction provided in this book allows access for ALL students in a practical, hands-on approach. So many worked examples, routines, and games to teach and support student reasoning with fraction and decimal operations. This is a go-to for all math educators, coaches, specialists, and interventionists!

Nichole DeMotte
K–5 Mathematics Coach, Atkinson Academy
Atkinson, NH

This book is such an eye-opener for providing interventions and strategies for students and supporting teachers that I coach. Fluency isn't about timed tests or "drill and kill" but providing students with rich discourse, games, tasks, routines, and more. I'm so excited to delve into this much-needed resource more.

Tomika R. Altman
Math/Science Specialist
Chapel Hill-Carrboro City Schools, NC

A needed addition to mathematics education! This book establishes a broader definition of fluency and emphasizes the importance of helping students develop and use relationships and strategies to solve problems. Bay-Williams, SanGiovanni, Martinie, and Suh outline which major relationships and strategies students need to develop stronger mathematical reasoning!

Pam Harris
Texas State University
San Marcos, TX

Oftentimes, fractions and decimals evoke fear in students and also may test a teacher's confidence with how to teach addition and subtraction of fractions and decimals beyond a rote procedure. This book is a must-have resource filled with activities and resources to foster mathematicians' flexibility, accuracy, and efficiency. It provides ideas that will help mathematicians have a true understanding and become what it really means to be proficient.

Dawn Jacobs
K–5 Math Coach
Lexington School District One
Lexington, SC

Where was this book when I taught students in 4th and 5th grade? From the Preface to the References, *Figuring Out Fluency—Addition and Subtraction With Fractions and Decimals: A Classroom Companion* summarizes the key ideas about fluency, teaches the reader about the "must know" strategies, and gives specific games, routines, and centers to develop students' fluency. This book is a must-have for anyone who teaches addition and subtraction of decimals and fractions!

Laura Vizdos Tomas
Math Coach
School District of Palm Beach County
Cofounder of LearningThroughMath.com
West Palm Beach, FL

This book places mathematical thinking front and center! The authors make the compelling case using myriad examples that fluency requires reasoning and relies on conceptual understanding. They provide a treasure trove of engaging activities teachers can use to help their students develop fluency with adding and subtracting fractions and decimals. If you want your students to confidently choose and flexibly use a range of strategies when working with fractions and decimals, you must read this book!

Grace Kelemanik
Cofounder Fostering Math Practices
Natick, MA

Some students can do magic! At least that's what it seems like to their classmates who don't have the "secret" strategies for calculating with fractions and decimals. Isn't this true for adults as well? But it isn't magic. There is no secret! All of the games and activities primary students learn to make sense of whole number computation are in this book, refashioned to develop the same number sense and skills with fractions and decimal fractions. Can your students play Make 100? Yes? Then they can also play Make a Whole. Read this book, reveal the "secret" strategies for your students, and soon you and your students will be the ones asked to make magic.

Kimberly Morrow-Leong
Senior Content Manager, The Math Learning Center
Salem, OR

Figuring Out Fluency—Addition and Subtraction With Fractions and Decimals: A Classroom Companion
The Book at a Glance

Building off of *Figuring Out Fluency*, this classroom companion dives deep into five of the Seven Significant Strategies that relate to procedural fluency when adding and subtracting fractions and decimals, beyond basic facts.

FIGURE 12 ● Reasoning Strategies for Adding and Subtracting Fractions and Decimals

REASONING STRATEGIES	RELEVANT OPERATIONS
1. Count On/Count Back (Module 2)	Addition and Subtraction
2. Make a Whole (Module 3)	Addition
3. Think Addition (Module 4)	Subtraction
4. Compensation (Module 5)	Addition and Subtraction
5. Partial Sums and Differences (Module 6)	Addition and Subtraction

Strategy overviews and family briefs communicate how each strategy helps students develop flexibility, efficiency, accuracy, automaticity, and reasonableness.

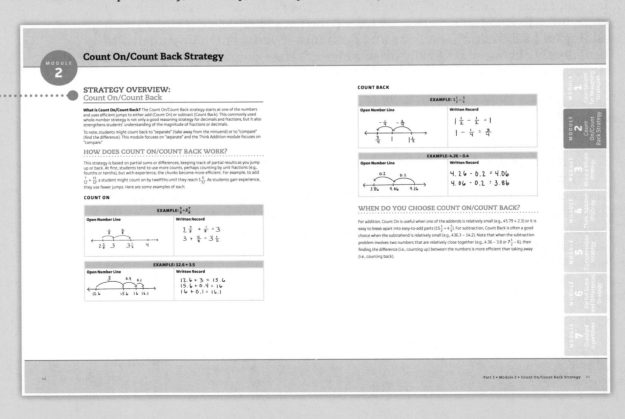

Each strategy module starts with teaching activities that help you explicitly teach the strategy.

(Continued)

The 100 beaded number line can readily be adapted to hundredths, with the strand labeled from 0 to 1 and each color group representing a tenth and each bead representing a hundredth. In this example, 0.73 – 0.38, a student starts at 73 hundredths. Then, the student slides 3 hundredths, to 7 tenths, then 3 tenths, then the remaining 5 hundredths (taking away a total of 0.38). The remaining beads are how much is left (0.35).

Students then record their work on a number line. For example, the student might count back 3 beads (–0.03), then count back 30 beads (–0.3), and then count back 5 more beads (–0.05).

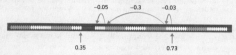

As it appears here, this number line could be used for fraction tenths. Alternatively, number lines can be made with eight beads in alternating colors to show eighths (and fourths and halves).

ACTIVITY 2.4
NUMBER BONDS FOR COUNT ON/COUNT BACK

Number bonds let students decompose numbers in useful ways. Students use the number bond to show how they want to decompose a number into convenient parts. Number bonds provide a nice visual to show that fractions, like whole numbers, can be decomposed in a variety of ways!

Let's start with $5\frac{3}{4} + 3\frac{5}{12}$. To count on from $5\frac{3}{4}$, $3\frac{5}{12}$ needs to be decomposed. The student must notice an equivalency, that $\frac{1}{4} = \frac{3}{12}$. Then they can split that into $\frac{5}{12}$ into $\frac{3}{12}$ and $\frac{2}{12}$.

Another option is to find common denominators and then count on or back, which is illustrated in the second example, $6\frac{1}{6} - 1\frac{3}{4}$.

COUNT ON FRACTION EXAMPLE	COUNT BACK FRACTION EXAMPLE
$5\frac{3}{4} + 3\frac{5}{12}$	$6\frac{1}{6} - 1\frac{3}{4} = 6\frac{2}{12} - 1\frac{9}{12}$
$3 \quad \frac{3}{12} \quad \frac{2}{12}$	$1 \quad \frac{2}{12} \quad \frac{7}{12}$
$5\frac{3}{4} + \frac{1}{4} = 6$	$6\frac{2}{12} - 1\frac{2}{12} = 5$
$6 + 3\frac{2}{12} = 9\frac{1}{6}$	$5 - \frac{7}{12} = 4\frac{5}{12}$

Each strategy shares worked examples for you to work through with your students as they develop their procedural fluency.

ACTIVITY 2.6
COUNT ON/COUNT BACK WORKED EXAMPLES

Worked examples can be used as a warmup, a focus of a lesson, at a learning center, or on an assessment. Here we share examples and ideas for preparing worked examples to support student understanding of the Count On/Count Back strategy. There are different ways to pose worked examples, and they each serve a different fluency purpose.

TYPE OF WORKED EXAMPLE	PURPOSE: COMPONENT (FLUENCY ACTIONS)	QUESTIONS FOR DISCUSSIONS OR FOR WRITING RESPONSE
Correctly Worked Example	Efficiency (selects an appropriate strategy) and flexibility (applies a strategy to a new problem type)	What did ____ do? Why does it work? Is this a good method for this problem?
Partially Worked Example	Efficiency (selects an appropriate strategy; solves in a reasonable amount of time) and accuracy (completes steps accurately; gets correct answer)	Why did ____ start the problem this way? What does ____ need to do to finish the problem?
Incorrectly Worked Example	Accuracy (completes steps accurately; gets correct answer)	What did ____ do? What mistake does ____ make? How can this mistake be fixed?

With Count On/Count Back, correctly and partially worked examples help students see different options for chunking (skip-counting) and incorrect examples highlight common errors (as well as successful steps). Another excellent practice is to ask students to compare two correctly worked examples:

- How are they alike? How are they different?
- How do they compare in terms of efficiency?
- When would you use each method?

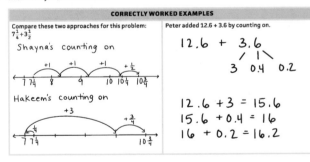

(Continued)

ACTIVITY 3.9

Name: "Say It As a Make a Whole"   **Type:** Routine

About the Routine: This routine explicitly charges students with renaming expressions in a variety of ways (SanGiovanni, 2019). In this particular version, the focus is on an equivalent expression after applying the Make a Whole idea.

Materials: prepared sets of expressions (examples follow)

Directions:
1. Pose three expressions to students and have them discuss another way to say each one. When you first launch this routine or when this strategy is new, pose the expressions one at a time. Later, they can be posed together.

2. Give students time to mentally think about a way to rewrite the expression (or rethink the expression) applying the Make a Whole idea.

3. Pair students to discuss their new expressions; then discuss options as a whole group.

4. With options on the board, ask students (a) the answer and (b) which expression they used to find the answer.

Here are a few sample sets of problems with fractions and with decimals:

Say It As a Make a Whole (Fractions, Same Denominators)

$2\frac{3}{4}+4\frac{1}{4}$	$7\frac{3}{8}+6\frac{7}{8}$	$9\frac{5}{6}+2\frac{5}{6}$
$3\frac{3}{4}+5\frac{2}{4}$	$\frac{6}{8}+4\frac{7}{8}$	$2\frac{5}{6}+3\frac{2}{6}$

Say It As a Make a Whole (Fractions, Mixed Denominators)

$5\frac{7}{8}+1\frac{1}{4}$	$\frac{7}{12}+\frac{1}{2}$	$5\frac{5}{6}+5\frac{1}{3}$

Say It As a Make a Whole (Tenths)

9.8 + 25.8	7.9 + 12.3	5.1 + 8.9

Say It As a Make a Whole (Hundredths)

2.18 + 7.98	0.55 + 3.88	0.41 + 5.89
4.58 + 5.43	38.92 + 4.46	6.15 + 8.83

Say It As a Make a Whole (Mixed Decimals)

4.8 + 6.35	5.276 + 21.9	8.75 + 3.30

Routines, Games, and Centers for each strategy offer extensive opportunity for student practice.

ACTIVITY 3.14

Name: Roll to Make a Whole   **Type:** Center

About the Center: This center activity has students create their own expressions (based on dice rolls) and then apply the Make a Whole strategy to solve. This means students will want to create expressions that lend to the strategy. You can modify this activity by offering different or fewer options on the placemat.

Materials: four 10-sided dice, a Roll to Make a Whole laminated placemat, and a dry-erase marker (optional: number lines or other physical tools to support reasoning)

Directions:
1. Students roll four dice.

2. Students decide which of the four options they want to use to write their expression (A–D on the placemat). *Note:* Students can place the dice right on the placemat and move them around to help select an option.

3. Students use a dry-erase marker to record the expression in the selected box.

4. Students rewrite the expression in a way that shows they applied the Make a Whole strategy.

5. Students solve the problem.

6. They roll the dice again and repeat the process, but this time there are just three options remaining on the placemat.

7. Students try to create four expressions, rewrite them using Make a Whole, and solve.

RESOURCE(S) FOR THIS ACTIVITY

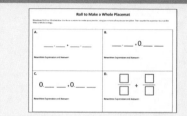

This resource can be downloaded at **resources.corwin.com/FOF/addsubtractdecimalfraction**.

Download the resources you need for each activity at this book's companion website.

FIGURING OUT
Fluency

ADDITION & SUBTRACTION
With Fractions and Decimals

Grades 4–8

A Classroom Companion

FIGURING OUT
Fluency

ADDITION & SUBTRACTION

With Fractions and Decimals

Grades 4–8

A Classroom Companion

Jennifer M. Bay-Williams
John J. SanGiovanni
Sherri Martinie
Jennifer Suh

CORWIN Mathematics

For information:

Corwin
A SAGE Company
2455 Teller Road
Thousand Oaks, California 91320
(800) 233–9936
www.corwin.com

SAGE Publications Ltd.
1 Oliver's Yard
55 City Road
London, EC1Y 1SP
United Kingdom

SAGE Publications India Pvt. Ltd.
B 1/I 1 Mohan Cooperative
Industrial Area
Mathura Road, New Delhi 110 044
India

SAGE Publications
Asia-Pacific Pte. Ltd.
18 Cross Street #10–10/11/12
China Square Central
Singapore 048423

President: Mike Soules
Associate Vice President and Editorial
    Director: Monica Eckman
Publisher: Erin Null
Content Development Editor:
    Jessica Vidal
Senior Editorial Assistant:
    Caroline Timmings
Editorial Assistant: Nyle De Leon
Production Editor: Tori Mirsadjadi
Copy Editor: Christina West
Typesetter: Integra
Proofreader:
Indexer: Integra
Cover Designer: Rose Storey
Marketing Manager:
    Margaret O'Connor

Printed in the United States of America.

Library of Congress Cataloging-in-Publication Data

Names: Bay-Williams, Jennifer M., author. | SanGiovanni, John, author. |
    Martinie, Sherri L., author. | Suh, Jennifer M., 1971- author
Title: Figuring out fluency -- addition and subtraction with fractions and
    decimals : a classroom companion / Jennifer M. Bay-Williams, John J.
    SanGioviann, Sherri Martinie, Jennifer Suh.
Description: Thousand Oaks, : Corwin, 2022. | Series: Corwin mathematics
    series
Identifiers: LCCN 2021041800 | ISBN 9781071825983 (paperback) | ISBN
    9781071862162 (epub) | ISBN 9781071862179 (epub) | ISBN 9781071825976
    (adobe pdf)
Subjects: LCSH: Mathematical fluency. | Addition--Study and teaching
    (Elementary) | Subtraction--Study and teaching (Elementary)
Classification: LCC QA135.6 .B384 2022 | DDC 372.7/2--dc23
LC record available at https://lccn.loc.gov/2021041800

This book is printed on acid-free paper.

22 23 24 25 26 10 9 8 7 6 5 4 3 2 1

Contents

Visit the companion website at
resources.corwin.com/FOF/
addsubtractdecimalfraction
for downloadable resources.

Preface

Fluency with fraction addition and subtraction is *not the same* as becoming proficient at adding using the standard algorithm. The same thing can be said for fraction and decimal addition and subtraction. We wanted to say this first because, well, oftentimes the standard algorithms are all that get taught. This denies students access to developing number sense, using quicker methods for some problems, and developing a sense of agency in doing mathematics. In other words, a sole focus on algorithms is an equity issue. If we don't teach ways to reason about rational numbers, our students are denied access to these methods. Fractions and decimals are rarely well liked or well understood. All that memorizing of steps leaves students bewildered and ill prepared for the flexibility and understanding they will need for success in algebra as well as in manipulating such numbers in their own life experiences.

In standards documents and in our daily work, we (mathematics teachers and leaders) communicate that every student must be *fluent* with decimal subtraction, for example. But we haven't even come close to accomplishing this for each and every student. The most recent National Assessment of Educational Progress data, for example, find that about two-fifths (41%) of the nation's Grade 4 students are at or above proficient and about one-third (34%) of our nation's Grade 8 students are at or above proficient (National Center for Education Statistics, 2019). We can and must do better! One major reason we haven't been able to develop fluent students is that there are misunderstandings about what fluency really means.

FIGURING OUT FLUENCY

In order to ensure every student develops fluency, we first must

- understand what procedural fluency is (and what it isn't),
- respect fluency, and
- plan to explicitly teach and assess reasoning strategies.

If you have read our anchor book *Figuring Out Fluency in Mathematics Teaching and Learning*—which we recommend in order to get the most out of *this* classroom companion—you'll remember an in-depth discussion of these topics.

WHAT PROCEDURAL FLUENCY IS AND ISN'T

Like fluency with language, wherein you decide how you want to communicate an idea, fluency in mathematics involves decision-making as you decide how to solve a problem. In our anchor book, we propose the following visual as a way to illustrate the full meaning of fluency.

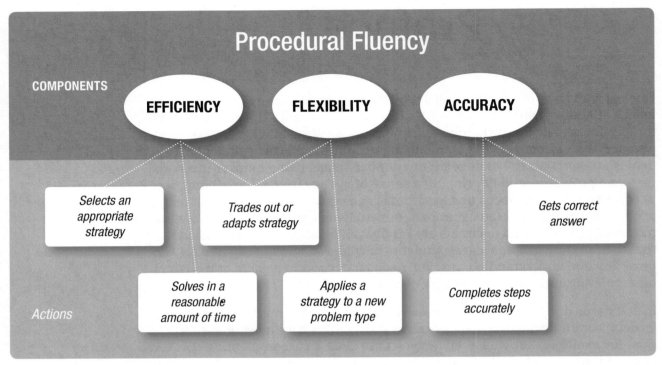

Procedural Fluency

COMPONENTS

EFFICIENCY   FLEXIBILITY   ACCURACY

Actions

Selects an appropriate strategy

Trades out or adapts strategy

Gets correct answer

Solves in a reasonable amount of time

Applies a strategy to a new problem type

Completes steps accurately

Part 1 of this book explains the elements of this procedural fluency graphic. In brief, procedural fluency is much more than knowing facts and standard algorithms. Fluency involves higher-level thinking, wherein a person analyzes a problem, considers options for how to solve it, selects an efficient strategy, and accurately enacts that strategy (trading it out for another if it doesn't go well). Decision-making is key, and that means you need to have good options to choose from. This book provides instructional and practice activities so that students learn different options (Part 2) and then provides practice activities to help students learn to choose options (Part 3).

RESPECT FLUENCY

We are strong advocates for conceptual understanding. We all must be. But there is not a choice here. Fluency relies on conceptual understanding, and conceptual understanding alone cannot help students fluently navigate computational situations. They go together and must be connected. Instructional activities throughout Part 2 provide opportunities for students to discuss, critique, and justify their thinking, connecting their conceptual understanding to their procedural knowledge and vice versa.

EXPLICITLY TEACH AND ASSESS REASONING STRATEGIES

If every student is to be fluent in fraction and decimal addition and subtraction, then every student needs access to the significant strategies for these operations. And there must be opportunities for students to learn how to select the best strategy for a particular problem. For example, students may learn that the Make a Whole strategy works well when one of the addends can become a whole number by moving some over. For example, $5.73 + 6.9$ can be rewritten or reimagined as $5.63 + 7$, moving 1 tenth over. Similarly, $5\frac{3}{4} + 4\frac{3}{4}$ can be rewritten or reimagined as $6 + 4\frac{1}{2}$ by moving $\frac{1}{4}$ over. If students only learn the standard algorithms for decimal and fraction addition, they will use regrouping to solve these, which is not the most efficient method. Thus, the Make a Whole strategy must be taught so that students have access to the strategy. And then, students need to learn when the strategy is a good option and when it is not. To accomplish this, all three fluency components must have equitable attention in instruction and assessment. This is a major shift from traditional teaching and assessing, which privileges standard algorithms and accuracy over flexibility and strategy selection.

Let's unpack the phrase *explicit strategy instruction*. According to the *Merriam-Webster Dictionary*, *explicit* means "fully revealed or expressed without vagueness" ("Explicit," 2021). In mathematics teaching, being *explicit* means making mathematical relationships visible. A *strategy* is a flexible method to solve a problem. *Explicit strategy instruction*, then, is engaging students in ways to clearly see how and why a strategy works. For example, with addition, students might compare $3.8 + 1.9$ and $4 + 2$ with base-10 pieces or on a number line as a way to reveal how the Compensation strategy works. With subtraction, students might be asked to compare a Count Back strategy (take-away interpretation) to a Count Up strategy (compare or find-the-difference interpretation) to solve $12\frac{1}{2} - 10\frac{3}{4}$ on a number line. With more examples, students notice that when the numbers are close together, a find-the-difference interpretation is more efficient than a take-away interpretation. Learning how to use and how to choose strategies *empowers* students to be able to decide how they want to solve a problem, developing a positive mathematics identity and a sense of agency.

USING THIS BOOK

This book is a classroom companion book to *Figuring Out Fluency in Mathematics Teaching and Learning*. In that anchor book, we lay out what fluency is, identify the fallacies that stand in the way of a true focus on fluency, and elaborate on necessary foundations for fluency. We also propose the following:

- Seven Significant Strategies across the operations, five of which apply to fraction and decimal addition and subtraction

- Eight "automaticities" *beyond* automaticity with basic facts

- Five ways to engage students in meaningful practice

- Four assessment options that can replace (or at least complement) tests and that focus on real fluency

- Many ways to engage families in supporting their child's fluency

In Part 1 of this book, we revisit some of these ideas in order to connect specifically to fraction and decimal addition and subtraction. This section is not a substitute for the anchor book but rather a brief revisiting of central ideas that serve as reminders of what was fully illustrated, explained, and justified in *Figuring Out Fluency in Mathematics Teaching and Learning*. Hopefully, you have had the chance to read and engage with that content with colleagues *first*, and then Part 1 will help you think about those ideas as they apply to fraction and decimal addition and subtraction. Finally, Part 1 includes suggestions for how to use the strategy modules.

Part 2 is focused on explicit instruction of each significant strategy for fraction and decimal addition and subtraction. Each module includes the following:

● An overview for your reference and to share with students and colleagues

● A strategy brief for families

● A series of instructional activities, with the final one offering a series of questions to promote discourse about the strategy

● A series of practice activities, including worked examples, routines, games, and center activities that engage students in meaningful and ongoing practice to develop proficiency with that strategy

As you are teaching and find your students are ready to learn a particular strategy, pull this book off the shelf, go to the related module, and access the activities and ready-to-use resources. While the modules are sequenced in a developmental order overall, the order and focus on each strategy may vary depending on your grade and your students' experiences. Additionally, teaching within or across modules does not happen all at once; rather, activities can be woven into your instruction regularly, over time.

Part 3 is about becoming truly fluent—developing flexibility and efficiency with addition and subtraction of fractions and decimals. Filled with more routines, games, and centers, the focus here is on students *choosing* to use the strategies that make sense to them in a given situation. Part 3 also provides assessment tools to monitor students' fluency. As you are teaching and find your students are needing opportunities to choose from among the strategies they are learning, pull this book off the shelf and select an activity from Part 3.

In the Appendix, you will find lists of all the activities in order to help you easily locate what you are looking for by strategy or by type of resource.

This book can be used to complement or supplement any published mathematics program or district-created program. As we noted earlier, elementary mathematics has tended to fall short in its attention to efficiency and flexibility with rational numbers (and the related Fluency Actions illustrated in the earlier graphic). This book provides a large collection of activities to address these neglected components of fluency. Note that this book is part of a series that explores other operations and other numbers. You may also be interested in *Figuring Out Fluency in Multiplication and Division With Whole Numbers* as well as the classroom companion books for whole-number operations.

WHO IS THIS BOOK FOR?

With over 110 activities and a companion website with resources ready to download, this book is designed to support classroom teachers as they advance their students' fluency with fraction and decimal addition and subtraction.

Special education teachers will find the explicit strategy instruction, as well as the additional practice, useful in supporting their students. Mathematics coaches and specialists can use this book for professional learning and to provide instructional resources to the classroom teachers they support. Mathematics supervisors and curriculum leads can use this book to help them assess fluency aspects of their mathematics curriculum and fill potential gaps in resources and understanding. Teacher preparation programs can use this book to galvanize preservice teachers' understanding of fluency and provide teacher candidates with a wealth of classroom-ready resources to use during internships and as they begin their career.

Acknowledgments

Just as there are many components to fluency, there are certainly many components to having a book like this come to fruition. The first component is the researchers and advocates who have defined procedural fluency and effective practices that support it. Research on student learning is hard work, as is defining effective teaching practices, and so we want to begin by acknowledging this work. We have learned from these scholars, and we ground our ideas in their findings. It is on their shoulders that we stand. Second are the teachers and their students who have taken up "real" fluency practices and shared their experiences with us. We would not have taken on this book had we not seen firsthand how a focus on procedural fluency in classrooms truly transforms students' learning and shapes their mathematical identities. It is truly inspiring! Additionally, the testimonies from many teachers about their own learning experiences as students and as teachers helped crystalize for us the facts and fallacies in this book. A third component to bringing this book to fruition was the family support to allow us to actually do the work. We are all grateful to our family members—expressed in our personal statements that follow—who supported us 24/7 as we wrote during a pandemic.

From Jennifer: I am forever grateful to my amazing husband, Mitch, who is supportive and helpful in every way. I also thank my children, MacKenna and Nicolas, who endure a lot of extra math in their lives while also giving me insights into learning. And that leads to my gratitude to my extended family—my parents and my siblings for their decades of support. To John, I am grateful to you for taking on this book series with me. And to Sherri and Jenn, thank you for agreeing to be part of a team to figure out fluency with rational numbers. You are each amazing educators and collaborators!

From John: I want to thank my family—especially my wife—who, as always, endure and support the ups and downs of taking on a new project. Thank you to Jenny, Sherri, and Jenn for being exceptional partners. And thank you for dealing with my random thoughts, tangent conversations, and fantastic humor. As always, a heartfelt thank you to certain math friends and mentors for opportunities, faith in me, and support over the years. And thank you to my own math teachers who let me do math "my way," even if it wasn't "the way" back then.

From Sherri: Thank you to my children—Curtis, Peter, and Lucy—who have patiently waited on me while I finish "one more thing" and whose math thoughts and math work have provided me great insight. Thank you to my husband, Brian, who is encouraging and supportive. Thank you to my colleagues and mentors, especially Jenny and John for including me in this project, and to Jenn for being an amazing writing buddy. Finally, a special thank-you to all of my students over the years who continue to inspire me to always be a better math teacher.

From Jenn: I would like to thank my husband, Tim, for his everlasting support in all my life adventures and endeavors. I thank my two sons, Jeremy and Zach, who always entertained me with "math happenings" in our everyday life and shared interesting ways to be flexible with numbers and develop into "number engineers" who can break apart and put numbers back together and, in general, become flexible thinkers and problem-solvers. Thanks to Sherri for being my thought partner, Rosalba for her artful math drawings, and Jenny and John for inviting me to contribute to this awesome series. I look forward to sharing this work with many teachers for years to come with you all as a team.

A fourth component is vision and writing support. We are so grateful to Corwin for recognizing the importance of defining and implementing procedural fluency in the mathematics classroom. Our editor and publisher, Erin Null, has gone above and beyond as a partner in the work, ensuring that our ideas are as well stated and useful as possible. The entire editing team at Corwin has been creative, thorough, helpful, and supportive.

As with fluency, no component is more important than another, and without any component, there is no book, so to the researchers, teachers, family, and editing team, thank you. We are so grateful.

PUBLISHER'S ACKNOWLEDGMENTS

Corwin gratefully acknowledges the contributions of the following reviewers:

Jamie Fraser
Math Consultant
Developer and Educational Distributer
Bound2Learn

Sarah Gat
Instructional Coach
Upper Grand District School Board

Christina Hawley
Grade 1 and Grade 2 Teacher
Rockcliffe Park Public School

Cathy Martin
Associate Chief of Academics
Denver Public Schools

Margie Pearse
Math Coach

Nicole Rigelman
Professor of Mathematics Education
Portland State University

About the Authors

Jennifer M. Bay-Williams is a professor of mathematics education at the University of Louisville, where she teaches preservice teachers, emerging elementary mathematics specialists, and doctoral students in mathematics education. She has authored numerous books as well as many journal articles, many of which focus on procedural fluency (and other aspects of effective mathematics teaching and learning). Jennifer is a frequent presenter at national and state conferences and works with schools and districts around the world. Her national leadership includes having served as a member of the National Council of Teachers of Mathematics (NCTM) Board of Directors, on the TODOS: Mathematics for All Board of Directors, and as president and secretary of the Association of Mathematics Teacher Educators (AMTE).

John J. SanGiovanni is a mathematics supervisor in Howard County, Maryland. There, he leads mathematics curriculum development, digital learning, assessment, and professional development. John is an adjunct professor and coordinator of the Elementary Mathematics Instructional Leadership graduate program at McDaniel College. He is an author and national mathematics curriculum and professional learning consultant. John is a frequent speaker at national conferences and institutes. He is active in state and national professional organizations, recently serving on the board of directors for the NCTM and currently as the president of the Maryland Council of Supervisors of Mathematics.

Sherri Martinie is an associate professor of curriculum and instruction at Kansas State University, where she teaches undergraduate and graduate courses in mathematics education. Prior to taking her position at Kansas State, she taught elementary, middle, and high school mathematics for a combined 20 years. Sherri is an author, professional development leader, grant writer, and conference speaker. She is continually seeking innovative ways to support preservice and inservice teachers in their development and refinement of effective mathematics teaching practices.

Jennifer Suh is a mathematics educator in the Graduate School of Education at George Mason University. She teaches mathematics methods courses in the Elementary Education Program and mathematics leadership courses for the Mathematics Specialist Master's and PhD Programs. Jennifer directs the Center for Outreach in Mathematics Professional Learning and Educational Technology (COMPLETE) and provides professional development focused on mathematics content and teaching practices. Her research focuses on using lesson study with school-based teams to develop high-leverage mathematics teaching practices and deepen teachers' content knowledge through an understanding of children's development of mathematics learning trajectories. Jennifer's project is called EQSTEMM, or Advancing Equity and Strengthening Teaching with Elementary Mathematical Modeling, which aims to develop K–8 problem-based modeling tasks to promote equitable access to 21st-century skills for diverse student populations in STEM disciplines.

PART 1

FIGURING OUT FLUENCY
Key Ideas

WHAT IS FLUENCY WITH FRACTION AND DECIMAL ADDITION AND SUBTRACTION?

Perhaps the best way to talk about fluency is to explore some examples. Take a moment to solve each of these problems:

$\frac{7}{8}+\frac{7}{8}$	$7\frac{3}{5}-3\frac{2}{3}$	$3\frac{1}{2}+2\frac{3}{4}$
3.63 − 1.80	14.99 + 7.07	14.00 − 12.68

How did you find the sums and differences? Did you use the same approach or strategy for each? Did you change out a strategy based on the numbers within the problem? Did you start with one strategy and shift to another? For fraction and decimal addition and subtraction, the answer to "Did you use the same approach?" is too often "yes." And that approach is the standard algorithm. But let's look at just the first example. You can just move an eighth over and see that the answer is $1\frac{6}{8}$ or $1\frac{3}{4}$; you don't need to "add the numerators and sim- plify." Rather than this Make a Whole strategy, you may have just thought of the first number as 1 whole, added to get $1\frac{7}{8}$, and then compensated, subtract- ing the extra eighth to equal $1\frac{3}{4}$.

Let's look at one of the decimal examples: 14.99 + 7.07. If you added using the standard algorithm, ask yourself how you could add it using Make a Whole or Compensation. Make a Whole involves moving one-hundredth from one addend to the other, changing the expression to 15 + 7.06. The Compensation strategy involves just changing 14.99 to 15.00 (add 0.01), adding the two num- bers 15.00 + 7.07 (22.07), and then compensating (subtract 0.01) to get 22.06. Adding partial sums is another option. Which method is closer to your way of thinking. Or did you think about it differently?

Real fluency is the ability to select efficient strategies; to adapt, modify, or change out strategies; and to find solutions with accuracy. Real fluency is *not* the act of replicating someone else's steps or procedures for doing mathemat- ics. It is the act of thinking, reasoning, and doing mathematics on one's own. Before fluency can be taught well, you must understand what fluency is and why it matters.

Procedural fluency is an umbrella term that includes basic fact fluency and computational fluency (see Figure 1). *Basic fact fluency* attends to fluently adding, subtracting, multiplying, and dividing single-digit numbers. *Computational fluency* refers to the fluency in four operations across number types (whole numbers, fractions, etc.), regardless of the magnitude of the number. Procedural fluency encompasses both basic fact fluency and com- putational fluency, plus other procedures like finding equivalent fractions. This book focuses on computational fluency for addition and subtraction of fractions and decimals.

FIGURE 1 ● The Relationship of Different Fluency Terms in Mathematics

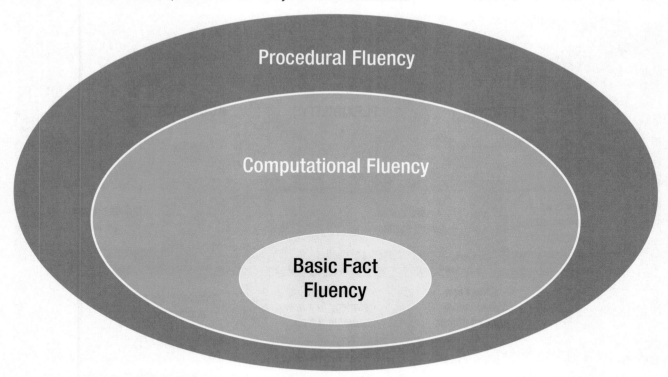

Beyond being an umbrella term that encompasses basic fact and computational fluency, procedural fluency is well defined as solving procedures efficiently, flexibly, and accurately (Kilpatrick et al., 2001; National Council of Teachers of Mathematics, 2014). These three components are defined as follows:

1. *Efficiency:* solving a procedure in a reasonable amount of time by selecting an appropriate strategy and readily implementing that strategy

2. *Flexibility:* knowing multiple procedures and can apply or adapt strategies to solve procedural problems (Baroody & Dowker, 2003; Star, 2005)

3. *Accuracy:* correctly solving a procedure

Strategies are not the same as algorithms. Strategies are general methods that are flexible in design, compared to algorithms that are established steps implemented the same way across problems.

To focus on fluency, we need specific observable actions that we can look for in what students are doing in order to ensure they are developing fluency. We have identified six such actions. The three components and six Fluency Actions, and their relationships, are illustrated in Figure 2.

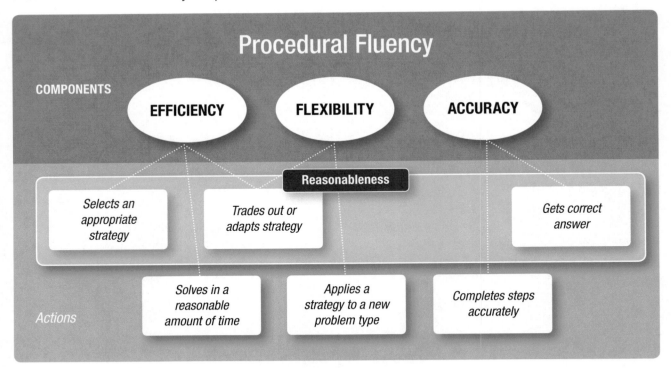

Three of the six Fluency Actions (should) attend to reasonableness. Fluency Actions and reasonableness are described later in Part 1, but first, it is important to consider why this "bigger" (comprehensive) view of fluency matters.

WHY FOCUS ON FLUENCY FOR FRACTION AND DECIMAL ADDITION AND SUBTRACTION?

There are two key reasons why it's important to focus on fluency with adding and subtracting fractions and decimals. First, it is a critical foundation for ensuring that students fully realize procedural fluency in general, with all kinds of numbers. Fluency with addition and subtraction is a *necessity* for developing fluency with multiplication and division. For example, an efficient way to solve 0.9×4 is to think 1×4 (4) and subtract 0.4. This should be a natural mental process. Additionally, being fluent with fractions and decimal operations supports student learning in algebra and beyond. These connections are a focus of our anchor book, *Figuring Out Fluency in Mathematics Teaching and Learning* (hereafter titled *Figuring Out Fluency*).

Second and most important, developing fluency is an equity issue. Students must have access to efficient ways to solve problems and must be positioned as capable "choosers" of methods. Equipping students with options for how to solve addition and subtraction problems and explicitly teaching students to choose a method that works best for them develops a positive mathematics identity and sense of agency. Conversely, trying to remember algorithms and feeling anxiety about being correct or fast develops a negative mathematics identity and a lack of agency.

WHAT DO FLUENCY ACTIONS LOOK LIKE FOR FRACTION AND DECIMAL ADDITION AND SUBTRACTION?

The six Fluency Actions are observable and therefore form a foundation for assessing student progress toward fluency. Let's take a look at what each of these actions looks like in the context of fraction and decimal addition and subtraction.

FLUENCY ACTION 1: Select an Appropriate Strategy

Selecting *an* appropriate strategy does not mean selecting *the* appropriate strategy. Many problems can be solved efficiently in more than one way. Here is our operational definition: Of the available strategies, the one the student opts to use gets to a solution in about as many steps and/or about as much time as other appropriate options.

Consider 4.79 + 2.41. One could Count On from 4.79 (Figure 3a), Use Partials (Figure 3b), or Make a Whole (Figure 3c). Each of these strategies is appropriate for this problem but may not be as appropriate for other problems such as 5.00 + 3.63 or 2.99 + 4.76.

TEACHING TAKEAWAY

Selecting *an* appropriate strategy does not mean selecting *the* appropriate strategy. Many problems can be solved efficiently in more than one way.

FIGURE 3 ● Some Appropriate Strategies for Adding 4.79 + 2.41

a. Count On

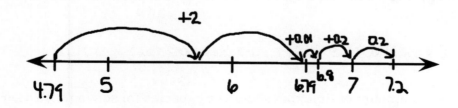

b. Partial Sums

$$4 + 2 = 6$$
$$0.7 + 0.4 = 1.1$$
$$0.09 + 0.01 = 0.1$$
$$\overline{7.2}$$

c. Make a Whole

$$4.79 + 2.41$$
$$0.21 \quad 2.2$$
$$5.0 + 2.2 = 7.2$$

These same strategies are appropriate options for adding $3\frac{1}{2} + 2\frac{3}{4}$. One way to count on is to start at $3\frac{1}{2}$ and add on 2, then $\frac{1}{2}$, then $\frac{1}{4}$ (Figure 4a). Another option is to add wholes and parts separately (i.e., Partial Sums; Figure 4b), or move $\frac{1}{2}$ over to make a whole (Figure 4c).

FIGURE 4 ● Some Appropriate Strategies for Adding $3\frac{1}{2}+2\frac{3}{4}$

a. Count On

b. Partial Sums

c. Make a Whole

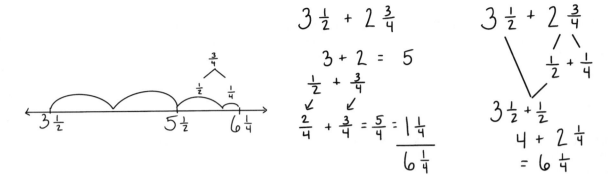

While these two examples had several appropriate options, this is not the case with all problems. For example, consider 28.425 + 3.9. Using partials in this case is more cumbersome than just adding 4 and subtracting 0.1 (Compensation). Count On is an appropriate strategy for 5.00 + 3.70 or 14.50 + 3.22 but not for 3.99 + 3.76.

A student who knows the significant reasoning strategies for addition and subtraction will find them more efficient than the standard algorithm in many cases. A strategy cannot be used until it is understood and practiced. The modules in Part 2 provide resources for developing student competency with each strategy, and Part 3 focuses on this fluency action, selecting an appropriate strategy.

FLUENCY ACTION 2: Solve in a Reasonable Amount of Time

There is no set amount of time that should be expected for solving a fraction or decimal problem. The observable action here is that students can readily work their way through a selected strategy or algorithm without getting bogged down, stuck, or lost. Additionally, appropriate strategies can be selected (Fluency Action 1) but carried out in inefficient ways. For example, the Count On examples in the earlier figures are implemented with efficient chunking, but students may not chunk and simply count by tenths or fourths.

FLUENCY ACTION 3: Trade Out or Adapt a Strategy

As strategies are better understood, students are able to adapt them or swap them out for another more efficient strategy and even combine strategies. Adapting a strategy is using the strategy in a different way. A student might start subtracting 45.3 – 19.5 with a Count Back strategy, counting back by tens, ones, and tenths, and realize they would rather count back 20 and count up 5 tenths. Or they might abandon Count Back altogether, trading out this strategy for Compensation and rethinking the problem as 45.3 – 20, subtracting (25.3), and adding 0.5 to compensate (25.8).

Let's consider a fraction example: $10\frac{1}{5} - 8\frac{7}{10}$. Students have learned both a Count Back strategy (take-away interpretation) and a Think Addition strategy (find-the-difference interpretation; see Figure 5). To begin, Lucy finds the common denominator, $10\frac{2}{10} - 8\frac{7}{10}$, and her first thought is to use a Count Back strategy. Then, she notices that these numbers are close together and decides instead to use a Think Addition strategy.

FIGURE 5 ● Two Strategies for Subtracting $10\frac{1}{5} - 8\frac{7}{10}$

Count Back Strategy

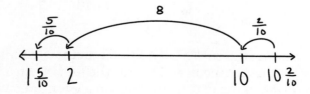

Think Addition Strategy

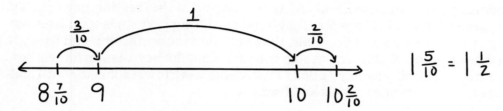

As strategies are better understood, students are able to adapt them or trade them out as they seek an efficient way to add or subtract. As this statement implies, students need to be adept at using strategies so they can become adept at working flexibly within and across strategies.

FLUENCY ACTION 4: Apply a Strategy to a New Problem Type

As its name suggests, this action involves seeing how a strategy learned for one type of numbers can be applied to others. This fluency action is necessary for students to make sense of strategies for decimals and fractions, as they have already learned the strategies for whole numbers. For example, students have learned Make Tens and Make Hundreds and can apply that strategy to decimals and fractions, which becomes Make a Whole. Students may learn Make a Whole first with fraction addition and then see how it can also be applied to decimals.

FLUENCY ACTIONS 5 AND 6: Complete Steps Accurately and Get Correct Answers

These two Fluency Actions relate to the accuracy component. The goal is for both to be in place. A student may make an error in the process itself, in particular with standard algorithms. Other times, a computational error may undercut a correctly executed strategy. The student's work in Figure 6 is a good example of this.

FIGURE 6 ● Think Addition (Counting Up) Strategy With a Computational Error

Problem: 7.10 – 4.79 =

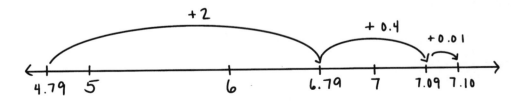

Here, a student uses an efficient Think Addition method (chunking by wholes, tenths, and hundredths) but incorrectly notes the jump from 6.79 to 7.09 as 0.4 (rather than the correct jump of 0.3), resulting in a wrong answer.

Decimal and fraction addition and subtraction must move beyond only implementing standard algorithms. As the examples in this section have shown, strategies have many benefits: They build on and support student understanding of the fractions and decimals, they are often more efficient, and they are less error-prone. An important step to figuring out fluency, then, is for teachers to attend to all six Fluency Actions as students work toward fluency with adding and subtracting decimals and fractions.

Fluency Action 6 is one of three connected to reasonableness. Within this action is noticing if your answer makes sense. While reasonableness has been woven into the discussion of Fluency Actions, it is critical to fluency and warrants more discussion.

REASONABLENESS

A fluent student determines if their strategies and results are reasonable. Checks for reasonableness occur in three of the six Fluency Actions, as shown in Figure 2. Traditionally, reasonableness has only been considered in regard to the solution, but it also applies to strategy selection and enactment. It takes time to develop reasonableness. It should be practiced and discussed as often as possible. Students can develop reasonableness by practicing these three moves (a match to the Fluency Actions 1, 3, and 6).

THREE "Cs" OF REASONABLENESS

Choose: Choose a strategy that is efficient based on the numbers in the problem.
Change: Change the strategy if it is proving to be overly complex or unsuccessful.
Check: Check to make sure the result makes sense.

Let's explore how reasonableness plays out for Francie in solving 5.89 + 4.5.

1. Francie decides to use the Make a Whole strategy, because this seems efficient for these numbers.

2. She starts trying to move some over to add 0.11 to 5.89 to make a whole and gets bogged down. She realizes this isn't going smoothly, and she decides to go the other way and move 0.5 over to 4.5. She rewrites the expression as 5.39 + 5.

3. She adds, gets 10.39, and looks back to see if, in fact, the answer should be a little over 10.

You can encourage and support student thinking about reasonableness by providing Choose, Change, Check reflection cards (see Figure 7). These cards can be adapted into anchor charts for students to use while working on problems or during class discussions about adding and subtracting.

FIGURE 7 ● Choose, Change, Check Reflection Card for Students

CHECKS FOR REASONABLENESS		
Choose	Change	Check
Is this something I can do in my head? What strategy makes sense for these numbers?	Is my strategy going well or should I try a different approach? Does my answer so far seem reasonable?	Is my answer close to what I anticipated it might be? How might I check my answer?

Icon sources: Choose by iStock.com/Enis Aksoy; Change by iStock.com/Sigit Mulyo Utomo; Check by iStock.com/Indigo Diamond.

 This resource can be downloaded at **resources.corwin.com/FOF/addsubtractdecimalfraction**.

WHAT FOUNDATIONS DO STUDENTS NEED TO DEVELOP FLUENCY WITH FRACTION AND DECIMAL ADDITION AND SUBTRACTION?

This section attends to three categories of foundations: conceptual understanding, foundational skills, and automaticities. Students need certain conceptual understandings as foundations for learning the strategies for addition and subtraction of fractions and decimals presented in Part 2. Rushing students to strategy instruction before these foundations are firmly in place can be disastrous. In addition to conceptual understanding, emerging student automaticities contribute to their facility with strategies for adding and subtracting fractions and decimals. To begin, students must have automaticity with their basic facts. But there are other skills for which having automaticity supports reasoning (e.g., knowing equivalencies of $\frac{1}{2}$). These automaticities are not pre-requisites for strategy instruction but develop side by side with strategies.

CONCEPTUAL UNDERSTANDING

Fractions are numbers. This may sound obvious, but many students come to understand fractions as a number over a number or shaded parts over total parts. Instead, conceptual understanding must focus on the relative size of fractions (including fractions less than, equal to, and greater than 1). Researchers include the following significant fraction concepts (Cramer & Whitney, 2010; Empson & Levi, 2011; Lamon, 2020; Van de Walle et al., 2019):

- Fractions are equal shares of a whole or a unit.

- Fractions have a location on a number line; unlike shading part of a region, locating fractions on a number line requires reasoning about the size of the fraction (in other words, understanding the fraction as a number in and of itself).

- Fractions may represent part of an area, part of a length, or part of a set.

- Just like 5 can be decomposed into 3 + 2 or 1 + 1 + 1 + 1 + 1 or other ways, fractions can be decomposed in a variety of ways. For example, $\frac{5}{8}$ can be decomposed into $\frac{3}{8} + \frac{2}{8}$ or $\frac{1}{8} + \frac{1}{8} + \frac{1}{8} + \frac{1}{8} + \frac{1}{8}$. Partitioning and iterating are strategies students can use to understand the meaning of fractions. Partitioning can be thought of as splitting the whole equally (e.g., splitting a whole into fourths), and iterating can be thought of as making a copy of each piece and counting them (e.g., one-fourth, two-fourths, etc.).

- When working with fractions, they can only be compared, added, or subtracted if the fractions are part of the same-sized whole (this is often implied but needs to be explicit).

- Equivalent fractions are ways of describing the same quantity, the difference being in how the same-sized whole is partitioned.

These fraction concepts develop through exploring contextual problems and using manipulatives and visuals. For example, sharing tasks help students make sense of fractions, including such things as knowing that $\frac{1}{6}$ of a whole is less than $\frac{1}{3}$ of that whole (in fact, $\frac{1}{6}$ is half of $\frac{1}{3}$; Empson & Levi, 2011).

Decimals are sometimes considered "easier" than fractions, perhaps because the algorithms parallel whole number algorithms. But the conceptual understanding of decimals is, in fact, at least as challenging as fractions (Hurst & Cordes, 2018; Lortie-Forgues et al., 2015; Martinie, 2014); conceptual understanding of decimals and their connections to fractions must be carefully developed.

While we use the term "decimals," the full name for these numbers is "decimal fractions," as they are fractions that happen to have denominators of 10, 100, 1,000, and so forth, so decimals are a special case of fractions that fit within our place value system. Number sense with decimals is therefore dependent on an understanding of place value *and* fractions. The following are important conceptual understandings to support student fluency:

- Decimals are a way of writing fractions within the base-10 system (denominators of 10, 100, 1,000, and so on).

- The position to the left of the decimal point is the units place; the position to the right of the decimal point tells how many tenths.

- The value to the right of the decimal point is a quantity between 0 and 1, regardless of how long the decimal is.

A developmental progression to building a strong connection between fractions and decimals includes the following:

1. Explore tenths in fraction form and learn to notate the quantities both as fractions and as decimals (this should become an automaticity).

2. Explore hundredths, again in both fraction and decimal form, seeing the connection to fractions and to the place value system.

3. Explore other fractions for which the decimal equivalent is within hundredths and is commonly used: halves, fourths, and fifths.

Using appropriate language (tenths and hundredths) throughout the process further supports both the connection between fractions and decimals and the fundamental idea that these numbers are parts of a whole.

TEACHING TAKEAWAY

Using appropriate language (tenths and hundredths) throughout the process further supports both the connection between fractions and decimals and the fundamental idea that these numbers are parts of a whole.

REPRESENTATIONS

Students develop a deeper conceptual understanding of fractions and decimals by using multiple modes of representations. More specifically, it is the connection between the multiple physical models that is critical to representational fluency (Cramer et al., 2002; Monson et al., 2020). For fractions, there are area models (fraction circles or bars), measurement models (fraction number lines), and set models (counters; Van de Walle et al., 2019). For decimals, common models include Unifix or multilink cubes, base-10 blocks, decimal grids, money, and number lines.

Use of multiple representations helps students develop a solid foundation for critical concepts like equivalencies. Beginning with an area model and then translating the same fraction or decimal to a number line can help students see the relative size of the numbers. This is particularly important in developing automaticity with equivalencies, which is one of the most important foundations to adding and subtracting fractions. As stated in *Figuring Out Fluency*, "recognizing and recalling fraction equivalence with minimal effort contributes to strategy selection and efficiency" (Bay-Williams & SanGiovanni, 2021, p. 123).

PROBLEM SITUATIONS

Story problems provide another means of developing conceptual understanding by helping students make sense of situations and quantities. It is a mistake to save story problems as an application, as stories give students a context

TEACHING TAKEAWAY

Developing fluency *begins* with stories because stories give students a context from which they can reason.

from which they can reason. Stories need to be *relevant* to students, meaning that students are familiar with the context and it is interesting to students. Stories must also vary in two ways:

1. Type of situation (a join story, a part–part–whole story)

2. What is unknown in the story (the initial quantity, the change, or the result)

In recent standards documents, much attention has been given to these two ideas but they are typically mentioned only with whole numbers. Yet these ideas are at least as important with fraction and decimal stories.

Audit a page of "word problems" for adding and subtracting decimals and/or fractions. Chances are good you will find that "join" stories for addition and "separate" stories for subtraction are plentiful, and "part–part–whole" and "compare" stories are missing or barely represented. Look again for what is unknown in the story and you will likely find that most or all of the stories read as "result unknown." For example, consider this "join" story template:

Leo runs ____ miles. He runs ____ more. In all, Leo has run ____ miles.

It usually appears this way (result unknown):

Leo runs $1\frac{1}{2}$ miles and takes a water break. Then, he runs $1\frac{3}{4}$ more. How far did Leo run in all?

Students overgeneralize that "in all" means "add." But here are the other two ways this story can be told, for example:

Leo runs for a while and stops for a water break. Then, he runs $1\frac{3}{4}$ miles more. In all, he ran $3\frac{1}{4}$ miles. How far did Leo run before his water break?

This story is part unknown and is solved by using subtraction. Varying story types helps students learn to interpret stories; it also helps students understand important ideas, such as the relationship between addition and subtraction (which is essential to fluency strategies). Figure 8 can be used as a resource to be sure you are varying your story types.

FIGURE 8 ● Addition and Subtraction Situations

ADDITION AND SUBTRACTION SITUATIONS			
Join	**Separate**	**Compare**	**Part–Part–Whole**
Story is about something being added to an original amount.	Story is about something being removed from the original amount.	Story compares two quantities.	Story is about combining different types of objects.
Ex: AJ had ____ brownies. She got ____ brownies. She has a total of ____ brownies.	Ex: AJ had ____ brownies. She gave away ____ brownies. Now she has a total of ____ brownies.	Ex: AJ has ____ brownies. Ian has ____ brownies. AJ has ____ more/less than Ian.	Ex: AJ has ____ chocolate brownies and ____ peanut butter brownies. The total of her brownies is ____.

EQUIVALENCIES

Knowing equivalencies is both a conceptual foundation and an automaticity. As a conceptual foundation, it means that students "see" that two-tenths is the same as 20 hundredths, perhaps using base-10 pieces. And they know they can write this equivalency in any of these ways:

$$0.2 \qquad 0.20 \qquad \frac{2}{10} \qquad \frac{20}{100}$$

Of course, there are infinitely many other ways as well. Students also understand that if they have any fraction and they want to represent it as a decimal, the goal is to find an equivalent fraction with a denominator of 10, 100, and so forth. To find the decimal equivalent to $\frac{1}{4}$, for example, students might reason that there is no equivalent fraction in the form $\frac{?}{10}$, so they look for an equivalency in the form $\frac{?}{100}$, which turns out to be $\frac{25}{100}$ or 0.25. These ideas can be explored with Unifix Cubes, base-10 pieces, and number lines.

NOTATIONS

Despite their equivalence, notations for values can look very different. Perhaps because we (as adults) are very familiar with the notations, we forget how very different they are to someone who has spent their whole life working with whole numbers. Time spent attending to notations is essential to being able to later focus on computational fluency.

A fraction is written with a line separating the numerator, representing parts of a whole, and a denominator, representing the number of parts in the whole. As the whole is sectioned into more or less equal-sized pieces, the number of parts represented by the numerator changes to reflect this as well. The meaning of the fraction bar must be understood, including its connections to division. The fraction $\frac{1}{4}$, for example, may be interpreted as one part of four parts, but it is also one shared four ways, or 1 divided by 4, with the resulting fair-share being $\frac{1}{4}$. An actual division operation of this fraction results in 0.25, the decimal equivalent.

A decimal is a fraction with implied denominators of 10, 100, 1,000, and so on. Decimals do not explicitly show the denominator; instead, it is implied by the location relative to the decimal point. With decimal notation, students need to understand that there are infinitely many ways to represent the same number. For example, 0.2 = 0.20 = 0.200. Because students *know* that $2 \neq 20 \neq 200$, this differing meaning to the right of the decimal point requires attention. Fraction equivalencies can help build this meaning.

Finally, it is not uncommon for students to overgeneralize fraction or decimal notation and confuse the two. For example, they may write $\frac{1}{6} = 1.6$ *or* $\frac{1}{6} = 0.6$.

PROPERTIES AND UTILITIES FOR STRATEGIC COMPETENCE

In addition to conceptual foundations, fluency is grounded in using properties of the operations and knowing a few other important things, which we refer to as "utilities" because students must utilize them in their reasoning.

TEACHING TAKEAWAY

Knowing properties does not equal using properties. Instruction must focus on applying properties, not identifying them.

It is important to note that knowing properties does not equal using properties. It is *not* useful to have students name the associative property. It is absolutely necessary that students *use* properties in solving problems efficiently, finding numbers that add to benchmarks, like these two examples:

$$5.42 + 7.02 + 2.58 + 4.98 = \underline{\hspace{1cm}}$$

$$\frac{1}{8} + \frac{1}{4} + \frac{5}{16} + \frac{3}{4} = \underline{\hspace{1cm}}$$

Fluency with addition relies heavily on students using the commutative and associative properties of addition. Additionally, the identity property is central to working with fraction operations. The identity property of 1 says that any number multiplied by 1 keeps its identity. The number 1 has infinitely many forms: $\frac{2}{2}, \frac{3}{3}, \ldots, \frac{8}{8}$, and so on. We pick the form that helps us generate an equivalent fraction. The visual in Figure 9 can remind students of the value of fractions equivalent to 1.

FIGURE 9 ● Highlighting the Identity Property of Multiplication in Finding Equivalent Fractions

$$\frac{3}{5} \times \frac{2}{2} = \frac{6}{10}$$

See Chapter 3 (pp. 47–75) of *Figuring Out Fluency* for more about foundations and good beginnings for fluency.

Beyond the properties, a short list of utilities that support fluency is presented in Figure 10.

FIGURE 10 ● Utilities That Support Procedural Fluency

UTILITY	WHAT IT IS	RELATIONSHIP TO FLUENCY
Distance From a Whole	Knowing how many parts a given fraction is from a whole (i.e., understanding that $\frac{8}{10}$ is $\frac{2}{10}$ away from 1, the unit being $\frac{1}{10}$).	Knowing how far a fraction or decimal number is from a whole is necessary to implement reasoning strategies, as many of them make use of using benchmarks.
Decomposing Numbers Flexibly	Knowing that a number can be decomposed in a number of ways. Example 1: $\frac{3}{4} = \frac{1}{2} + \frac{1}{4}$ or $\frac{1}{4} + \frac{1}{4} + \frac{1}{4}$ Example 2: $1.8 = 1 + 0.8$ or $1.4 + 0.4$	Decomposing in flexible ways supports efficiency with strategy implementation. Example 1: $3\frac{1}{2} + 4\frac{3}{4} = 3\frac{1}{2} + 4\frac{1}{2} + \frac{1}{4} = 8\frac{1}{4}$ Example 2: $3.4 - 1.8 = 3.4 - 1.4 - 0.4 = 1.6$

UTILITY	WHAT IT IS	RELATIONSHIP TO FLUENCY
Part–Part–Whole	Knowing that a whole is composed of parts. While the label has two parts and one whole, it could be three or more parts.	Understanding this model will enable students to easily move back and forth between addition and subtraction and better understand their inverse relationship.
Iterating (Extension of Skip-Counting)	Counting by a fractional amount, such as fourths (1 fourth, 2 fourths, 3 fourths, etc.) or tenths (1 tenth, 2 tenths, etc.). Understanding that a fraction is made of iteration of a unit fraction $\frac{1}{n}$ is key to being able to skip-count by a fraction.	Reasoning strategies often involve counting on or back by fractional parts. Efficiency comes from counting in chunks, which could be counting by wholes and then by parts (e.g., eighths, tenths, hundredths).

COMPUTATIONAL ESTIMATION
. . . .

Computational estimation is finding an approximate answer to a computation problem. Historically students have struggled more to estimate with rational numbers than to actually compute. Here is a classic example from the National Assessment of Educational Progress:

Estimate $\frac{12}{13} + \frac{7}{8}$

a. 1   b. 2   c. 19   d. 21

In this example, only 24% of 13-year-olds estimated correctly, and 55% chose either 19 or 21 (Carpenter et al., 1980). Try this item with your students and see how they do!

Just like exact computation, there are strategies for computational estimation and the use of those strategies should be *flexible*. For addition and subtraction with fractions and decimals, students must understand and be able to flexibly use these three methods:

1. *Rounding*: Flexible rounding means that one or both numbers might be rounded. Students may round to the nearest number or they may round so that one number rounds up and the other one rounds down. Rounding is a well-known strategy but is often approached in a step-by-step manner, which can interfere with the point of estimating—getting a quick idea of what the answer will be close to. Use conceptual language, such as "Which whole number is this closest to?" Help students understand that they aren't always going to use rounding rules. For example, for 24.4 + 34.452, rounding both down to the nearest whole number will give a very low estimate, whereas rounding one up and one down gives a closer estimate.

2. *Front-end estimation*: In its most basic form, students just add or subtract the largest place value. More flexibly, though, students may use the largest two place values or adjust their estimate because of what they notice with the rest of the numbers. Front-end estimation is *quick* and doesn't require rounding. For example, to estimate 7.4 – 3.6, a student subtracts 7 – 3. For 38.7 + 63.5, front-end estimation results in an estimate of 90. A quick look to the right shows there is another 10 there, so a final

adjusted estimate would be 100. For mixed numbers, front-end estimation works like with whole numbers (ignoring the fraction).

3. *Compatible numbers*: In this strategy, students change one or both of the numbers to a nearby number so that the numbers are easy to add or subtract. Compatibles take advantage of making whole numbers or making tens. The beauty of this strategy is its flexibility. For example, in estimating the sum of $2\frac{3}{4} - \frac{7}{8}$, changing one of the fractions to be the same as the other results in an estimate of 2. Consider estimating $34.56 - 18.90$.

WHAT AUTOMATICITIES DO STUDENTS NEED?

Automaticity is the ability to complete a task with little or no attention to process. Little thought, if any, is given to skills that are automatic (Chein & Schneider, 2012). They appear intuitive or reflexive. Automaticities help students select strategies, move between strategies, and carry out a strategy. To begin, automaticity with basic facts warrants special attention. Students must know their facts (i.e., be automatic) and know the strategies that come with basic fact fluency (Bay-Williams & Kling, 2019; O'Connell & SanGiovanni, 2015). These strategies grow into useful strategies for adding and subtracting fractions and decimals, as illustrated in Figure 11.

FIGURE 11 ● How Basic Fact Reasoning Strategies Grow Into Strategies for Fractions and Decimals

REASONING STRATEGY: MAKING 10 [BASIC FACTS] → MAKE TENS (HUNDREDS, ETC.) [WHOLE NUMBERS] → MAKE A WHOLE (TENTHS, ETC.) [FRACTIONS AND DECIMALS].		
Whole Number Examples	**Decimal Examples**	**Fraction Examples**
$8 + 6 = 10 + 4 = 14$ $39 + 28 = 40 + 27$ $395 + 784 = 381 + 800$	$3.9 + 2.8 = 4.0 + 2.7$ $9.7 + 3.5 = 10.0 + 3.2$	$3\frac{3}{4} + 2\frac{1}{2} = 4 + 2\frac{1}{4} = 6\frac{1}{4}$ $\frac{2}{3} + \frac{11}{12} = \frac{8}{12} + \frac{11}{12}$ $= \frac{7}{12} + 1 = 1\frac{7}{12}$
REASONING STRATEGY: PRETEND-A-TEN BECOMES COMPENSATION, IN GENERAL PRETENDING THERE IS ONE WHOLE NUMBER OR MORE AND COMPENSATING.		
Whole Number Example	**Decimal Example**	**Fraction Example**
$39 + 28 \rightarrow 40 + 30$ $\rightarrow 70 - 3 = 67$	$5.7 + 9.8 \rightarrow 6 + 10$ $\rightarrow 16 - 0.5 = 15.5$	$3\frac{4}{5} + 1\frac{4}{5} \rightarrow 4 + 2$ $\rightarrow 6 - \frac{2}{5} = 5\frac{3}{5}$
REASONING STRATEGY: THINK ADDITION BECOMES COUNTING UP, IN GENERAL, FINDING THE DIFFERENCE BETWEEN THE TWO NUMBERS.		
Whole Number Example	**Decimal Example**	**Fraction Example**
$615 - 582 \rightarrow 582$ to 600 (Jump of 18) $\rightarrow 600$ to 615 (Jump of 15) $\rightarrow$ jumps add to 33	$8.9 - 7.5 \rightarrow 7.5$ to 8.5 (Jump of 1.0) $\rightarrow 8.5$ to 8.9 (Jump of 0.4) $\rightarrow$ jumps add to 1.4	$2\frac{3}{8} - 1\frac{7}{8} \rightarrow 1\frac{7}{8}$ to $2\left(\text{Jump of } \frac{1}{8}\right)$ $\rightarrow 2$ to $2\frac{3}{8}\left(\text{Jump of } \frac{3}{8}\right)$ $\rightarrow$ jumps add to $\frac{4}{8}$ *or* $\frac{1}{2}$

REASONING STRATEGY: DOWN UNDER 10 BECOMES COUNTING BACK.		
Whole Number Example	**Decimal Example**	**Fraction Example**
$3{,}450 - 1{,}650 \rightarrow 3{,}450 - 1{,}450$ (to 2,000) $\rightarrow 2000 - 200 = 1{,}800$	$5.2 - 0.8 \rightarrow 5.2 - 0.2$ (to 5) $\rightarrow 5 - 0.6 = 4.4$	$8\frac{1}{4} - 1\frac{3}{8} \rightarrow 8\frac{1}{4} - 1\frac{1}{4}$ (to 7) $\rightarrow 7 - \frac{1}{8} = 6\frac{7}{8}$

REASONING STRATEGY: TAKE FROM 10 BECOMES PARTIAL DIFFERENCES, WITH THE SUBTRAHEND TAKEN FROM THE LARGEST PLACE VALUE. (THIS BLENDS IN COMPENSATION, TOO.)		
Whole Number Example	**Decimal Example**	**Fraction Example**
$52 - 28 \rightarrow 50 - 28 = 22$ $\rightarrow 22 + 2$ $= 24$	$45.6 - 28.0 \rightarrow 40.0 - 28.0 = 12$ $\rightarrow 12.0 + 5.6$ $= 17.6$	$4\frac{1}{8} - 1\frac{3}{8} \rightarrow 4 - 1\frac{3}{8} = 2\frac{5}{8}$ $\rightarrow \frac{1}{8} + 2\frac{5}{8}$ $= 2\frac{6}{8}$ or $2\frac{3}{4}$

There are automaticities beyond the basic facts, skills that students need to be able to do effortlessly so that they can employ reasoning strategies with fractions and decimals. In brief, those automaticities are the following:

- Flexible decomposition
- Combinations that equal 1 (base-10 combinations)
- Fraction and decimal benchmarks
- Estimating the location of fractions and decimals on a number line
- Multiples and factors
- Equivalencies of one-half
- Common fraction equivalencies

See Chapter 5 (pp. 107– 129) of *Figuring Out Fluency* for more about automaticities for fluency.

Moving these critical skills to automaticity means providing significant and meaningful practice. That is the focus of Module 1. These automaticities, including basic facts, are not prerequisites for strategy instruction, but they do support using strategies and algorithms (and conversely, using strategies strengthens these automaticities).

TEACHING TAKEAWAY

Automaticities, including basic facts, are not prerequisites for strategy instruction, but they do support using strategies and algorithms.

WHAT ARE THE SIGNIFICANT STRATEGIES FOR ADDING AND SUBTRACTING FRACTIONS AND DECIMALS?

Teaching strategies beyond the standard algorithms is necessary for fluency, yet these unfamiliar methods can lead to pushback from families and other stakeholders. Two questions require solid responses:

1. Why do students need strategies when they can use the standard algorithm?

One way to quickly respond to this question is to share an example for which the standard algorithm takes much more time than an alternative.

For example, 5.9 + 12.6 or $11\frac{1}{8} - 10\frac{5}{8}$. Why learn other methods? Because many problems can be solved more efficiently another way. Fluent students look for the most efficient method.

2. What strategies are worthy of attention?

Let's just take some pressure off here. The list is short, and we must help students see that they are not necessarily learning a new strategy, but they are applying a strategy they learned with basic facts and transferring it to other numbers. In *Figuring Out Fluency*, we propose Seven Significant Strategies. Of these, five relate to adding and/or subtracting with fractions and decimals, and they are listed in Figure 12.

FIGURE 12 ● Reasoning Strategies for Adding and Subtracting Fractions and Decimals

REASONING STRATEGIES	RELEVANT OPERATIONS
1. Count On/Count Back (Module 2)	Addition and Subtraction
2. Make a Whole (Module 3)	Addition
3. Think Addition (Module 4)	Subtraction
4. Compensation (Module 5)	Addition and Subtraction
5. Partial Sums and Differences (Module 6)	Addition and Subtraction

Representations are not strategies! Using base-10 pieces, fraction circles, Cuisenaire rods, or a number line are ways to represent ones' thinking. The thinking is the strategy. For example, if a student subtracts on a number line, they may be using a Count Back strategy or a Compensation strategy, among others. When a student says, "I used a number line," ask *how* they used it—then you will learn what strategy they used.

Teaching for fluency means that each of these strategies is explicitly taught to students. This is an issue of access. We teach students to *use* the strategy, and then we give students many opportunities to engage in *choosing* strategies (Part 3 of this book). Explicitly teaching a strategy does not mean turning the strategy into an algorithm. Strategies require flexible thinking. Each module provides instructional ideas and practice to ensure students become adept at using each strategy flexibly. There is also a module on algorithms (Module 7) so that they are integrated into the use of strategies.

HOW DO I USE THE PART 2 MODULES TO TEACH, PRACTICE, AND ASSESS STRATEGIES?

Part 2 is a set of modules, each one focused on understanding why a specific reasoning strategy works and learning how to use it well. The first module has its own style, as it provides activities to support conceptual foundations and automaticities to set students up for success with the other modules. The remaining modules have a consistent format, described in brief here.

EXPLICIT STRATEGY INSTRUCTION

Each module begins with an overview that explains the strategy, why it works, and when it is a good option. These are written to you, the teacher. Next is a series of strategy briefs, shorter strategy overviews written for families. Either the overview or the brief can also be shared with students for their reference.

Each module provides approximately five instructional activities. Any one of these activities might form the focus of a lesson or series of lessons. These activities focus on making sense of the strategy and lend to opportunities for small group interactions. After students engage in the activities, a summarizing conversation can focus on why the strategy works and when it is useful.

The final instructional activity in each module is a collection of discourse prompts that can be used for a summarizing conversation, as a classroom activity in and of itself, or as an assessment.

QUALITY PRACTICE

It takes practice to become proficient at enacting a strategy or algorithm. Students need access to quality practice that is not a worksheet. Quality practice is focused on a strategy, varied in type of engagement, processed by the student to make sense of what they did, and connected to what they are learning. Each module provides four types of quality practice: (1) worked examples, (2) routines, (3) games, and (4) centers.

See Chapter 6 (pp. 130–153) of *Figuring Out Fluency* for more about quality practice.

Each practice section begins with **worked examples**. Worked examples are opportunities for students to attend to the thinking involved with a strategy, without solving the problem themselves. We feature three types to get at all components of fluency:

1. *Correctly worked example*: efficiency (selects an appropriate strategy) and flexibility (applies strategy to a new problem type)

2. *Partially worked example*: efficiency (selects an appropriate strategy) and accuracy (completes steps accurately; gets correct answer)

3. *Incorrectly worked example*: accuracy (completes steps accurately; gets correct answer)

Also, comparing two correctly worked examples is very effective in helping students learn to choose efficient methods. Throughout the modules are dozens of examples, any of which can be used as worked examples (and adapted to other similar worked examples). Your worked examples can be from a fictional "student" or be authentic student work. Some of the prompts from teaching the strategy section are, in fact, worked examples.

The remaining practice activities include routines, games, and centers. Each activity provides a brief "About the Activity" statement to help you quickly match what your students need with a meaningful activity. General resources, including number cards, mini ten-frame cards, addition charts, and more, are also available for download on the companion website.

Collectively, these four ways to practice provide ongoing opportunities for students to practice strategies even when your focus lesson is on a different topic. Routines and games allow for discussions and peer interactions, while centers provide individual, independent think time. Ongoing, engaging practice of strategies is necessary for students to truly become fluent in adding and subtracting fractions and decimals.

ASSESSING STRATEGY USE

As you have just read, each module offers a collection of instructional and practice activities. As students are engaged in these activities, you can be assessing the extent to which they are able to apply the selected strategy. **Observation tools** help you keep track of where each student is at and monitor their progress. An observation tool can be simple, such as a class list with an extra column. Your observations can be codes:

+ Is regularly implementing the strategy adeptly

✔ Understands the strategy, takes time to think it through

− Is not implementing the strategy accurately

A note-taking observation tool provides space for you to insert notes about how a student is doing (see Figure 13). You can laminate the tool and use dry-erase markers to update as needed, use sticky notes, or just write in the boxes.

FIGURE 13 ● Example Note-Taking Observation Tool

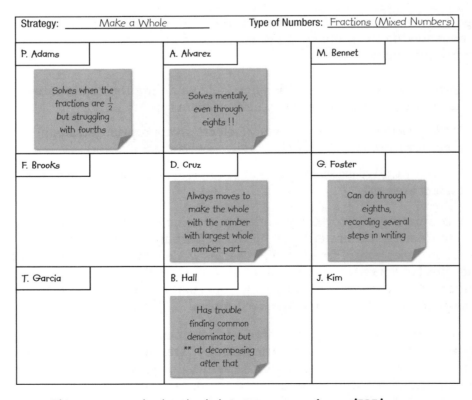

 This resource can be downloaded at **resources.corwin.com/FOF/ addsubtractdecimalfraction**.

Some days, you collect data on some students; other days, you collect data on other students. The data can help in classroom discussions and in planning for instructional next steps.

Journal prompts provide an opportunity for students to write about their thinking process. Each module provides a collection of prompts that you might use for journaling. You can modify those or craft your own. The prompt can specifically ask students to explain how they used the strategy:

> **Explain and show how you can use Make a Whole to solve this problem: 6.8 + 1.53**

Or a prompt can focus on identifying when that strategy is a good idea:

> **Circle the problems that lend themselves to the Make a Whole strategy. When you are finished, explain how you decide when to use this strategy:**
>
> Set 1: $1\frac{5}{8}+\frac{7}{8}$ $2\frac{3}{4}+1\frac{1}{5}$ $3\frac{7}{9}+1\frac{1}{3}$ $4\frac{2}{3}+1\frac{1}{4}$
>
> Set 2: 8.6 + 1.45   0.55 + 0.08   5.35 + 6.95   7.9 + 2.98

Interviewing is an excellent way to really understand student thinking. You can pick any problem that lends to the strategy you are working on and write it on a notecard (or record two or three on separate notecards). While students are engaged in an instructional or practice activity, you can have students come to you one-by-one or, in the case of short interviews, you can do a quick check at their desk. Have task(s) ready on cards, show the student the problem, and ask them (1) to solve it and (2) explain how they thought about it. You can pair this with an observation tool to keep track of how each student is progressing. If you ask eight students to solve the same problem, you can gain valuable formative assessment data (and if you want to gather data on every student, you can continue to interview on subsequent days).

HOW DO I USE PART 3 TO SUPPORT STUDENTS' FLUENCY?

As soon as students know more than one way, it is time to integrate routines, tasks, centers, and games that focus on choosing when to use a strategy. That is where Part 3 comes in. As you read in Fluency Action 1, students need to be able to choose efficient strategies. The strategy modules provide students *access* to those strategies, ensuring the strategies make sense and giving students ample opportunities to practice those strategies and become adept at using them. However, if you stop there, students are left on their own when it comes to choosing which strategy to use when. It is like having a set of knives in the kitchen but not knowing which ones to use for slicing cheese or bread, cutting meat, or chopping vegetables. Like with food, some items can be cut with various knives, but other food really needs a specific knife.

Do not wait until after all strategies are learned to focus on when to use a strategy—instead weave in Part 3 activities regularly. Each time a new strategy is learned, it is time to revisit activities that engage students in making choices from among the strategies in their repertoire. Students must learn what to look for in a problem to decide which strategy they will use to solve the problem *efficiently* based on the numbers in the problem. This is *flexibility* in action and thus leads to fluency.

IN SUM, MAKING A DIFFERENCE

Part 1 has briefly described ideas that make a difference in developing fluency, and these ideas are important as you implement activities from the modules. We sum up Part 1 with these key takeaways:

1. Be clear on what fluency means (three components and six actions). This includes communicating the full meaning to students and their parents.

2. Attend to readiness skills: conceptual understanding, properties, computational estimation, and automaticities (see Module 1).

3. Reinforce student reasoning, rather than focus on speed and accuracy. Getting the strategies down initially takes more time but eventually will become more efficient.

4. Help students connect the features of a sum or difference to strategies. In other words, help them determine when to choose a strategy.

5. Assess fluency, not just accuracy.

Time invested in strategy work has big payoffs—confident and fluent students! That is why we have so many activities in this book. Teach the strategies as part of core instruction, *and* continue to practice throughout the year, looping back to strategies that students might be forgetting to use (with Part 2 activities) and offering ongoing opportunities to choose from among strategies (with Part 3 activities).

PART 2

STRATEGY MODULES

Foundations for Reasoning Strategies

OVERVIEW: Foundations for Strategies

See Chapter 3 (pp. 47–75) of *Figuring Out Fluency* for more about good beginnings and utilities.

Students' fluency with fractions and decimals is built on a foundation of conceptual understanding (National Council of Teachers of Mathematics, 2014). In addition to conceptual understanding, good beginnings include "utilities"—skills that students use when adding or subtracting fractions and decimals, such as knowing how far 0.8 is from 1.0 and, of course, the properties of the operations. Specific to adding and subtracting fractions and decimals, this module attends to these foundational skills:

- Flexible decomposition

- Combinations that equal 1 (base-10 combinations)

- Fraction and decimal benchmarks

- Estimating the location of fractions and decimals on a number line

- Multiples and factors

- Equivalencies of one-half

- Common fraction equivalencies

See Chapter 5 (pp 107–129) of *Figuring Out Fluency* for more about automaticities.

Some skills, such as identifying fractions equivalent to half, will become automatic for students over time (i.e., automaticities). Being able to work with these skillfully and efficiently greatly supports students' learning of the fluency strategies in the upcoming modules. But these skills are *not* to be gatekeepers. Ongoing experiences with these skills coincide with strategy instruction. They support each other. However, if a student is struggling with equivalencies for $\frac{1}{2}$, for example, additional experiences in becoming adept or automatic with this skill will be very helpful to their overall fluency with addition and subtraction.

TEACHING UTILITIES AND AUTOMATICITIES

Initial conceptual development, while critical, is not the focus of this book. Based on a student's conceptual knowledge, this module focuses on developing utilities and automaticities that will support the significant reasoning strategies in Modules 2 through 6 and the standard algorithms in Module 7. This module is a collection of activities for you to provide multiple, meaningful experiences to practice foundational skills. You can schedule practice with these weekly or biweekly.

REVISITING UTILITIES AND AUTOMATICITIES

Not being able to adeptly use properties and other foundational skills can interfere with using strategies. Thus, when you notice students are having difficulty with a skill needed to enact a strategy (e.g., breaking apart decimals or finding equivalent fractions), use related activities in this module to make sense of and practice that skill. In addition, these activities can serve as an introductory activity to a strategy.

VERSATILITY

Students develop skills in different ways and at different paces. Most of the routines, games, and centers in this module can be learning centers or a choice activity. Many of these activities can grow into ones that involve the reasoning strategies, and conversely, many activities in later modules can be easily modified to feature these utilities. It may be most important to remember that the idea here is to provide opportunity and exposure or, in other words, quality practice. So when students engage with these activities, make sure that the tenets of quality practice are in place.

See Chapter 6 (pp. 130– 153) of *Figuring Out Fluency* for more about quality practice.

REFLECTING

Students need opportunities to process what they learned within an activity through discussion or a writing reflection. Parts 1 and 3 offer assessment ideas, such as journal writing prompts. Being explicit about the importance of understanding and using these skills sets students up for self-reflection: What skills am I adept at? Which ones do I still struggle to use? What do I need to do to become better at ____ skill?

NOTES

_____

_____

_____

_____

_____

_____

_____

MODULE 1 Foundations for Reasoning Strategies

MODULE 2 Count On/Count Back Strategy

MODULE 3 Make a Whole Strategy

MODULE 4 Think Addition Strategy

MODULE 5 Compensation Strategy

MODULE 6 Partial Sums and Differences Strategy

MODULE 7 Standard Algorithms

FLEXIBLE DECOMPOSITION

Decomposing numbers flexibly and with automaticity helps students select and carry out a strategy. Applying this skill to decimals and fractions is grounded in whole-number understanding of composition and decomposition. It begins with being able to readily decompose any number through 10, which includes breaking the number into more than two parts. It develops into breaking apart numbers by place value and eventually decomposing any number in a variety of ways. Because of this, many decomposition activities from primary grades can be easily modified to work with decimals and fractions. In fact, to build on students' experiences, you can do an activity with whole numbers first and then repeat the activity with fractions or decimals. This can help students transfer their thinking to the new number type.

ACTIVITY 1.1

Name: "The Find"   **Type:** Routine

About the Routine: "The Find" is an interactive, engaging way to discuss decomposition with other students. After finding their own way to decompose a number, students stand up and try to find a partner who decomposed the number in the same way. The benefit is that while students mingling with other students, they are exposed to a variety of ways that the number might have been decomposed.

Materials: sticky notes

Directions:
1. Give students a number to decompose, such as $3\frac{3}{4}$, and a direction for how they should decompose the number (e.g., decompose it into two numbers greater than 1).

2. Students decompose the number and record each of their numbers on different sticky notes. For $3\frac{3}{4}$, a student might use $2\frac{2}{4}$ and $1\frac{1}{4}$.

3. At the signal, students walk around the room and try to find a partner that made the same decomposition. When they find a partner, they sit down.

4. After time is called for finding a partner, the class is brought together to share matching decompositions and share some ways that others decomposed the number (without matches). During this discussion, it is wise to spotlight convenient or useful decompositions as well as the patterns within decompositions.

5. The process can be repeated, as time permits, with the same or a different number.

As a way to encourage less familiar ways to decompose, this activity can be adapted so that students find others with their same method, forming small groups that have the same decomposition. The number of students in the group is the score for that number. The lowest score wins.

ACTIVITY 1.2

Name: "Express It"　　　　　　　　　　**Type:** Routine

About the Routine: When students are skilled in manipulating numbers, they can do so in seemingly endless ways. When students are asked to show only one or two ways to break apart a number, they may only decompose by place value rather than think more flexibly about their options. "Express It" (SanGiovanni, 2019) develops students' capacity to decompose numbers flexibly. Over several days, students are pressed to find yet more unique ways to decompose a number.

Materials: student journals, chart paper

Directions:　1. Pose a number to students, like 53.75.

2. Students work to express the number in as many ways as possible in their journal.

3. After a minute or so, stop students and have them share their decompositions with a partner.

4. Solicit and record a handful of ideas from the class on the chart paper, ending the routine.

5. On day 2, ask students to decompose the same number (53.75) in new ways that don't appear in their journal already and don't appear on the chart paper from the day before.

6. Give students time to share with a partner before recording new ideas on the chart.

7. Repeat the routine for a third day before moving to a new number.

This routine can be adapted so that the three opportunities to express the number occur within the same day, as a full lesson focused on decomposing (and composing) decimals and/or fractions. In the following, the left image shows how the teacher recorded different expressions for 53.75 over the course of the first two days. The right image shows how "Express It" can be used with fractions.

53.75		
Day 1	Day 2	Day 3
53.00 + 0.75	52.50 + 1.25	
52.00 + 1.75	52.25 + 1.50	
51.00 + 2.75	46.50 + 7.25	
54.00 − 0.25	60 − 6.25	
55.00 − 1.25	63.75 − 10	
	73.75 - 20	

$3\frac{6}{8}$		
Day 1	Day 2	Day 3
$3 + \frac{6}{8}$	$4 - \frac{2}{8}$	
$1\frac{3}{8} + 2\frac{3}{8}$	$6 - 2\frac{2}{8}$	
$2\frac{7}{8} + \frac{7}{8}$	$4\frac{1}{8} - \frac{3}{8}$	
$3 + \frac{1}{8} + \frac{3}{8} + \frac{2}{8}$	$6 - 2\frac{1}{4}$	

ACTIVITY 1.3

Name: Math Chatter   **Type:** Game

About the Game: *Math Chatter* is a take on the old game show *$20,000 Pyramid* or the current board game *Hedbanz*. In this routine, one student faces the board and their partner faces away from it. The student facing the board gives clues about each number in a list so that their partner can guess each number. The twist is that each clue must be a decomposition of the given number. You can choose to put restrictions on the clues requiring students to avoid place value or clues like "one more than" or "one less than."

Materials: Prepare a list of fractions or decimals.

Directions:
1. Have students stand and determine who will be giving clues and who will be guessing.

2. Share any restrictions you have for clues. For example, "You cannot use a decomposition that is the whole number and the fraction/decimal part. In other words, for $3\frac{1}{2}$ you cannot give 3 and $\frac{1}{2}$." Here is another example for decimals: "No place value decompositions. For example, for 4.25, you cannot give 4 and 0.25 or 3 and 1.25."

3. Reveal the list of numbers to be identified.

4. When a partner gets through the list, they sit down.

5. After all groups are seated, solicit different examples of decompositions that were used by partner groups.

   The following table illustrates examples of fractions and decimals with example clues a student might give.

LIST OF FRACTIONS	EXAMPLES OF CLUES	LIST OF DECIMALS	EXAMPLES OF CLUES
$3\frac{1}{2}$	$2\frac{1}{4}$ and $1\frac{1}{4}$	4.25	3.5 and 0.75
$4\frac{3}{4}$	$2\frac{1}{2}$ and $2\frac{1}{4}$	7.3	4.1 and 3.2
$1\frac{7}{8}$	$1\frac{3}{8}$ and $\frac{4}{8}$	8.66	4.33 and 4.33
$2\frac{9}{10}$	$1\frac{5}{10}$ and $1\frac{4}{10}$	12.04	10.02 and 2.02

COMBINATIONS THAT EQUAL 1 (BASE-10 COMBINATIONS)

Recognizing combinations that equal 1 is necessary for most of the strategies in this book, in particular the Make a Whole strategy. In kindergarten and first grade, students work with combinations of 10. They build on that idea by finding combinations of 100 and 1,000 as they work with adding and subtracting whole numbers. You can extend this understanding to helping students see combinations of 1 (0.3 + 0.7 or 0.64 + 0.36) or even combinations of 0.1 (0.03 + 0.07). And, of course, combinations of 1 are applicable to working with fractions (e.g., $\frac{1}{4} + \frac{3}{4}$). Fraction combinations might be extended to combinations of unlike fractions for common fractions such as halves, fourths, and eighths (e.g., $\frac{4}{8} + \frac{2}{4}$).

ACTIVITY 1.4

Name: Take Ten   **Type:** Game

About the Game: *Take Ten* is a game for practicing making 1 with combinations of hundredths. It can easily be modified for making 10 with combinations of tenths using a decimal chart with tenths. Here the game is described for two players, but three players can also play (10 more of a different color cube is needed).

Materials: *Take Ten* game board; digit cards (0–9) or playing cards (queens = 0 and aces = 1; remove tens, kings, and jacks); 20 centimeter cubes (or similar objects), 10 each in two different colors for each player

Directions: 1. Each player places 10 cubes anywhere on the *Take Ten* game board.

2. Players then take turns generating two digits to make hundredths. (.__ __)

3. If the number they make combines with a number covered by one of the pieces on the game board to equal 1, they remove the piece. If it doesn't, they lose their turn.

4. The first player to remove 10 game pieces (placed by them or their opponent) wins.

In the following example, Player 1 generates a 5 and a 7. They could make 0.57 or 0.75. The player notes that 0.57 combines with 0.43 to make 1, but they have no counter on 0.43. She then tries 0.75 and notices she has a counter on 0.25 and removes it.

(Continued)

Take Ten

Directions: Each player places ten game pieces on the board. Take turns making hundredths. If the hundredth you make combines to make 1 with a hundredth covered, remove the piece. The first player to remove ten pieces wins.

0.01	0.02	0.03	0.04	0.05	0.06	0.07	0.08	0.09	0.10
0.11	□	0.13	0.14	0.15	0.16	□	0.18	□	0.20
0.21	0.22	0.23	□	□	0.26	0.27	□	0.29	□
0.31	□	0.33	0.34	□	0.36	0.37	□	0.39	0.40
0.41	0.42	□	0.44	0.45	0.46	0.47	0.48	0.49	0.50
□	0.52	□	0.54	0.55	□	0.57	0.58	□	0.60
0.61	□	0.63	0.64	0.65	0.66	□	0.68	0.69	0.70
0.71	0.72	0.73	0.74	0.75	0.76	0.77	□	0.79	0.80
0.81	0.82	□	0.84	0.85	0.86	□	0.88	0.89	0.90
0.91	0.92	0.93	0.94	0.95	0.96	0.97	0.98	0.99	1.00

Take Ten also works with fractions. Each player places 10 game pieces anywhere on the game board. Players take turns rolling two digits to make a fraction. For example, a 2 and a 3 would make $\frac{2}{3}$ and the player would remove $\frac{1}{3}$ from the game board because the two make a whole.

Take Ten

Directions: Each player places ten game pieces on the board. Take turns making fractions. If the fraction you make combines to make one whole a fraction covered, remove the piece. The first player to remove ten pieces wins.

$\frac{1}{2}$	$\frac{1}{3}$	$\frac{2}{3}$	$\frac{1}{4}$	$\frac{2}{4}$	$\frac{3}{4}$	$\frac{1}{5}$	$\frac{2}{5}$
$\frac{3}{5}$	$\frac{4}{5}$ □	$\frac{1}{6}$	$\frac{2}{6}$ □	$\frac{3}{6}$ □	$\frac{4}{6}$	$\frac{5}{6}$ □	$\frac{1}{8}$ □
$\frac{2}{8}$	$\frac{3}{8}$ □	$\frac{4}{8}$ □	$\frac{5}{8}$	$\frac{6}{8}$ □	$\frac{7}{8}$	$\frac{1}{10}$	$\frac{1}{10}$ □
$\frac{2}{10}$ □	$\frac{3}{10}$	$\frac{4}{10}$ □	$\frac{5}{10}$	$\frac{6}{10}$	$\frac{7}{10}$	$\frac{8}{10}$ □	$\frac{9}{10}$
$\frac{1}{2}$	$\frac{1}{3}$ □	$\frac{2}{3}$	$\frac{1}{4}$	$\frac{2}{4}$	$\frac{3}{4}$ □	$\frac{1}{5}$ □	$\frac{2}{5}$ □
$\frac{3}{5}$	$\frac{4}{5}$	$\frac{1}{6}$ □	$\frac{2}{6}$	$\frac{3}{6}$	$\frac{4}{6}$ □	$\frac{5}{6}$ □	$\frac{1}{8}$
$\frac{2}{8}$	$\frac{3}{8}$	$\frac{4}{8}$ □	$\frac{5}{8}$	$\frac{6}{8}$	$\frac{7}{8}$	$\frac{1}{10}$	$\frac{1}{10}$
$\frac{2}{10}$	$\frac{3}{10}$	$\frac{4}{10}$	$\frac{5}{10}$ □	$\frac{6}{10}$	$\frac{7}{10}$	$\frac{8}{10}$	$\frac{9}{10}$

ACTIVITY 1.5

Name: Closer To . . . 0 or 1?　　　　　　　　　　**Type:** Game

About the Game: *Closer To . . .* is a game that practices making combinations of 1. This game also involves comparisons and estimation as students try to construct numbers closer to the goal than their opponent.

Materials: *Closer To . . .* cards; two decks of digit cards (0–9) or playing cards (queens = 0 and aces = 1; remove tens, kings, and jacks)

Directions:　1. Players are each dealt two cards.

2. Player 1 flips over a *Closer To . . .* card.

3. Each player makes a two-digit number with hundredths (e.g., 0.58), trying to be the closest to the goal on the *Closer To . . .* card (0 or 1).

4. Each player shares how far away they are from the *Closer To . . .* card. The player closest to the benchmark on the card wins the card.

5. The first player to get seven *Closer To . . .* cards wins the game.

In the fraction version of the game, players draw three cards and use two or three of them to form a fraction that is closest to the *Closer To . . .* card. The player who is closest to the benchmark on the card wins the card.

Closer to 0	Closer to 0	Closer to 1	Closer to 1
Closer to 0	Closer to 0	Closer to 1	Closer to 1
Closer to 0	Closer to 0	Closer to 1	Closer to 1
Closer to 0	Closer to 0	Closer to 1	Closer to 1
Closer to 0	Closer to 0	Closer to 1	Closer to 1

online resources 🔎　This resource can be downloaded at **resources.corwin.com/FOF/addsubtractdecimalfraction**.

FRACTION AND DECIMAL BENCHMARKS

Knowing the relative size of fractions (and decimals) and using benchmarks enables one to estimate for determining reasonableness and contributes to using the Compensation or the Make a Whole strategy. Benchmarks are common values. For fractions, $\frac{1}{2}$ is a major benchmark, yet students struggle with understanding the relative size of fractions. Take a look at the National Assessment of Educational Progress (2019) Grade 4 released assessment item pictured here. What percentage of students were successful on this item?

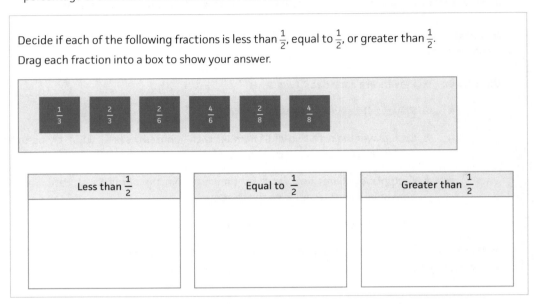

Source: National Assessment of Educational Progress. (2019). *NAEP Report Card: Mathematics.* https://www.nationsreportcard.gov/mathematics/sample-questions/?grade=4.

About half of students (48%) were not able to solve this problem at all, and only a third (32%) could complete it correctly. The implication is that students need more experiences estimating and using fraction benchmarks. Students need to understand the benchmark of $\frac{1}{2}$ in order to estimate and establish reasonableness. Over time, students can also use other benchmarks, such as $\frac{1}{4}$ and $\frac{3}{4}$ or perhaps even thirds or eighths. Decimal benchmarks, in parallel, include 0.5 and eventually 0.25 and 0.75.

ACTIVITY 1.6

Name: High/Low   **Type:** Game

About the Game: *High/Low* is a game for practicing comparison of fractions and reasoning about fractions as numbers. The game is a take on an old card game in which players determine if the next card in the deck will be higher or lower than the card showing. This version is played with fraction cards and the goal is to get seven correct predictions in a row.

Materials: deck of fraction cards (Use our downloadable ones or make your own with index cards. Just use a wide variety of numerators and denominators such as $\frac{8}{15}$, $\frac{3}{10}$, $\frac{5}{6}$, $\frac{19}{20}$, etc.)

Directions: 1. Shuffle a set of fraction cards.

2. Players flip over the first card and predict if the next card will be more or less (higher or lower) than the facing card.

3. The card is flipped. If correct, the players determine if the next card will be more or less than the second card. If incorrect, the cards are shuffled and the game begins again. (If the player is not sure, they can check with a calculator, but first they should use benchmarks to decide.)

4. The goal is to get seven cards in a row correct.

In the following example, the player has three correct in a row. They predict the next card will be less because $\frac{8}{15}$ is a little more than half.

$\frac{19}{20}$	$\frac{1}{9}$	$\frac{3}{7}$	$\frac{8}{15}$	

RESOURCE(S) FOR THIS ACTIVITY

$\frac{1}{9}$	$\frac{2}{3}$	$\frac{6}{7}$	$\frac{7}{12}$	$\frac{?}{?}$	$\frac{?}{?}$
$\frac{3}{7}$	$\frac{4}{5}$	$\frac{9}{10}$	$\frac{19}{20}$	$\frac{?}{?}$	$\frac{?}{?}$
$\frac{1}{5}$	$\frac{1}{11}$	$\frac{12}{13}$	$\frac{8}{20}$	$\frac{?}{?}$	$\frac{?}{?}$
$\frac{2}{6}$	$\frac{8}{15}$	$\frac{6}{9}$	$\frac{6}{12}$	$\frac{?}{?}$	$\frac{?}{?}$
$\frac{4}{9}$	$\frac{5}{10}$	$\frac{3}{4}$	$\frac{1}{3}$	$\frac{?}{?}$	$\frac{?}{?}$

ACTIVITY 1.7

Name: Three Close Covers   **Type:** Game

About the Game: *Three Close Covers* is a game for practicing with benchmarks. It can be played with fractions or decimals.

Materials: *Three Close Covers* game board; two sets of digit cards (1–9) or playing cards (aces = 1; remove tens and face cards); two-color counters or multicolored cubes for game pieces (a different color for each player)

Directions:

1. Players take turns generating a fraction (or decimal) with their cards, placing the smaller of the two numbers as the numerator (unless the digits are the same).

2. The player determines the fraction to be close to 0, $\frac{1}{2}$, or 1. The player places a game piece on a space on the game board that matches. The opponent can check their answer with a calculator if they disagree.

3. Players try to make their own three-in-a-row while also trying to block their opponent.

4. The first player to get 3 three-in-a-rows (horizontal, vertical, diagonal) wins.

Three Close Covers

Directions: Take turns making a fraction or decimal. Determine if the number you make is close to 0, ½, or 1. Place a game piece on a spave that matches. Be the first player to get three-in-a-row, three times.

Close to 0	Close to $\frac{1}{2}$	Close to 1	Close to 0	Close to $\frac{1}{2}$	Close to 1	Close to 1
Close to 1	Close to $\frac{1}{2}$	Close to $\frac{1}{2}$	Close to $\frac{1}{2}$	Close to 0	Close to $\frac{1}{2}$	Close to 1
Close to $\frac{1}{2}$	Close to 1	Close to 0	Close to $\frac{1}{2}$	Close to 1	Close to 0	Close to $\frac{1}{2}$
Close to 0	Close to $\frac{1}{2}$	Close to 1	Close to 0	Close to $\frac{1}{2}$	Close to 1	Close to 0
Close to 1	Close to 0	Close to $\frac{1}{2}$	Close to 1	Close to 0	Close to $\frac{1}{2}$	Close to 1
Close to $\frac{1}{2}$	Close to 1	Close to 0	Close to $\frac{1}{2}$	Close to 1	Close to 0	Close to $\frac{1}{2}$
Close to 0	Close to $\frac{1}{2}$	Close to 1	Close to 0	Close to $\frac{1}{2}$	Close to 1	Close to 0

In the example, player 1 (orange) went first, making $\frac{1}{9}$. The player said that $\frac{1}{9}$ is closer to 0 and placed their piece on a "Close to 0" space. Player 2 (gray) made $\frac{3}{5}$ and said it was close to half, putting their piece on a corresponding space on the game board.

online resources 🔍 This resource can be downloaded at **resources.corwin.com/FOF/addsubtractdecimalfraction.**

ESTIMATING THE LOCATION OF FRACTIONS AND DECIMALS ON A NUMBER LINE

The benefit of being able to estimate the locations of fractions and decimals on a number line is twofold. First, students who estimate the location of fractions and decimals on a number line are more successful with computation (Deliyianni et al., 2016; Fuchs et al., 2021; Siegler et al., 2010). Second, the number line is a very useful tool in enacting significant reasoning strategies, such as Count On/Count Back and Think Addition.

ACTIVITY 1.8

Name: "Guess My Point"   **Type:** Routine

About the Routine: In "Guess My Point," the class works together to identify up to three points on a number line. As described here, this routine focuses on common fractions (halves, fourths, eighths, thirds, sixths). To implement this routine with decimals, use common decimal values like tenths (0.1, 0.2, etc.) and fourths (0.25). Share with students that the mystery value is a common fraction (or decimal).

Materials: There are no materials required for this routine.

Directions:
1. The teacher identifies a common fraction, writes it on a sticky note or small whiteboard, and keeps it hidden.

2. The teacher shows an open number line (showing only whole number values such as 0 and 1) with their mystery point marked.

3. Students think–pair–share what fraction they think the point might represent and why.

4. After a few moments, the whole group shares what they think the fraction might be.

5. The teacher records guesses and then asks students to select their top three (and why).

6. The teacher reveals the sticky note to see if one of the three guesses is correct.

7. That point on the number line is labeled.

8. Repeat steps 1–6 with a new point (leaving the original labeled point).

9. Repeat a third or fourth time, as time allows.

In the following example, the teacher started with $\frac{1}{3}$ (left image). After students successfully identified it, the teacher moved to $\frac{1}{2}$, leaving $\frac{1}{3}$ on the number line (middle example). Then the third prompt was given with the previously identified fractions on the number line (right example).

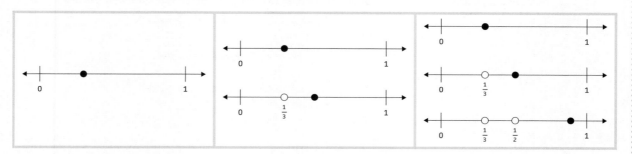

ACTIVITY 1.9

Name: "The Dynamic Number Line"   **Type:** Routine

About the Routine: A number's position on a number line is dynamic. It changes as the endpoints on the number line change. This routine is an opportunity to deepen students' understanding of the relationship between numbers through number lines. Early use with this routine may call for using just two number lines instead of three. "The Dynamic Number Line" works well with fractions or decimals.

Materials: There are no materials needed for this routine.

Directions:

1. The teacher posts a number line with given endpoints and a point on the number line.

2. With partners, students discuss what value the point represents.

3. The class discusses their ideas and comes to an agreement.

4. The teacher draws a second number line directly below the first number line with a point placed at the same location as the original number line. This second number line has *new* endpoints, but the point is in the same location on the line.

5. Students (a) determine the value of the point on this second number line and then (b) identify where the value from the first number line belongs on this second line.

6. The teacher draws a third number line with yet another change in the endpoints.

7. Students (a) determine the value of the point on this third number line and then (b) identify where the values from the first two number lines belong on this third line.

In this example, the first line has endpoints of 0 and 1. Students determine that the point represents $\frac{3}{4}$.

Then another number line is drawn right below it with the unknown in approximately the same location and new endpoints of 0 and 2. The students decide that the point of the second number line now has a value of $1\frac{1}{3}$ and then they locate $\frac{3}{4}$ a little less than halfway between the endpoints (marked with an X).

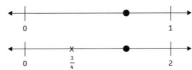

A third number line is presented with an unknown placed in a similar location and endpoints of 0 and $1\frac{1}{2}$. Students estimate the value of the new unknown point to be about 1. They then determine where $\frac{3}{4}$ (the point from the first number line) and $1\frac{1}{3}$ (from the second number line) would be placed on this third number line.

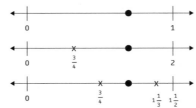

MULTIPLES AND FACTORS

Recognizing multiples and factors is useful for many skills in mathematics, including adding and subtracting fractions. With adding and subtracting fractions, knowing multiples and factors is helpful in finding common denominators and simplifying fractions. Quality practice uses known facts, patterns, and relationships to help students reason about common denominators (rather than rote processes for finding common factors or multiples). Because the focus of this section is on readiness for fraction addition, the multiples used in the following examples are within 100.

ACTIVITY 1.10

Name: "The Stand" (Factors and Multiples)   **Type:** Routine

About the Routine: "The Stand" is a whole-class routine or game to practice multiples or factors. It plays out like the iconic television show *Survivor*. Students who meet conditions "survive" the round, but those who don't may be better positioned to win in the long run.

Materials: one deck of digit cards (0–9) or playing cards (queens = 0 and aces = 1; remove tens, kings, and jacks) for each student

Directions:
1. The leader (teacher or a selected student) asks all students to stand and announces a factor (e.g., 4).

2. Each student deals themselves three digit cards and attempts to make a multiple of the called number (in this case, 4).

3. Using a random way to call on students, the leader calls on a student. Here are the stakes:
   - If the student did not make a multiple of 4, they sit down (temporarily).
   - If the student did form a multiple of 4, they remain standing.

4. All students discard their three cards.

5. The leader again identifies a factor (e.g., 5) and students (both sitting and standing) draw three cards and try to form a multiple (of 5). The stakes above apply and this "new rule" can be used:
   - If a sitting student is selected and they have a multiple of 5, they stand back up *and* pick three students (or randomly draw three names) to sit down.
6. Repeat with new factors and/or new cards until only one student is left standing—the survivor of "The Stand."

ACTIVITY 1.11

Name: The Connects   **Type:** Game

About the Game: *The Connects* is an engaging game for students to practice finding multiples. It is played something like the classic board game *Boggle* as students find examples by connecting digits.

Materials: *The Connects* game board (one per player); digit cards (4–9) or playing cards (remove twos, threes, tens, aces, and face cards); paper for recording solutions

Directions: 1. Players fill out a game board by randomly placing digits in each grid as shown in the example.

2. One player flips a digit card to identify a factor (e.g., 6).

3. Both players look for multiples of that factor on their *Connects* game board. The digits must be connected horizontally, vertically, or diagonally, but direction does not matter.

4. Players get 1 point for each multiple they find. They record their equations in their journal (e.g., 6 × 5 = 30).

5. The first player to reach a set goal (e.g., 10 points) or to have the most when time is up wins.

For example, 6 was the digit card flipped. On this game board, the player found 30 (going down), 132 (making an L), 48 (diagonally), and 54 (backward horizontally).

The Connects

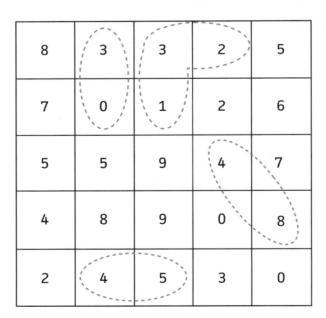

To work with two-digit factors, just name a factor for which it is useful for students to explore multiples (e.g., 10, 12, 15, 20, or 25) after students have created their game boards and play in the same way.

 The Connects game board can be downloaded at **resources.corwin.com/FOF/ addsubtractdecimalfraction**.

EQUIVALENCIES OF ONE-HALF

One-half is a major benchmark. Readily knowing how to generate equivalent versions supports computation and estimation. You want students to be able to identify or generate fractions equivalent to one-half as practiced in the first center, Halvsies. This stems from the skill of halving or doubling numbers reinforced in the game *The Splits*.

ACTIVITY 1.12

Name: Halvsies   **Type:** Center

About the Center: As the name implies, students use cards to create fractions equivalent to $\frac{1}{2}$. As students participate in this activity, it is interesting to listen and watch to see if they are finding numerators and doubling them to determine a denominator, or vice versa. After playing, have students share the strategies they used to find fractions equivalent to $\frac{1}{2}$.

Materials: three decks of digit cards (1–9) or two decks of playing cards (aces = 1; remove tens and face cards)

Directions:
1. Deal eight cards to each player.

2. Students use their cards to make fractions equivalent to $\frac{1}{2}$. For example, they may use a 4 and an 8 to form $\frac{4}{8}$; a 7, 1, and 4 to form $\frac{7}{14}$; or 1, 2, 4, and 8 to form $\frac{14}{28}$.

3. The goal is to clear all eight cards. If a player clears all eight in one round, they win!

4. If no player uses all eight cards, players keep their cards they used to create fractions and put them aside, and play continues to Round 2.

5. In Round 2, players are dealt new cards to fill in what was used in the last round (if a player used four cards, they receive four new cards).

6. Repeat Step 2–5 until (a) someone wins (clears all cards in one round) or (b) the deck is gone or time is up. In the second case, the player who has the most cards from creating fractions wins.

For example, the player's first deal of eight cards is shown on the left. They take 9, 1, and 8 because $\frac{9}{18}$ is equivalent to $\frac{1}{2}$. They also take the 2 and 4 $\left(\frac{2}{4}\right)$ as well as the 3 and 6 $\left(\frac{3}{6}\right)$. They deal seven more cards to use with the "1" remaining from the first deal. Now, they can use 7, 1, and 4 to make $\frac{7}{14}$ and a 3 and 6 again $\left(\frac{3}{6}\right)$. After the second deal, the player has a 3, 5, and 2 remaining. They will deal five new cards for their third deal.

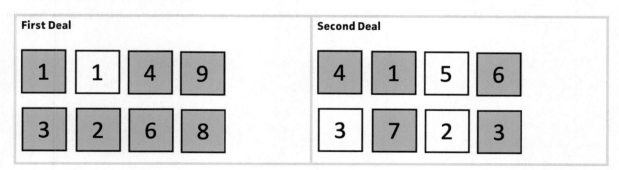

First Deal

1	1	4	9
3	2	6	8

Second Deal

4	1	5	6
3	7	2	3

ACTIVITY 1.13

Name: The Splits   **Type:** Game

About the Game: *The Splits* focuses on finding half of a number, a skill that helps students determine if fractions are less than, greater than, or equal to $\frac{1}{2}$. For example, knowing that 14 is half of 28 helps a student recognize that $\frac{14}{28}$ is equivalent to $\frac{1}{2}$.

Materials: *The Splits* game board (one per student); tools for generating numbers, such as a 10-sided die, digit cards (0–9), or playing cards (queens = 0 and aces = 1; remove tens, jacks, and kings)

Directions:

1. Players take turns dealing two cards (or rolling the die two times) to generate a two-digit number. Players arrange the cards in any order (e.g., a 3 and a 6 can be 36 or 63).

2. Players "split" that number in half and record it in one of their available boxes on their game board. Notice that, in the end, the numbers must be in order from least to greatest, so students must strategize where to place their number.

3. If the player cannot halve the number (or does so incorrectly), they lose their turn.

4. If the player can halve the number but it turns out to be too big or too small to fit on their game board, they also lose a turn.

5. The first player to fill all six boxes wins the game.

For example, the player's first number was 64 and they recorded half (32). On their next turn, they made 28 and recorded 14. Then they made 50 and recorded 25. On their fourth turn, they made 60. The player can't use their roll of 60 because half is 30 and there is no space for 30 on the board.

The Splits

Directions: Use digit cards to make a two-digit number. Find half of the number. Record the number in one of the boxes. The numbers in the boxes must be in order from least to greatest. First to fill all six boxes wins!

	14	25	32		

online resources — This resource can be downloaded at **resources.corwin.com/FOF/addsubtractdecimalfraction**.

COMMON FRACTION EQUIVALENCIES

Recognizing and recalling fraction equivalence with minimal effort contributes to strategy selection and efficiency. You want to build skill with equivalencies of these fraction families: halves, fourths, and eighths (possibly sixteenths); thirds, sixths, and twelfths; fifths and tenths. Multiplication charts are useful in showing equivalent fractions. First, they can be modified to include facts through 12 × 12 as shown. In the top image, you see how the multiplication chart identifies fractions equivalent to $\frac{1}{2}$. The middle image shows fractions equivalent to $\frac{4}{5}$. The bottom image shows how the chart can be used to find equivalents of any fraction, such as equivalents of $\frac{3}{5}$. To do this, simply ignore the rows in between.

x	0	1	2	3	4	5	6	7	8	9	10	11	12
0	0	0	0	0	0	0	0	0	0	0	0	0	0
1	0	1	2	3	4	5	6	7	8	9	10	11	12
2	0	2	4	6	8	10	12	14	16	18	20	22	24
3	0	3	6	9	12	15	18	21	24	27	30	33	36
4	0	4	8	12	16	20	24	28	32	36	40	44	48
5	0	5	10	15	20	25	30	35	40	45	50	55	60
6	0	6	12	18	24	30	36	42	48	54	60	66	72
7	0	7	14	21	28	35	42	49	56	63	70	77	84
8	0	8	16	24	32	40	48	56	64	72	80	88	96
9	0	9	18	27	36	45	54	63	72	81	90	99	108
10	0	10	20	30	40	50	60	70	80	90	100	110	120
11	0	11	22	33	44	55	66	77	88	99	110	121	132
12	0	12	24	36	48	60	72	84	96	108	120	132	144

x	0	1	2	3	4	5	6	7	8	9	10	11	12
0	0	0	0	0	0	0	0	0	0	0	0	0	0
1	0	1	2	3	4	5	6	7	8	9	10	11	12
2	0	2	4	6	8	10	12	14	16	18	20	22	24
3	0	3	6	9	12	15	18	21	24	27	30	33	36
4	0	4	8	12	16	20	24	28	32	36	40	44	48
5	0	5	10	15	20	25	30	35	40	45	50	55	60
6	0	6	12	18	24	30	36	42	48	54	60	66	72
7	0	7	14	21	28	35	42	49	56	63	70	77	84
8	0	8	16	24	32	40	48	56	64	72	80	88	96
9	0	9	18	27	36	45	54	63	72	81	90	99	108
10	0	10	20	30	40	50	60	70	80	90	100	110	120
11	0	11	22	33	44	55	66	77	88	99	110	121	132
12	0	12	24	36	48	60	72	84	96	108	120	132	144

x	0	1	2	3	4	5	6	7	8	9	10	11	12
0	0	0	0	0	0	0	0	0	0	0	0	0	0
1	0	1	2	3	4	5	6	7	8	9	10	11	12
2	0	2	4	6	8	10	12	14	16	18	20	22	24
3	0	3	6	9	12	15	18	21	24	27	30	33	36
	0	4	8	12	16	20	24	28	32	36	40	44	48
5	0	5	10	15	20	25	30	35	40	45	50	55	60
6	0	6	12	18	24	30	36	42	48	54	60	66	72
7	0	7	14	21	28	35	42	49	56	63	70	77	84
8	0	8	16	24	32	40	48	56	64	72	80	88	96
9	0	9	18	27	36	45	54	63	72	81	90	99	108
10	0	10	20	30	40	50	60	70	80	90	100	110	120
11	0	11	22	33	44	55	66	77	88	99	110	121	132
12	0	12	24	36	48	60	72	84	96	108	120	132	144

ACTIVITY 1.14

Name: Fraction Tile Take   **Type:** Game

About the Game: Students begin this game with a full set of fraction tiles, and they remove pieces based on the numbers they roll (draw). As they try to remove fraction tiles that are different-sized pieces, they must consider fraction equivalencies. For example, if they roll (draw) $\frac{3}{4}$, they may choose to remove 3 fourths, or they may choose to remove 6 eighths or any other combination that is equivalent to (same length as) $\frac{3}{4}$.

Materials: fraction tile set; digit cards (1–10), playing cards (aces = 1; remove face cards), or a 10-sided die, with the 0 adapted to be a 10

Directions:
1. Players put their fraction tile sets together in same-sized rows.

2. On a player's turn, they generate a proper fraction (the larger value in the denominator) or whole number by drawing two digit cards or rolling the die twice.

3. The player removes tiles to represent the fraction they formed.

4. If a player rolls a fraction for which they cannot make an equivalency, they lose their turn. For example, a player rolling $\frac{2}{7}$ would lose their turn.

5. The first player to remove all of their tiles wins the game.

In the example, the player removed $\frac{1}{2}$ on their first turn because they rolled a 1 and a 2. They also rolled $\frac{7}{8}, \frac{2}{3}, \frac{2}{5}$ and $\frac{1}{4}$. When they roll $\frac{1}{4}$ again, they decide to remove 3 twelfths because it is equivalent to $\frac{1}{4}$.

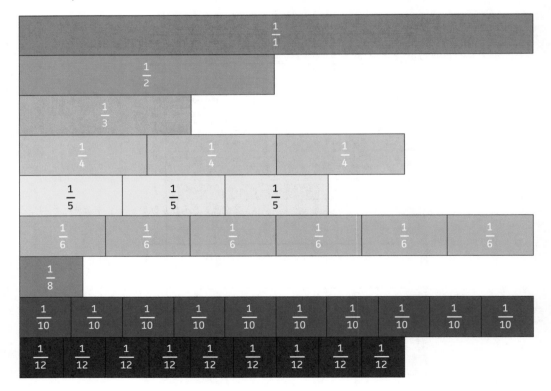

ACTIVITY 1.15

Name: Fill the Charts   **Type:** Game

About the Game: *Fill the Charts* is a game for finding equivalent fractions and noticing patterns within equivalent fraction sets. Students may benefit from using a multiplication chart initially but will hopefully begin to see patterns that help them find equivalent fractions through reasoning.

Materials: *Fill the Charts* game board (one per player); two decks of digit cards (0–9), playing cards (queens = zero and aces = 1; remove tens, kings, and jacks), or a 10-sided die

Directions:
1. Players take turns generating a number and completing one of the corresponding columns for one of the three charts.

2. If a player can't use the number that they generate (because they have filled all three columns), they lose their turn.

3. If a player incorrectly records the equivalent fraction, they lose their turn.

4. The first player to fill all three charts wins the game.

For example, the player first rolled a 3 and completed the 3 column on the third chart (the $\frac{3}{4}$ chart) by recording an equivalent fraction, $\frac{9}{12}$, that is related by ×3. On their next turn, they rolled a 5 and completed the 5 column on their $\frac{1}{4}$ chart.

Fill the Charts

Directions: Choose a number. Find the related numerator and denominator on one of the charts. Be the first to fill the charts.

	1	2	3	4	5	6	7	8	9	10
1					5					
4					20					

	1	2	3	4	5	6	7	8	9	10
2								16		
4								32		

	1	2	3	4	5	6	7	8	9	10
3			9							
4			12							

You can download the game board and modify it in a variety of ways by changing the fractions within the chart (e.g., $\frac{3}{8}$, $\frac{5}{8}$, and $\frac{7}{8}$) or by removing some of the columns so that certain numbers rolled cannot be used.

online resources ⏵ This resource can be downloaded at **resources.corwin.com/FOF/addsubtractdecimalfraction**.

Count On/Count Back Strategy

STRATEGY OVERVIEW:
Count On/Count Back

What is Count On/Count Back? The Count On/Count Back strategy starts at one of the numbers and uses efficient jumps to either add (Count On) or subtract (Count Back). This commonly used whole-number strategy is not only a good reasoning strategy for decimals and fractions, but it also strengthens students' understanding of the magnitude of fractions or decimals.

To note, students might count back to "separate" (take away from the minuend) or to "compare" (find the difference). This module focuses on "separate" and the Think Addition module focuses on "compare."

HOW DOES COUNT ON/COUNT BACK WORK?

This strategy is based on partial sums or differences, keeping track of partial results as you jump up or back. At first, students tend to use more counts, perhaps counting by unit fractions (e.g., fourths or tenths), but with experience, the chunks become more efficient. For example, to add $\frac{7}{12} + \frac{11}{12}$, a student might count on by twelfths until they reach $1\frac{6}{12}$. As students gain experience, they use fewer jumps. Here are some examples of each.

COUNT ON

EXAMPLE: $\frac{5}{8} + 2\frac{7}{8}$	
Open Number Line	**Written Record**
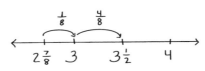	$2\frac{7}{8} + \frac{1}{8} = 3$ $3 + \frac{4}{8} = 3\frac{1}{2}$

EXAMPLE: 12.6 + 3.5	
Open Number Line	**Written Record**
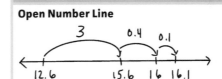	$12.6 + 3 = 15.6$ $15.6 + 0.4 = 16$ $16 + 0.1 = 16.1$

COUNT BACK

EXAMPLE: $1\frac{1}{2} - \frac{3}{4}$	
Open Number Line	**Written Record**
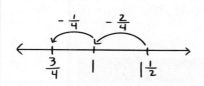	$1\frac{1}{2} - \frac{1}{2} = 1$ $1 - \frac{1}{4} = \frac{3}{4}$

EXAMPLE: 4.26 – 0.4	
Open Number Line	**Written Record**
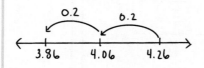	$4.26 - 0.2 = 4.06$ $4.06 - 0.2 = 3.86$

WHEN DO YOU CHOOSE COUNT ON/COUNT BACK?

For addition, Count On is useful when one of the addends is relatively small (e.g., 45.79 + 2.3) or it is easy to break apart into easy-to-add parts ($15\frac{1}{2} + 4\frac{3}{4}$). For subtraction, Count Back is often a good choice when the subtrahend is relatively small (e.g., 436.3 – 14.2). Note that when the subtraction problem involves two numbers that are relatively close together (e.g., 4.36 – 3.8 or $7\frac{1}{2} - 6$), then finding the difference (i.e., counting up) between the numbers is more efficient than taking away (i.e., counting back).

MODULE 1 Foundations for Reasoning Strategies

MODULE 2 Count On/Count Back Strategy

MODULE 3 Make a Whole Strategy

MODULE 4 Think Addition Strategy

MODULE 5 Compensation Strategy

MODULE 6 Partial Sums and Differences Strategy

MODULE 7 Standard Algorithms

COUNT ON AND COUNT BACK:
Strategy Briefs for Families

It is important that families understand the strategies and know how they work so that they can be partners in the pursuit of fluency. These strategy briefs are a tool for doing that. You can include them in newsletters for parents or caregivers, or at a school event like a Back to School Night. They are available for download so that you can adjust them as needed.

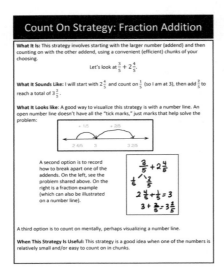

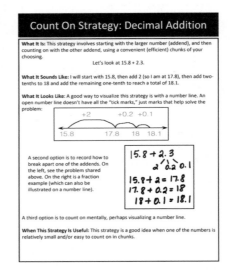

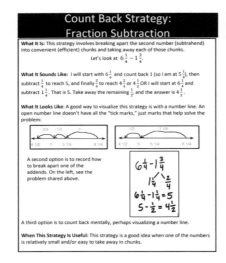

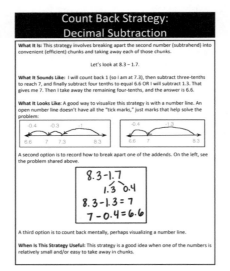

This resource can be downloaded at **resources.corwin.com/FOF/ addsubtractdecimalfraction**.

TEACHING ACTIVITIES for Count On/Count Back

Count On and Count Back are often the first strategies students learn. What begins as count on or back by ones becomes count on by tens, then larger chunks like 30 or 100, and then by equivalent fractional parts. In this section, you'll find instructional activities for helping students develop efficient ways to count on or count back. The goal is that students become adept at using counting strategies efficiently and accurately, and also consider when they will want to use a counting strategy.

 ACTIVITY 2.1
COUNTING ON: FROM AREAS TO NUMBER LINES

The Count On strategy is often modeled (physically or mentally) on a number line. The number line, however, is a more challenging model than area models. This activity bridges an area representation to the number line. Using either fraction tiles or rectangle sketches, ask students to sketch the larger fraction. Then continue to *count on* with the other addend.

Let's explore $2\frac{4}{5} + \frac{3}{5}$. Students use rectangles to solve the problem.

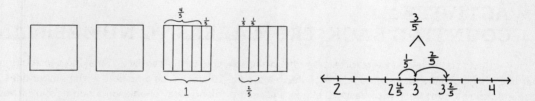

In both representations, you can reinforce counting on by having students count aloud the units they are adding.

This activity is also effective with decimals. Let's explore 2.28 + 1.05. This is 2 and 28 hundredths:

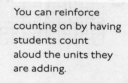

> **TEACHING TAKEAWAY**
>
> You can reinforce counting on by having students count aloud the units they are adding.

We add 1 whole:

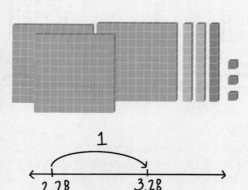

(*Continued*)

(Continued)

Now, we have 3 and 28 hundredths. We add on 5 hundredths, 2 hundredths (0.02), complete a tenth, and there are 3 more hundredths:

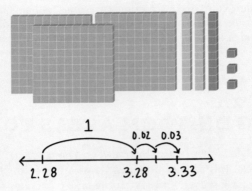

The answer is 3.33.

ACTIVITY 2.2
COUNTING BACK: FROM AREAS TO NUMBER LINES

Counting Back reflects the take-away interpretation of subtraction. Like with Activity 2.1, making sense of jumps on the number line is supported with area models. With decimals, base-10 blocks can be paired with number lines. In this activity, students show Count Back with base-10 blocks and record taking away chunks on a number line. These four steps show Count Back using base-10 blocks paired with the number line for the problem 2.45 – 1.32.

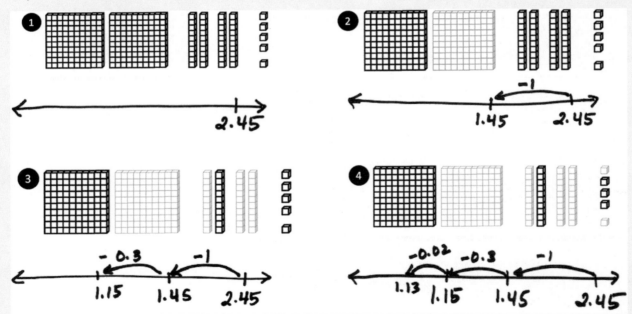

As students explain their process, they benefit from saying and/or writing the partial differences (e.g., "2 and 45 hundredths minus 1 is 1 and 45 hundredths . . ."). For fractions, fraction circles, fraction strips, or Cuisenaire rods can be paired with a number line to show Count Back.

ACTIVITY 2.3
BEADED DECIMAL NUMBER LINES

One way to develop the understanding of Count On and Count Back is to represent it with a 100 beaded number line and connect the work to a written number line. First, the beaded number line can be used as a number line representing 0 to 10 as illustrated next. In this situation, each bead represents one-tenth. To become familiar with the bead model, have students identify quantities on the beaded number line, such as 6.2.

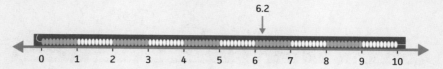

In this activity, students partition the beads to represent the addend they want to count on from. Students then shift beads to count on the amount of the second addend.

Here is an example: 4.5 + 1.7.

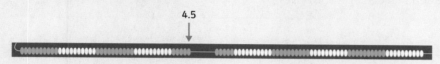

The student moves 45 beads to the left and says, "4 and five-tenths." Ask students what they notice about the set of beads (they should notice there are 4 groups of ten-tenths representing 4 and another group of 5 beads representing 0.5). Then the student reasons about how they might decompose 1.7 and moves the beads using that strategy.

TEACHING TAKEAWAY

Students can use a clip (clothespin, bag clip, bobby pin, or barrette) to mark the quantity they are starting with to separate it from the unused beads.

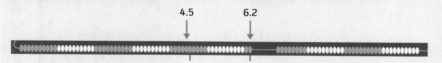

As students work, they record their reasoning on a bead counter number line. Here are three ways students might count on:

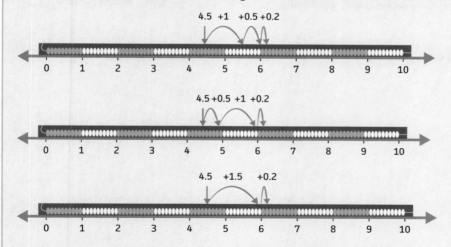

Count Back works in a similar manner, marking the starting point and then jumping back in chunks.

(Continued)

(Continued)

The 100 beaded number line can readily be adapted to hundredths, with the strand labeled from 0 to 1 and each color group representing a tenth and each bead representing a hundredth. In this example, 0.73 – 0.38, a student starts at 73 hundredths. Then, the student slides 3 hundredths, to 7 tenths, then 3 tenths, then the remaining 5 hundredths (taking away a total of 0.38). The remaining beads are how much is left (0.35).

Students then record their work on a number line. For example, the student might count back 3 beads (–0.03), then count back 30 beads (–0.3), and then count back 5 more beads (–0.05).

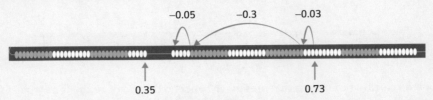

As it appears here, this number line could be used for fraction tenths. Alternatively, number lines can be made with eight beads in alternating colors to show eighths (and fourths and halves).

ACTIVITY 2.4
NUMBER BONDS FOR COUNT ON/COUNT BACK

Number bonds let students decompose numbers in useful ways. Students use the number bond to show how they want to decompose a number into convenient parts. Number bonds provide a nice visual to show that fractions, like whole numbers, can be decomposed in a variety of ways!

Let's start with $5\frac{3}{4}+3\frac{5}{12}$. To count on from $5\frac{3}{4}$, $3\frac{5}{12}$ needs to be decomposed. The student must notice an equivalency, that $\frac{1}{4}=\frac{3}{12}$. Then they can split that into $\frac{5}{12}$ into $\frac{3}{12}$ and $\frac{2}{12}$.

Another option is to find common denominators and then count on or back, which is illustrated in the second example, $6\frac{1}{6}-1\frac{3}{4}$.

COUNT ON FRACTION EXAMPLE	COUNT BACK FRACTION EXAMPLE
$5\frac{3}{4}+3\frac{5}{12}$ $3 \quad \frac{3}{12} \quad \frac{2}{12}$ $5\frac{3}{4}+\frac{1}{4}=6$ $6+3\frac{2}{12}=9\frac{1}{6}$	$6\frac{1}{6}-1\frac{3}{4}=6\frac{2}{12}-1\frac{9}{12}$ $1 \quad \frac{2}{12} \quad \frac{7}{12}$ $6\frac{2}{12}-1\frac{2}{12}=5$ $5-\frac{7}{12}=4\frac{5}{12}$

With decimals, this process is very similar, counting on by the whole numbers and then thinking about how to efficiently do jumps for the tenths and/or hundredths.

COUNT ON DECIMAL EXAMPLE	COUNT BACK DECIMAL EXAMPLE
$15.8 + 3.6$ $3 \quad 0.2 \quad 0.4$ $15.8 + 3 = 18.8$ $18.8 + 0.2 = 19$ $19 + 0.04 = 19.04$	$3.45 - 1.37$ $1 \quad 0.3 \quad 0.05 \quad 0.02$ $3.45 - 1 = 2.45$ $2.45 - 0.3 = 2.15$ $2.15 - 0.05 = 2.10$ $2.10 - 0.02 = 2.08$

As students decompose numbers, look for them to break a number into units (such as one-tenth) or chunks (such as two-tenths or four-tenths). In the Count Back example, 3.45 – 1.37, the student makes a jump of 0.3 instead of 3 jumps of one-tenth. You want to help students move from individual hundredths, tenths, or ones to groups of each. In this example, students may also chunk 0.35 together, subtracting it from 0.45.

ACTIVITY 2.5
PROMPTS FOR TEACHING COUNT ON/COUNT BACK

Use the following prompts as opportunities to develop understanding of and reasoning with the strategy. Have students use representations and tools to justify their thinking, including base-10 models, number lines, hundredth charts, rectangles, and so on. After students work with the prompt(s), bring the class together to exchange ideas. These could be useful for collecting evidence of student understanding. Any prompt can be easily modified to feature different numbers (e.g., three-digit or four-digit numbers) and any prompt can be offered more than once if modified.

Decimal Prompts

- Lihua counts on to solve 2.9 + 5.3. What number would you suggest she start with? How should she then count on from the number you suggest? Show your thinking with a manipulative, number line, or series of equations.

- Show or explain two different ways to count on to solve 0.35 + 0.7. Explain why the answer is the same.

- Show or explain two different ways to count back to solve 87.1 – 13.5. Tell which way you think is most efficient.

Fraction Prompts

- Shannel counts back to solve $15\frac{7}{12} - 5\frac{1}{2}$. What jump would you suggest she start with? How should she then count back from the number you suggest? Show your thinking with a number line or equations.

- Allen solved $51\frac{1}{2} + 15\frac{7}{8}$ by thinking $51+5+5+5+\frac{1}{8}+\frac{1}{8}+\frac{1}{8}+\frac{1}{8}+\frac{1}{8}+\frac{1}{8}+\frac{1}{8}$. What is another way he might have counted on?

General Prompts

- How are Count On and Count Back similar and how are they different?

- Give an example of when the Count On or Count Back strategy would not be the most efficient strategy to use.

PRACTICE ACTIVITIES for Count On/Count Back

Fluency is realized through quality practice that is focused, varied, processed, and connected. The activities in this section focus students' attention on how this strategy works and when to use it. The activities are a collection of varied engagements. Game boards, recording sheets, digit cards, and other required materials are available as online resources for you to download, possibly modify, and use.

As students practice, look for how well they are using the new strategy and assimilating it into their collection of strategies. Postactivity discussions help students reflect on *how* they reasoned and *when* that strategy was useful (and when it was not). Discussions can also help students reflect on how that strategy connects to recent instruction and to other strategies they have learned.

FLUENCY COMPONENT	WHAT TO LOOK FOR AS STUDENTS PRACTICE THIS STRATEGY
Efficiency	• Are students using Count On/Count Back efficiently? (e.g., Are they counting efficiently?) • Do they count by unit fractions when they could be adding in chunks? (e.g., Are they adding $\frac{7}{8}$ by adding $\frac{1}{8}$ seven times rather than adding a chunk of $\frac{1}{2}$ and then add $\frac{3}{8}$?) • Do they count by one-hundredths when one addend can be decomposed into tenths and hundredths and added in chunks? (e.g., For 0.21, do they count on 2 tenths and then add 1 hundredth?) • Are students using the strategy adeptly (not getting hung up)? Are students readily changing fraction denominators to support counting on or back? • Do students overuse the strategy (use it when it is not a good fit)?
Flexibility	• Are students carrying out the strategy in flexible ways? (Do they sensibly choose what number to count on from? Are they chunking efficiently, or always counting by unit fractions or tenths?) • Do they change their counting approach if it doesn't seem to be working? • Do they change to a different strategy when counting doesn't seem to be efficient? • Are students applying this strategy in "new" situations (e.g., applying to different fractional parts or to hundredths)?

Accuracy	• Are students thinking through the Count On/Count Back strategy correctly?
	     ○ Are they attending to the fractional parts?
	     ○ Are they attending to place value?
	
	 • Are students estimating before solving the problems?
	
	 • Are students considering the reasonableness of their solutions?
	
	 • Are students finding accurate solutions?

ACTIVITY 2.6
COUNT ON/COUNT BACK WORKED EXAMPLES

Worked examples can be used as a warmup, a focus of a lesson, at a learning center, or on an assessment. Here we share examples and ideas for preparing worked examples to support student understanding of the Count On/Count Back strategy. There are different ways to pose worked examples, and they each serve a different fluency purpose.

TYPE OF WORKED EXAMPLE	PURPOSE: COMPONENT (FLUENCY ACTIONS)	QUESTIONS FOR DISCUSSIONS OR FOR WRITING RESPONSE
Correctly Worked Example	Efficiency (selects an appropriate strategy) and flexibility (applies a strategy to a new problem type)	What did _____ do? Why does it work? Is this a good method for this problem?
Partially Worked Example	Efficiency (selects an appropriate strategy; solves in a reasonable amount of time) and accuracy (completes steps accurately; gets correct answer)	Why did _____ start the problem this way? What does _____ need to do to finish the problem?
Incorrectly Worked Example	Accuracy (completes steps accurately; gets correct answer)	What did _____ do? What mistake does _____ make? How can this mistake be fixed?

With Count On/Count Back, correctly and partially worked examples help students see different options for chunking (skip-counting) and incorrect examples highlight common errors (as well as successful steps). Another excellent practice is to ask students to compare two correctly worked examples:

- How are they alike? How are they different?

- How do they compare in terms of efficiency?

- When would you use each method?

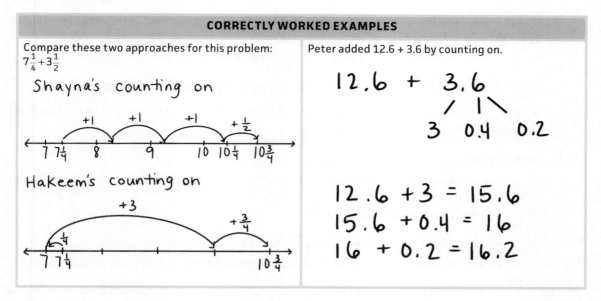

(Continued)

(Continued)

PARTIALLY WORKED EXAMPLES	
Jada's start for $10\frac{1}{2} - 3\frac{7}{8}$ $10\frac{1}{2} - \frac{1}{2}$ Aliyah's start for $10\frac{1}{2} - 3\frac{7}{8}$ $10\frac{1}{2} - 3$	Curtis's Start $13.6 + 1.85$ / | \ 1 0.4 0.45
INCORRECTLY WORKED EXAMPLES	
$9\frac{1}{4} - 2\frac{3}{4}$ 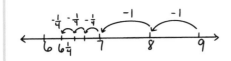	$7.05 - 1.83$ 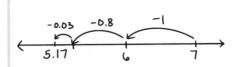

The following list of common challenges or errors can be used to create more worked examples.

1. The student loses track of how many jumps and makes too many or too few jumps.
    - 3.94 + 4.77: starts at 4 and counts on to 8.77, but forgets to count back 0.06.
    - $8\frac{7}{10} + 1\frac{9}{10}$: recognizes $1\frac{9}{10}$ is close to 2 and counts on 2 from $8\frac{7}{10}$, but forgets to count back $\frac{1}{10}$.

2. The student makes an error in breaking apart a number.
    - 8.7 + 7.1: from 8.7, counts on 2 to get to 10.7 and then 4 [rather than 5] to get to 14.7 and one more to 14.8.
    - $12\frac{5}{9} - 6\frac{7}{9}$: breaks $\frac{7}{9}$ into $\frac{5}{9}$ and $\frac{3}{9}$.

3. The student uses denominators incorrectly, either by adding/subtracting them or ignoring them when they do not match.
    - $\frac{3}{4} - \frac{1}{2}$: starts with 3 and counts back 1, then starts with 4 and counts back 2, resulting in $\frac{2}{2}$.

4. The student counts on the numerator and picks one of the denominators for the answer.
    - $2\frac{3}{4} - \frac{1}{8}$: ignores that taking away from fourths requires breaking fourths into eights and instead subtracts the numerators only and gets $2\frac{2}{4}$.

5. The student loses track of the place value.
    - 8.7 − 3.05: ignores the zero and counts back three 7.7, 6.6, 5.5, 4.4, then continues jumps for five-tenths 4.3, 4.2, 4.2, 4.0, 3.9.
    - 5.3 + 4: counts on from 0.3 resulting in 5.7.

6. The student misses a count when consecutive digits are the same.
    - 87.1 − 44.9: counts back 4 tens to 47.1, but overlooks 4 ones because a jump of 4 was just made.

Although it is not an error, students may continue to count by unit fractions or by tenths or hundredths instead of chunking their counts more efficiently. You can compare two worked examples, one that counts more efficiently than the other, and have students analyze the two (see also Activity 2.8, "Routine: Or You Could . . .").

ACTIVITY 2.7

Name: "The Count"   **Type:** Routine

About the Routine: "The Count" is a routine that has students estimate and skip-count. It is a good opportunity for practicing skip-counting by a variety of intervals, which is essential for using the Count On and Count Back strategies. You can use this routine with fractions or decimals.

Materials: identify a counting interval and a starting number; supporting decimal or fraction chart (optional)

Directions:

1. Set a clear counting path so that students know how they will count in the room. Having students gather in a large circle is a good option.

2. Identify a starting number, the student who will count first, and a counting interval such as skip-count forward by tens. Then, use the following questions to ask students about the impending count:

   - What are some numbers we will say as we count?

   - What number do you think you will say?

   - What will be the last number said?

As students count, you can record the numbers they say on the board or mark them on a related number chart or number line. After the count, use the numbers you record to discuss patterns within the numbers said, challenges with counting, and how student predictions compared with the results of the count.

The Count: Fractions

Start with $2\frac{1}{2}$ Count on by $\frac{1}{2}$	Start with 4 Count on by $\frac{1}{3}$	Start with $5\frac{1}{2}$ Count on by $\frac{1}{4}$	Start with 7 Count back by $\frac{2}{8}$

The Count: Decimals

Start with 10.5 Count on by 0.2	Start with 3.6 Count on by 0.02	Start with 51.75 Count back by 1.5	Start with 78.4 Count back by 0.05

The example shows a variety of prompts you can pose for both Count On and Count Back using a variety of intervals. Skip-counting by fourths, eighths, tenths, and hundredths helps students notice patterns that help them move from counting by singles to chunking their counts.

ACTIVITY 2.8

Name: "Or You Could . . .?"   **Type:** Routine

About the Routine: This routine helps students develop more efficient approaches for counting. Initially, it is reasonable for students to first learn and use Count On and Count Back by decomposing a number into unit fractions or tenths and counting by each. In fact, this strengthens students' understanding of place value and/or fractional parts. But, with experience, students need to chunk their jumps. In "Or You Could . . . ," students are shown a Count On or Count Back method by units and asked to think of another way they could count on or back. Flexibility is key (there is not one best way). For example, in 3.78 + 3.44, one might start with 3.78 and add on 3 (6.78), then 0.02 (6.80), then 0.2 (7) to make a whole number, and then add the remaining 0.22 (7.22).

Directions: 1. Provide completed Count On or Count Back problems such as the following:

- You can solve $5\frac{7}{8}+3\frac{5}{8}$ by thinking $5\frac{7}{8}+3+\frac{1}{8}+\frac{1}{8}+\frac{1}{8}+\frac{1}{8}+\frac{1}{8}$ **or you could . . .**

- You could solve $4\frac{3}{4}-1\frac{7}{8}$ by thinking of $4\frac{3}{4}$ as $4\frac{6}{8}$ and then thinking $4\frac{6}{8}-1-\frac{1}{8}-\frac{1}{8}-\frac{1}{8}-\frac{1}{8}-\frac{1}{8}-\frac{1}{8}$ **or you could . . .**

- You can solve 0.92 – 0.24 by thinking 0.92 – 0.1 – 0.1 – 0.01 – 0.01 – 0.01 – 0.01 **or you could . . .**

- You can solve 8.96 + 3.042 by thinking 8.96 + 3 + 0.01 + 0.01 + 0.01 + 0.01 + 0.001 + + 0.001 **or you could . . .**

2. Ask students to talk with a partner about another way to count on or back.

3. After a few moments, bring the group together to share their thinking.

4. As students share more efficient ways to chunk the skip counts, record their thinking on a number line or with an equation.

5. Reinforce to students how the different approaches yield the same sum or difference.

Open number lines are an excellent representation to support this routine! For example, you can say, "You can add $1\frac{3}{4}+7\frac{3}{4}$ like this," and show students the following:

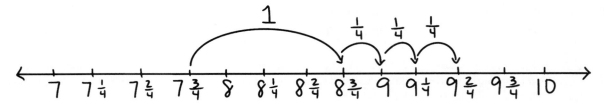

Then students might say, "Or you could add 1 to get to $8\frac{3}{4}$, add $\frac{1}{4}$ to get to 9, and add $\frac{2}{4}$ or $\frac{1}{2}$ to get to $9\frac{2}{4}$ or $9\frac{1}{2}$.

ACTIVITY 2.9

Name: Race to Zero   **Type:** Game

About the Game: *Race to Zero* helps students consider different ways to skip-count back to zero. This game helps students think about how to mark off equal-sized portions on a number line. The following description is for fractions. To adapt it to decimals, use a 10-sided die. The same recording sheet can be used and the number lines can be "open" so the student estimates where 3.4 is located, for example.

Materials: *Race to Zero* recording page (or a laminated number line such as the one shown here and a bean or other marker), a regular die (one per group), and a set of unit fraction cards labeled $\frac{1}{2}, \frac{1}{3}, \frac{1}{4}, \frac{1}{5},$ and $\frac{1}{6}$.

Directions:

1. Place students in triads.

2. Give each person a recording page (or a number line and a marker). Give each group a die and a set of unit fraction cards.

3. Students mix up the fraction cards and place them face down.

4. One of the students in each group draws a fraction card. Each student then marks their number lines to represent the fraction on the card. For example, if they draw $\frac{1}{4}$, they would make tick marks equal distance apart, between the whole numbers, to mark off fourths on their number lines.

5. Students take turns rolling a die and counting back out loud the number of times indicated by the dice. For example, if Leah rolls a 6, she counts back by 6 fourths. She may count by fourths, or she might notice that she can count 4 fourths to get to 4 and back 2 more fourths to $3\frac{2}{4}$. She places her marker on $3\frac{2}{4}$ on her number line. She records a related equation on her paper: $5 - \frac{6}{4} = 3\frac{2}{4}$ $\left(or\ 3\frac{1}{2}\right)$. The next player rolls the die and repeats.

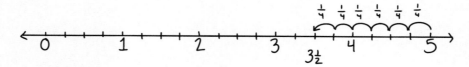

6. The first person to count back to zero wins.

Optional Rule: The last roll has to land exactly on zero. If the value they roll is too high, they skip their turn.

Have students repeat the whole process, rolling the dice to get a different fractional amount, partitioning a new number line, and playing again.

Questions to Ask While Students Play

1. What patterns are you noticing as you count back?

(Continued)

(Continued)

2. What shortcuts (chunks) help you count back efficiently?

3. What are you noticing about fractions and whole numbers?

Questions to Ask After Students Play

1. When you drew fourths on your number line, how many marks did you make between each whole number? Why?

2. How did the size of the fractional parts (e.g., fourths vs. sixths) impact the game?

3. What similarities and differences did you notice as you switched to different fractional parts?

RESOURCE(S) FOR THIS ACTIVITY

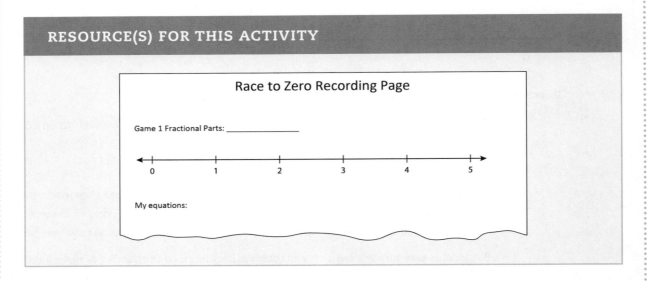

Race to Zero Recording Page

Game 1 Fractional Parts: _____

My equations:

online resources ↖ This resource can be downloaded at **resources.corwin.com/FOF/addsubtractdecimalfraction.**

ACTIVITY 2.10

Name: Count On Bingo—Decimals   **Type:** Game

About the Game: *Count On Bingo* helps students think about the jumps they make and how they might become more strategic with their jumps. Blank 5 × 5 bingo boards can be downloaded and students can then create their own boards by writing the numbers 1 through 9 and multiples of 10 randomly anywhere on their board.

Materials: *Count On Bingo* boards (one per student), counters, and expression cards (or a list of expressions)

Directions: 1. Players take turns pulling expression cards.

2. Players solve the expression on the card using the Count On strategy.

3. Players place a counter on each of the jumps/chunks they used to count on. As students need certain places on their bingo board, they can think strategically about their count on options to see if they can get Bingo!

4. The first players to get five in a row in any direction get Bingo (and win).

For example, students pull the expression card 4.8 + 2.3. Player 1's jumps are 1.0 + 1.0 + 0.3 (on the left board). They place a counter on those numbers. Player 2's jumps are 2.0 + 0.3 (on the right board). They place a counter on those numbers. Another option would be for a player to start at 2.3 and count on 4 and 0.8, marking out those places on their bingo board.

Count On Bingo

Directions: Choose from the numbers in the box. Write a number in each box. You can write a number more than once.

.1	.2	.3	.4	.5	.6	.7	.8	.9
1.0	2.0	3.0	4.0	5.0	6.0	7.0	8.0	9.0

(1.0)	.4	3.0	2.0	1.0
.6	(1.0)	4.0	1.0	(.3)
7.0	.2	9.0	.5	3.0
.6	2.0	.7	7.0	8.0
1.0	1.0	.1	.8	4.0

Count On Bingo

Directions: Choose from the numbers in the box. Write a number in each box. You can write a number more than once.

.1	.2	.3	.4	.5	.6	.7	.8	.9
1.0	2.0	3.0	4.0	5.0	6.0	7.0	8.0	9.0

4.0	.3	2.0	1.0	5.0
.8	1.0	(.3)	.1	2.0
.7	1.0	(2.0)	3.0	4.0
.6	.5	7.0	.6	.8
.1	1.0	1.0	9.0	.4

The following list of expressions might be used for playing the game, although it will work with any examples. Expressions can be written on index cards if you want small groups of students to play *Count On Bingo* without you.

(Continued)

(*Continued*)

EXAMPLE DECIMAL ADDITION EXPRESSIONS			
TENTHS		HUNDREDTHS	
2.1 + 4.6	3.1 + 1.7	1.83 + 3.55	8.80 + 1.14
4.1 + 3.1	5.2 + 3.4	3.39 + 1.40	1.35 + 5.43
5.5 + 3.8	3.9 + 4.2	5.14 + 3.99	6.82 + 1.70
5.3 + 1.8	4.4 + 3.7	1.40 + 2.67	5.39 + 3.70
9.8 + 5.6	8.7 + 4.5	4.83 + 4.52	9.30 + 1.13

EXAMPLE FRACTION ADDITION EXPRESSIONS			
TENTHS		HUNDREDTHS	
5.0 – 4.4	5.1 – 3.0	4.44 – 3.93	6.72 – 5.05
10.0 – 4.9	6.4 – 4.5	2.81 – 1.13	5.77 – 4.45
3.0 – 1.2	9.4 – 5.6	9.04 – 8.36	4.74 – 1.69
5.3 – 2.4	8.5 – 4.7	6.16 – 3.77	5.01 – 1.88
9.4 – 4.8	9.6 – 4.4	2.29 – 1.92	9.90 – 8.38

online resources ↖ *Count on Bingo* game boards can be downloaded at **resources.corwin.com/FOF/ addsubtractdecimalfraction.**

ACTIVITY 2.11

Name: Make It Close   **Type:** Game

About the Game: *Make It Close* is a target-based game for practicing addition and developing number sense. The goal is to create a sum as close to the target as possible. The unique twist in this game is that the target changes from round to round. While the following example focuses on tenths, this can be adapted to hundredths. This game can be played with two to four players.

Materials: four decks of digit cards (0–9) or playing cards (queens = 0 and aces = 1; remove tens, kings, and jacks); *Make It Close* recording sheet

Directions:

1. To set the target, deal four cards to the "leader" for that round. The leader makes two 2-digit decimal addends (see the following image). The leader uses the Count On strategy to find the sum, which becomes the target for the round. The other players confirm the sum is correct. In the example, the target for round 1 is 9.5.

2. The leader then deals four cards to each player (including themselves).

3. The players arrange the four digits so that their sum is close to the target, as shown here.

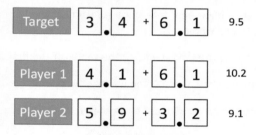

4. The player with the sum closest to the target for round 1 gets 1 point (Player 2 in the example). *Optional Rule:* If a player hits the target exactly, they earn a bonus point.

5. Rotate who is the leader to set the target for the next game.

6. The first player to earn 5 points wins the game.

RESOURCE(S) FOR THIS ACTIVITY

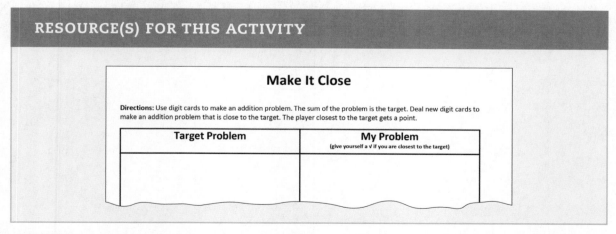

Make It Close

Directions: Use digit cards to make an addition problem. The sum of the problem is the target. Deal new digit cards to make an addition problem that is close to the target. The player closest to the target gets a point.

Target Problem	My Problem
	(give yourself a √ if you are closest to the target)

online resources ☞ This resource can be downloaded at **resources.corwin.com/FOF/addsubtractdecimalfraction.**

ACTIVITY 2.12

Name: Find the Value of the Shape   **Type:** Center

About the Center: This center uses pattern blocks to engage students in adding and subtracting with unlike denominators. Building the creature builds background in fraction equivalencies. Then when students are asked to create a new larger (or smaller) creature, they are engaged in counting on (or back).

Materials: a set of pattern blocks (four to six of each of these pieces: hexagons, trapezoids, blue rhombuses, and triangles; no orange or white pieces); a pattern block design using a combination of these pieces (two examples are provided here, but you can create others on virtual manipulative sites); triangle graph paper (optional, downloadable)

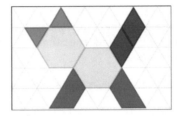 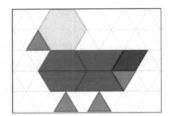

Directions:

1. Build the shape and determine its value if the yellow hexagon is equal to one whole.

2. Write an expression for adding the values of the first shape.

3. Add the equivalent of $1\frac{1}{3}$ and create your own shape.

   a. Sketch it on the pattern block paper.

   b. Tell the value of your new shape.

4. Subtract the equivalent of $1\frac{1}{2}$ and create your own shape.

   a. Sketch it on the pattern block paper.

   b. Tell the value of your new shape.

> **TEACHING TIP**
>
> This center is easily updated by changing the designs that are provided and/or changing the fractional values in steps 3 and 4.

RESOURCE(S) FOR THIS ACTIVITY

online resources ▷ This resource can be downloaded at **resources.corwin.com/FOF/addsubtractdecimalfraction.**

ACTIVITY 2.13

Name: Logical Leaps   **Type:** Center

About the Center: Logical Leaps engages students in representing their thinking with number lines and equations. It also works well as an instructional activity because students can compare the equations they wrote for a given number line. This center is designed for partners.

Materials: Logical Leaps equation cards and Logical Leaps recording sheet (partners share)

Directions: 1. Partner 1 draws an addition (or subtraction) card and keeps it a secret from partner 2. Partner 1 uses the number line on their recording sheet to use Count On (or Count Back) to solve the addition (or subtraction) problem.

2. Partner 1 then hands the number line to partner 2. Partner 2 uses the number line to determine the original equation and records it next to the number line.

3. Partner 2 hands the number line back to partner 1 and partner 1 checks the equation with the card they have drawn.

4. Partners switch roles.

For example, Juan draws the card 17.37 + 2.44 = 19.81. He starts by marking 17.37 on the open number line and draws the jumps he would make to add 2.44 (see the following illustration). Tina sees the jumps and records the amount of each jump above the arrows. Then she adds up all the jumps and writes the equation in the equation box.

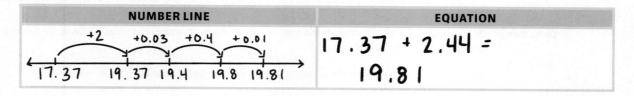

NUMBER LINE	EQUATION
+2 +0.03 +0.4 +0.01 17.37 19.37 19.4 19.8 19.81	17.37 + 2.44 = 19.81

RESOURCE(S) FOR THIS ACTIVITY

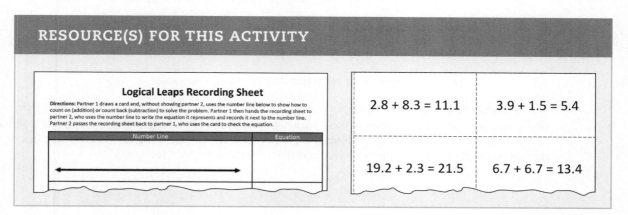

Logical Leaps Recording Sheet

Directions: Partner 1 draws a card and, without showing partner 2, uses the number line below to show how to count on (addition) or count back (subtraction) to solve the problem. Partner 1 then hands the recording sheet to partner 2, who uses the number line to write the equation it represents and records it next to the number line. Partner 2 passes the recording sheet back to partner 1, who uses the card to check the equation.

Number Line	Equation

2.8 + 8.3 = 11.1	3.9 + 1.5 = 5.4
19.2 + 2.3 = 21.5	6.7 + 6.7 = 13.4

online resources This resource can be downloaded at **resources.corwin.com/FOF/addsubtractdecimalfraction**.

ACTIVITY 2.14

Name: Largest and Smallest Sums   **Type:** Center

About the Center: This center reinforces Count On or Count Back strategies for decimals while also focusing on number sense and reasoning. As a center it encourages students to notice and think about place value and the value of the digits to make the largest or smallest sum. Largest and Smallest Sums can be used as a game where students earn points for finding the largest or smallest sum within a group.

Materials: digit cards (0–9) or playing cards (queens = 0 and aces = 1; remove tens, kings, and jacks); Largest and Smallest Sums recording sheet (decimal or fraction version); decimal numbers to use as the second addend that are appropriate for counting on or counting back (e.g., 3.24)

First addend	Second addend	Sum
☐.☐☐	+3.24	
☐.☐☐	+3.24	
☐.☐☐	+3.24	

Directions:

1. Students pull three digit cards and arrange them to make the first addend (a decimal to the hundredths place) and record it.

2. Students use the Count On strategy to add the numbers and record the sum.

3. Students rearrange the same three cards to make a new addend and record it.

4. Students use the Count On strategy to add the numbers and record the sum.

5. Repeat steps 3 and 4 a third time.

6. Students complete the reflection questions (see thumbnail).

This center can be adapted in many ways. For decimals, the decimal point can be relocated (rather than moving the digits; e.g., count on from 24.6, 2.46, or 0.246). Fractions can be used by simply having the template look like a mixed number rather than a decimal and students place the cards to form the starting value. In this case, you may want to remove sevens from the deck (because students don't need to work with sevenths).

Largest and Smallest Sums – Decimals

Pull three digit cards and arrange them to make the first addend, and then record it below. Use counting on to add this addend to the second addend (provided by the teacher) and record your sum. Rearrange your digit cards to make a new addend. Use Counting On to add it to the second addend and record your sum. Repeat the process a third time.

First addend	Second addend	Sum

Look at and think about your addends and sums and answer the questions.

1. Which sum is the largest? How do you know this is the largest?

2. Which sum is the smallest? How do you know it is the smallest?

3. For which of the three sums was Counting On a good strategy?

4. In general, when is Counting On a good strategy?

Largest and Smallest Sums – Fractions

Pull three digit cards and arrange them to make the first addend, and then record it below. Use counting on to add this addend to the second addend (provided by the teacher) and record your sum. Rearrange your digit cards to make a new addend. Use Counting On to add it to the second addend and record your sum. Repeat the process a third time.

First Addend	Second Addend	Sum

Look at and think about your addends and sums and answer the questions.

1. Which sum is the largest? How do you know this is the largest?

2. Which sum is the smallest? How do you know it is the smallest?

3. For which of the three sums was Counting On a good strategy?

4. In general, when is Counting On a good strategy?

online resources

This resource can be downloaded at **resources.corwin.com/FOF/addsubtractdecimalfraction.**

Make a Whole Strategy

STRATEGY OVERVIEW:
Make a Whole

What is Make a Whole? This strategy builds on the Make Tens (or Hundreds) strategy with whole number addition. The strategy involves decomposing one of the addends to make a whole with the other. Here are two examples:

$$4\tfrac{7}{8} + 3\tfrac{5}{8}$$

$$\tfrac{1}{8} \quad 3\tfrac{4}{8}$$

$$4\tfrac{7}{8} + \tfrac{1}{8} + 3\tfrac{4}{8}$$

$$5 + 3\tfrac{4}{8}$$

$$8\tfrac{1}{2}$$

$$\overset{+\,0.2}{\overbrace{}}$$
$$0.8 + 0.5 = 1.0 + 0.3$$
$$\underset{-\,0.2}{\underbrace{}}$$

In both examples, the student could have made a whole with the other addend. This strategy also extends to Make a Tenth:

$$\overset{+\,0.02}{\overbrace{}}$$
$$0.58 + 0.05 = 0.60 + 0.03$$
$$\underset{-\,0.02}{\underbrace{}}$$

HOW DOES MAKE A WHOLE WORK?

This strategy involves breaking apart (decomposing) one of the addends and associating it with another addend with the intent of making a whole. As with many strategies, Make a Whole begins with finding the common denominator so that you are adding liked-sized pieces.

Fraction Example: $\tfrac{2}{3} + \tfrac{5}{12} = \tfrac{8}{12} + \tfrac{5}{12}$

With Visuals

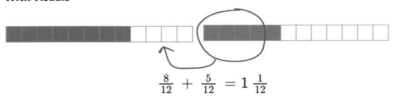

$$\tfrac{8}{12} + \tfrac{5}{12} = 1\tfrac{1}{12}$$

With Equations

$$\frac{8}{12} + \frac{5}{12} = \frac{8}{12} + \left(\frac{4}{12} + \frac{1}{12}\right)$$

$$= \left(\frac{8}{12} + \frac{4}{12}\right) + \frac{1}{12}$$

$$= 1\frac{1}{12}$$

Decimal Examples

4.98 + 5.45	1.671 + 6.9
Notice that 4.98 is 0.02 away from 5.	Notice that 6.9 is 0.1 away from 7.

Break apart   4.98 + 5.45
           / \\
       0.02   5.43
 	
Make a Whole   4.98 + 0.02 + 5.43
              \\ /
         5   + 5.43
 	
Sum = 10.43
	1.671 + 6.9
	             ⌢
	Break apart 1.571 + 0.1 + 6.9
	                    \\ /
	Make a Whole 1.571 + 7
	
	Sum = 8.571

Make a Whole may be a mental or written process. As numbers get larger, students may wish to write down their adjusted addends so they don't have to keep it all in their head. The written process can still be more efficient and accurate than the standard algorithm because it does not require regrouping.

WHEN DO YOU CHOOSE MAKE A WHOLE?

TEACHING TAKEAWAY

Writing down addends can help students track their thinking, eventually moving toward using a mental process.

Make a Whole is a great option when at least one of the addends is close to a benchmark. Conversely, it may not be an efficient strategy when it is difficult to make a whole (e.g., 6.58 + 3.77). It is also an excellent strategy to use when adding mixed numbers that would otherwise involve regrouping (e.g., $4\frac{7}{8} + 3\frac{5}{8}$).

MODULE 1 Foundations for Reasoning Strategies

MODULE 2 Count On/Count Back Strategy

MODULE 3 Make a Whole Strategy

MODULE 4 Think Addition Strategy

MODULE 5 Compensation Strategy

MODULE 6 Partial Sums and Differences Strategy

MODULE 7 Standard Algorithms

MAKE A WHOLE:
Strategy Briefs for Families

It is important that families understand the strategies and know how they work so that they can be partners in the pursuit of fluency. These strategy briefs are a tool for doing that. You can include them in newsletters for parents or caregivers, or at a school event like a Back to School Night. They are available for download so that you can adjust them as needed.

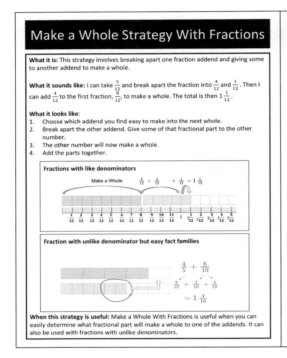

Make a Whole Strategy With Fractions

What it is: This strategy involves breaking apart one fraction addend and giving some to another addend to make a whole.

What it sounds like: I can take $\frac{5}{12}$ and break apart the fraction into $\frac{4}{12}$ and $\frac{1}{12}$. Then I can add $\frac{4}{12}$ to the first fraction, $\frac{8}{12}$, to make a whole. The total is then $1\frac{1}{12}$.

What it looks like:
1. Choose which addend you find easy to make into the next whole.
2. Break apart the other addend. Give some of that fractional part to the other number.
3. The other number will now make a whole.
4. Add the parts together.

Fractions with like denominators

Make a Whole $\frac{8}{12} + \frac{4}{12}$ $+ \frac{1}{13} = 1\frac{1}{12}$

Fraction with unlike denominator but easy fact families

$\frac{4}{5} + \frac{6}{10}$

$\frac{8}{10} + \frac{2}{10} + \frac{4}{10}$

$= 1\frac{4}{10}$

When this strategy is useful: Make a Whole With Fractions is useful when you can easily determine what fractional part will make a whole to one of the addends. It can also be used with fractions with unlike denominators.

Make a Whole Strategy With Decimals

What it is: This strategy involves breaking apart one addend and giving some to another addend to make a whole, a tenth, a hundredth, and so on.

What it sounds like: I will take 0.1 from 1.7 to make 3.9 into 4 wholes to make adding it easier to get a sum of 5.6.

What it looks like:
1. Choose which addend you find easy to make into the next whole.
2. Break apart the other addend. Give some of that number to the other number.
3. The other number will now make a whole.
4. Add the parts together.

In the left example, 3.9 is close to 4. To make it a 4, you break apart the tenths place, 0.7, to 0.1 and 0.6. Use 0.1 and add it to the 3.9 to make 4. Now add the 1.6 you have left to the 4. 3.9 + 1.7 becomes 4 + 1.6 = 5.6.

In the right example, 0.58 is close to 0.6. To make 0.60, you take 0.02 from the 0.06. Then add that to the 0.58. The new number sentence is 0.60 + 0.04 = 0.6 + 0.04 = 0.64.

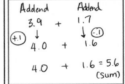
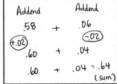

When this strategy is useful: Make a Whole With Decimals is useful when one of the addends is close to a whole, a tenth, or a hundredth.

online resources

This resource can be downloaded at **resources.corwin.com/FOF/ addsubtractdecimalfraction**.

TEACHING ACTIVITIES for Make a Whole

Before students are able to choose strategies, a key to fluency, they first must be able to understand and use relevant strategies. These activities focus specifically on the Make a Whole strategy. While students may employ other methods, which is appropriate, they also must learn this important strategy that employs and strengthens their understanding of decimals and fractions and flexible use of the properties for the operations.

ACTIVITY 3.1
POST-PARTY PIZZA LEFTOVERS

A common experience after ordering pizza is that some pizza in each box is left over. Pizzas are usually cut into eighths (but you can change this up to fourths, sixths, or twelfths). And if you cut the pizza into tenths, this can be a decimal activity, too. With leftover pieces from several pizzas, it is common to move slices over to fill a box (i.e., make a whole pizza). Thus, this context lends to the Make a Whole strategy.

Pose this problem to students:

The class ordered cheese pizzas and pepperoni pizzas for a Math Game Night at school. After the party, each grade combined the pizza boxes so that as many as possible were full. Can you figure out exactly how much pizza was left for each of these scenarios? How many full boxes were there? How much was in the partially filled box?

GRADE	CHEESE PIZZA LEFTOVERS	PEPPERONI PIZZA LEFTOVERS	TOTAL PIZZA LEFTOVER
1	$1\frac{7}{8}$	$1\frac{3}{8}$	
2	$2\frac{3}{4}$	$1\frac{3}{4}$	
3	$\frac{3}{4}$	$2\frac{1}{4}$	
4	$1\frac{1}{2}$	$1\frac{3}{4}$	
5	$2\frac{7}{8}$	$\frac{5}{8}$	

Distribute fraction circles or have students sketch them to illustrate the solution to each problem. Ask students to use the idea of making full boxes of pizza to figure out how much is left over. For example, a student might explain their solution to the first problem like this: "I moved 1 eighth (one piece) over to make 2 full boxes, then added to get 3 full boxes and $\frac{2}{8}$ of a pizza in the last box."

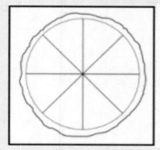 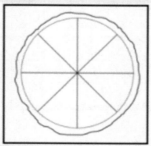 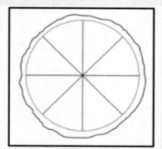 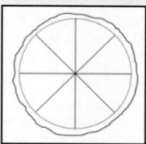

online resources — These pizza fraction circles can be downloaded at **resources.corwin.com/FOF/ addsubtractdecimalfraction**.

ACTIVITY 3.2
EGGS-ACTLY HOW MANY?

This activity uses egg cartons to engage students in the Make a Whole strategy. You can use egg cartons as is to work with twelfths. Or cut two off the end to work with tenths (decimals or fractions), or cut in other ways to have sixths or eighths. If you are working on fractions with like denominators, then use only like denominators. The following examples show a mix.

Like the previous activity, the focus is on how to fill a partially filled carton to make a whole. Pose this problem to students:

> *Two friends, Ani and Noah, have gathered eggs from the henhouse. When they come inside, they combine their eggs to get as many full egg cartons as possible so they can sell them.*
>
> *How many full egg cartons are there? What fraction of an egg carton is filled each day?*

	ANI	NOAH	TOTAL
Monday	$1\frac{11}{12}$	$2\frac{5}{12}$	
Tuesday	$3\frac{3}{4}$	$3\frac{3}{4}$	
Wednesday	$2\frac{3}{4}$	$1\frac{1}{2}$	
Thursday	$2\frac{10}{12}$	$3\frac{1}{4}$	
Friday	$2\frac{3}{4}$	$2\frac{1}{3}$	

To challenge students, they can use their Make a Whole strategy to figure out how many cartons were collected for the week. To support student reasoning with visual tools, consider these options:

- 2 × 6 rectangles to shade (or 2 × 3, if using sixths)

- Unifix cubes (the whole can be any quantity). These cubes allow students to "break apart" physically and make a whole, which is not possible with base-10 pieces or Cuisenaire rods.

- Ten-frame cards (for tenths) with two-color counters (or adapt the frames to the size you want)

As with many activities, also having students translate their thinking onto a number line strengthens both their conceptual understanding and procedural flexibility.

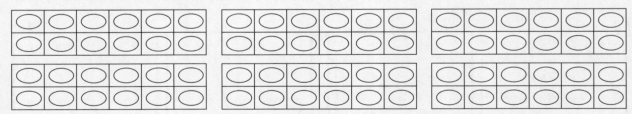

online resources These egg carton templates can be downloaded at **resources.corwin.com/FOF/ addsubtractdecimalfraction**.

ACTIVITY 3.3
TWO-CARD EQUATIONS

Provide decimal cards to students (pictured here and available for download). Have students select two cards and write an addition expression. Then, ask students to write an equivalent expression, using the Make a Whole strategy. Students should also record how they made the new equation. In the example, the student says they gave 0.2 to 0.8 to make 1.0 + 0.3 = 1.3.

0.8 + 0.5

I gave 0.2 to 0.8 to make

1.0 + 0.3 = 1.3

Once students become familiar with moving tenths to make a whole, focus on hundredths. As you move to hundredths, the thinking is more complex—students must think about tenths and hundredths to make the whole. In the example here, they may see 2 tenths and 5 hundredths or 25 hundredths. This is a great connection for students to see that both ways describe the missing part to one whole.

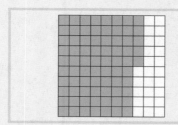 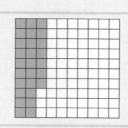

0.75 + 0.27

I gave 0.25 to 0.75 to make a whole:

1.00 + 0.02 = 1.02

Students can also translate their thinking onto a number line, which strengthens their conceptual understanding and procedural flexibility.

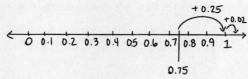

+ 0.25

+0.02

0   0.1   0.2   0.3   0.4   0.5   0.6   0.7   0.8   0.9   1

0.75

RESOURCE(S) FOR THIS ACTIVITY

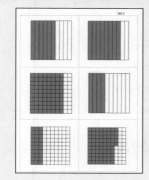 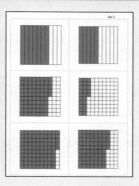 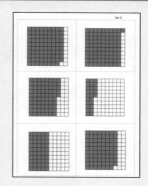 

online resources ➤ This resource can be downloaded at **resources.corwin.com/FOF/addsubtractdecimalfraction**.

ACTIVITY 3.4
BUILD THE FRACTION AND DECIMAL TRACK

Number lines are essential to developing fluency. Fraction tracks (pictured here) are a way to connect an area representation (fraction strip) to a number line. With fraction tracks (and decimal tracks), students shade a length above a number line rather than show jumps with arrows. For example, the following fraction track shows $\frac{8}{10} + \frac{5}{10}$.

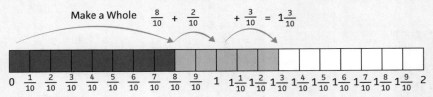

Ask students to estimate how long the two tracks will be when combined. Discuss how $\frac{2}{10}$ or 0.2 can be moved to the track of $\frac{8}{10}$ or 0.8 to make one whole. Ask students how this process connects to ways to add efficiently. An alternative to shading is to have students make physical sets of fraction tracks (like fraction strips) and physically lay down their fraction track on a master fraction track to see how long the tracks are when combined.

The process looks the same with decimals. The fraction track is simply labeled with decimal values rather than fraction values, as illustrated here for 0.7 + 0.5.

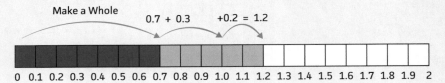

TEACHING TAKEAWAY

Fraction tracks, like many tools, also can be used for other strategies like Count On, Count Back, Think Addition, and so on.

Fraction tracks, like many tools, also can be used for other strategies like Count On, Count Back, Think Addition, and so on.

Repeat the activity with a variety of combinations. Here are some examples where both addends are less than 1:

$\frac{9}{10} + \frac{5}{10}$	$\frac{8}{10} + \frac{6}{10}$	0.9 + 0.05	0.8 + 0.6
$\frac{9}{10} + \frac{7}{10}$	$\frac{7}{10} + \frac{7}{10}$	0.9 + 0.7	0.7 + 0.7

Using decimal fractions allows students to naturally see how the Make a Whole strategy works for both decimals and fractions in the same way. Once students are comfortable with like denominators, these activities can be used with other like and unlike denominators.

$\frac{3}{5} + \frac{4}{5}$	$\frac{5}{8} + \frac{1}{2}$	$\frac{3}{4} + \frac{1}{2}$	$\frac{7}{8} + \frac{1}{4}$

Addends greater than 1 also can be solved with fraction tracks; the track just has to be long enough to represent the quantities. Also see Activity 3.13 for a fraction track center activity.

ACTIVITY 3.5
EXPRESSION MATCH

Use 3 × 5 notecards or print on cardstock to prepare a set of about 12 cards, which includes approximately six trios of equivalent expressions: one expression that lends to the Make a Whole strategy and two that pair with this expression (i.e., the Make a Whole strategy has been applied; see examples in the following table). Use similar-sized numbers across the 12 cards so that students focus on the details of the expressions and not just finding the same numbers. Have students work together to find the trio of cards. After students find their sets, they can record equations in their math journal, noting how the expression was changed. For example, a student might write the following:

$$4.7 + 0.8 = 5 + 0.5$$

These expressions are equivalent because 0.3 was moved from 0.8 to 4.7.

You can provide sentence frames to support reasoning:

I know _____ expression is the same as _____ expression because . . .

TEACHING TAKEAWAY

Provide time after the activity for students to reflect on and write about the strategy. Sentence frames can support reasoning.

Examples of decimal expressions you might use are as follows.

EXPRESSION	PAIRS WITH	PAIRS WITH
4.7 + 0.8	5 + 0.5	4.5 + 1
1.8 + 4.6	2 + 4.4	1.4 + 5
2.9 + 3.8	3 + 3.7	2.7 + 4
3.3 + 1.9	3.2 + 2	4 + 1.2

Examples of fraction expressions you might use include are as follows. (These examples are based on the assumption that students have automaticity with moving among halves, fourths, and eighths, but they can be adapted so that every fraction is written as eighths.)

EXPRESSION	PAIRS WITH	PAIRS WITH
$4\frac{7}{8} + \frac{7}{8}$	$5 + \frac{3}{4}$	$4\frac{3}{4} + 1$
$4\frac{5}{8} + 1\frac{7}{8}$	$5 + 1\frac{1}{2}$	$4\frac{1}{2} + 2$
$3\frac{5}{8} + 1\frac{1}{2}$	$4 + 1\frac{1}{8}$	$3\frac{1}{8} + 2$
$1\frac{3}{8} + 3\frac{3}{4}$	$1\frac{1}{8} + 4$	$2 + 3\frac{1}{8}$

Note that these expressions keep the addends in the same order. To increase the challenge, you can apply the commutative property.

ACTIVITY 3.6
PROMPTS FOR TEACHING MAKE A WHOLE

Use the following prompts as opportunities to develop understanding of and reasoning with Make a Whole and/or as assessments to determine whether students understand and can use the strategy. You can require students to use representations and tools to justify their thinking, including fraction circles, decimal grids, fraction tracks, number lines, and so on, or you can focus on mental math. If you use these prompts for whole-class discourse, first provide individual think time, then small-group (e.g., triads) talk time, and finally whole-group time. Any prompt can be easily modified to feature different decimals and fractions.

Decimal Prompts

- Alexa said she thinks in coins when adding. She says, "I break apart the numbers 0.89 + 0.45 using dimes, nickels, and pennies. Then I rearrange them to make a dollar." She writes this on the board:

  0.85 + 0.04 + 0.15 + 0.30 = 0.85 + 0.15 + 0.30 + 0.04

  - What do you notice about Alexa's method?

  - What other ways might you break apart these numbers to use this Make a Dollar strategy?

  - Explain how to use the Make a Dollar strategy to add 0.78 + 0.47.

- Christopher is adding 3.8 + 7.71 and wants to move some tenths to 3.8 to make a whole. Show him how to do this and explain whether or not you recommend this strategy for this problem.

- Carlos found two ways to rewrite the expression 5.8 + 3.94. He says they are different ways to get the same sum: (1) 6 + 3.74 and (2) 5.74 + 4.

  - Is option 1 equivalent? Show or explain.

  - Is option 2 equivalent? Show or explain.

  - Which option makes more sense to you (and why)?

Fraction Prompts

- How can you make a whole to solve $\frac{3}{4}+\frac{3}{4}$?

- Create three fraction problems that you would solve with the Make a Whole strategy. What do each of the problems have in common?

- Brylie says that you can make two whole numbers with $\frac{3}{4}+\frac{1}{2}+\frac{4}{8}+\frac{2}{8}$. Can you explain what Brylie is seeing? [Decimal option: 0.89 + 0.45 + 0.11 + 0.55]

- In measuring a ribbon border, you end up with these measurements for each side of your picture: $3\frac{7}{8}+6\frac{1}{4}+3\frac{7}{8}+6\frac{1}{4}$. How might you add these numbers using your Make a Whole strategy?

- Tell how the Make a Whole strategy works for fractions with like and unlike denominators.

PRACTICE ACTIVITIES for Make a Whole

Fluency is realized through quality practice that is focused, varied, processed, and connected. The activities in this section focus students' attention on how this strategy works and when to use it. The activities are a collection of varied engagements. Game boards, recording sheets, digit cards, and other required materials are available as online resources for you to download, possibly modify, and use.

As students practice, look for how well they are using the new strategy and assimilating it into their collection of strategies. Post-activity discussions help students reflect on *how* they reasoned and *when* that strategy was useful (and when it was not). Discussions can also help students reflect on how that strategy connects to recent instruction and to other strategies they have learned.

FLUENCY COMPONENT	WHAT TO LOOK FOR AS STUDENTS PRACTICE THIS STRATEGY
Efficiency	• Do they choose the Make a Whole strategy when it is a good fit for the problem?
	• Are they using the strategy adeptly (not getting hung up)? Are students readily changing fraction denominators to support Making a Whole?
	• Do students overuse the strategy (i.e., try to use it when it is not a good fit, such as 4.24 + 1.52)?
Flexibility	• Are students carrying out the strategy in flexible ways (sometimes making a whole with the first addend, sometimes the second one)?
	• Do they flexibly choose between which addend(s) they are using to make a whole?
	• Do they change their approach to or from this strategy as it proves inappropriate or overly complicated for the problem?
	• Are they seeing how to apply this strategy in "new" situations (e.g., applying to tenths, or to new denominators)?
Accuracy	• Are students thinking through the Make a Whole process correctly (decomposing accurately)?
	• Do they accurately make a whole, tenths, or hundredths?
	• Are students estimating before solving the problems?
	• Are students considering the reasonableness of their solutions?
	• Are students finding accurate solutions?

ACTIVITY 3.7
MAKE A WHOLE WORKED EXAMPLES

Worked examples can be used as a warm-up, as a focus of a lesson, at a learning center, or on an assessment. Here we share examples and ideas for preparing worked examples to support student understanding of the Make a Whole strategy. There are different ways to pose worked examples, and they each serve a different fluency purpose:

TYPE OF WORKED EXAMPLE	PURPOSES: COMPONENT (FLUENCY ACTIONS)	QUESTIONS FOR DISCUSSIONS OR FOR WRITING RESPONSES
Correctly Worked Example	Efficiency (selects an appropriate strategy) and flexibility (applies a strategy to a new problem type)	What did _____ do? Why does it work? Is this a good method for this problem?
Partially Worked Example (Implement the Strategy Accurately)	Efficiency (selects an appropriate strategy; solves in a reasonable amount of time) and accuracy (completes steps accurately; gets correct answer)	Why did _____ start the problem this way? What does _____ need to do to finish the problem?
Incorrectly Worked Example (Highlight Common Errors)	Accuracy (completes steps accurately; gets correct answer)	What did _____ do? What mistake does _____ make? How can this mistake be fixed?

With Make a Whole, correctly and partially worked examples help students see how the strategy works and notice that either addend can be decomposed to make the other one a whole.

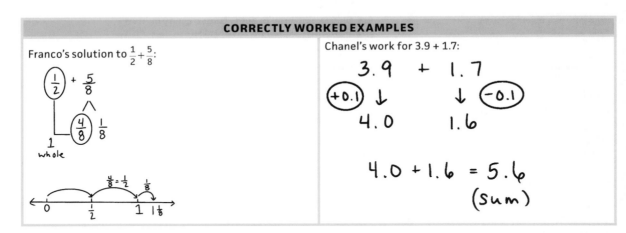

CORRECTLY WORKED EXAMPLES

Franco's solution to $\frac{1}{2} + \frac{5}{8}$:

Chanel's work for 3.9 + 1.7:

PARTIALLY WORKED EXAMPLES	
Theo and Andre are doing an activity where they do one step and trade papers; then their partner does the next step. Andre gave Theo this first step for $5\frac{3}{4}+3\frac{7}{8}$. What do you suggest Theo do next? $$5\frac{3}{4} + 3\frac{7}{8}$$ $$\diagdown$$ $$\frac{1}{4} \quad 3\frac{5}{8}$$	Nicole started to add these numbers. She was interrupted. What does she need to do to finish the problem? $$0.58 \; + \; 0.06$$ $\boxed{+0.02}$ $\quad\quad$ $\boxed{-0.02}$

INCORRECTLY WORKED EXAMPLES	
Colin's work for $2\frac{7}{8}+3\frac{3}{4}$: $$2\frac{7}{8} + 3\frac{3}{4}$$ $$\diagdown$$ $$\frac{1}{4} \quad \frac{2}{4}$$ $\boxed{6\frac{1}{2}}$	Can you find Jana's mistake and offer her a suggestion to avoid that mistake? $$8.28 \; + \; 5.8$$ $$8.26 + 6$$ $$14.26$$

A strength of the Make a Whole strategy is that it takes advantage of benchmarks and strengthens students' understanding of decimals and fractions. However, it is a strategy that can be error-prone if students lack this understanding. Ask students to *compare* two correctly worked examples—for example, comparing two different ways to make a whole (see Activity 3.5, "Expression Match"). Here are two challenges that students commonly encounter.

1. The student has trouble determining the distance to a whole.

   - For fractions, the student attends to the denominator (rather than thinking "make 10"). For example, for $\frac{8}{12}+\frac{5}{12}$, a student might think they need to add $\frac{2}{12}$ to make $\frac{10}{12}$ instead of the $\frac{4}{12}$ needed to make a whole.

   - To add $7\frac{5}{8}+5\frac{3}{4}$, the student moves over $\frac{1}{8}$ to make a whole with $\frac{3}{4}$ (instead of moving $\frac{2}{8}$).

   - For 3.87 + 2.34, the student sees the 8 in the tenths place and thinks they need 23 instead of 13 hundredths.

2. The student decomposes the other addend as they make a whole (tenths, hundredths).

   - To add $1\frac{5}{6}+5\frac{2}{3}$, the student breaks apart $\frac{2}{3}$ into $\frac{1}{6}+\frac{1}{6}$ rather than $\frac{1}{6}+\frac{1}{2}$.

   - To add 18.7 + 3.86, the student intends to move 3 tenths over but has place value confusion and removes 3 hundredths from the other addend: 19 + 3.83 (rather than 19 + 3.36).

The instructional prompts from Activity 3.5 can also be used for collecting worked examples. Throughout the module are various worked examples that you can use as fictional worked examples.

ACTIVITY 3.8

Name: "Paired Quick Looks"   **Type:** Routine

About the Routine: Fraction circles and bars help students see parts and wholes. This routine involves quick looks at two fraction images and challenges students to think about how much altogether. The visual images are designed to encourage students to employ the Make a Whole strategy to add the numbers mentally.

Materials: "Paired Quick Looks" cards and recording sheets

Directions: 1. Tell students that the circles are partitioned into tenths (or whatever fraction you are using).

2. Show two cards for a quick look (a few seconds), and then hide them. Give a second quick look.

3. On the third look, keep the visuals visible and ask students, "How many tenths altogether?" or "How many pieces in all?"

4. Invite students to share with a partner how they put the quantities together to find the total.

5. Discuss options with the whole group. As students share, you record the equation(s) that go with it.

6. Pairs can continue the routine with the recording sheets by using a cover sheet to quickly flash pairs and cover again. Ask a partner for a sum and reveal. The partners can confirm the quick look sums and record the equation in the column on the right.

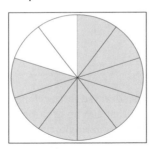 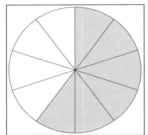

For this example with $\frac{8}{10}$ and $\frac{6}{10}$, you record $\frac{8}{10} + \frac{6}{10}$ and the new expression that students thought about, such as $\frac{10}{10} + \frac{4}{10}$ (moving 2 tenths to the left) or $\frac{4}{10} + 1$ (moving 4 tenths to the right). Then record the sum they found ($1\frac{4}{10}$ or $1\frac{2}{5}$).

"Paired Quick Looks" can be a routine with decimal addition as well. For example, in the following image, one might do a paired quick look with a decimal, such as 0.89 + 0.91. A student might decide to make the second decimal a whole by adding 0.09 to 0.91 and have 1 and 0.9 or 1.9.

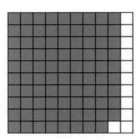 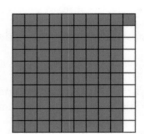

The "Paired Quick Looks" cards and recording sheets can be downloaded at **resources.corwin.com/FOF/addsubtractdecimalfraction**.

ACTIVITY 3.9

Name: "Say It As a Make a Whole"   **Type:** Routine

About the Routine: This routine explicitly charges students with renaming expressions in a variety of ways (SanGiovanni, 2019). In this particular version, the focus is on an equivalent expression after applying the Make a Whole idea.

Materials: prepared sets of expressions (examples follow)

Directions: 1. Pose three expressions to students and have them discuss another way to say each one. When you first launch this routine or when this strategy is new, pose the expressions one at a time. Later, they can be posed together.

2. Give students time to mentally think about a way to rewrite the expression (or rethink the expression) applying the Make a Whole idea.

3. Pair students to discuss their new expressions; then discuss options as a whole group.

4. With options on the board, ask students (a) the answer and (b) which expression they used to find the answer.

Here are a few sample sets of problems with fractions and with decimals:

Say It As Make a Whole (Fractions, Same Denominators)

$2\frac{3}{4}+4\frac{1}{4}$	$7\frac{3}{8}+6\frac{7}{8}$	$9\frac{5}{6}+2\frac{5}{6}$

$3\frac{3}{4}+5\frac{2}{4}$	$\frac{6}{8}+4\frac{7}{8}$	$2\frac{5}{6}+3\frac{2}{6}$

Say It As Make a Whole (Fractions, Mixed Denominators)

$5\frac{7}{8}+1\frac{1}{4}$	$\frac{7}{12}+\frac{1}{2}$	$5\frac{5}{6}+5\frac{1}{3}$

Say It As Make a Whole (Tenths)

9.8 + 25.8	7.9 + 12.3	5.1 + 8.9

Say It As Make a Whole (Hundredths)

2.18 + 7.98	0.55 + 3.88	0.41 + 5.89

4.58 + 5.43	38.92 + 4.46	6.15 + 8.83

Say It As Make a Whole (Mixed Decimals)

4.8 + 6.35	5.276 + 21.9	8.75 + 3.30

ACTIVITY 3.10

Name: "Same and Different"   **Type:** Routine

About the Routine: It is important to understand how a strategy works and that the strategy yields the same result as another strategy. In "Same and Different," you pose two expressions and ask students to compare the two (prior to adding). Here is an example: (Decimal) 0.35 + 0.38   0.33 + 0.4

(Fraction)

Materials: Prepare a collection of related expressions in one row as shown.

Directions:
1. Ask, "How are the expressions the *same*?" Record ideas.

2. Ask, "How are the expressions *different*?" Record ideas.

3. Ask students to solve the two problems (e.g., using base-10 pieces, a number line, or mentally, depending on their experiences).

4. After they have worked out the problems, ask, "How is adding 0.35 + 0.38 *the same as* 0.33 + 0.4? How is adding 0.35 + 0.38 *different from adding* 0.33 + 0.4?" Give students time to talk to a partner or trio about this question.

5. Share the same and different findings across groups in a whole-group discussion. Students noticings might include the following:
- Both yield the same sum of 0.73.
- The second expression is just adding a tenth with no hundredths.
- They are the same because "you" just made a tenth to show the second expression.

Other example paired expressions for decimals are provided here:

1.9 + 4.8 and 2 + 4.7	4.75 + 5.5 and 4.25 + 6	9.8 + 1.9 and 10 + 1.7
1.33 + 2.38 and 1.31 + 2.4	0.67 + 0.17 and 0.7 + 0.14	0.59 + 0.47 and 0.6 + 0.46
1.34 + 2.56 and 1.40 + 2.50	0.28 + 1.55 and 0.30 + 1.53	0.77 + 2.31 and 0.07 + 3.01

"Same and Different" is a great activity for fractions as well. You can work with common denominators or use the simplest form and help students work on their automaticity in recognizing equivalencies for common fractions (halves, fourths, and eighths or thirds and sixths). Fraction examples are shared here.

$\frac{3}{4}+\frac{3}{4}$ and $1+\frac{1}{2}$	$4\frac{1}{2}+12\frac{1}{2}$ and $5 + 12$	$4\frac{5}{6}+3\frac{5}{6}$ and $4\frac{4}{6}+4$
$\frac{4}{5}+\frac{4}{5}$ and $\frac{3}{5}+1$	$2\frac{1}{2}+1\frac{3}{4}$ and 3 and $1\frac{1}{4}$	$\frac{8}{12}+1\frac{1}{2}$ and $\frac{1}{6}+2$
$2\frac{3}{4}+\frac{3}{4}$ and $3+\frac{1}{2}$	$3\frac{1}{2}+\frac{3}{4}$ and 4 and $\frac{1}{4}$	$\frac{5}{8}+\frac{5}{8}$ and $\frac{1}{4}+1$

Following this activity, ask students to "find the pair":

(Decimals) 9.8 + 6.8 and _____

(Fractions) and _____

ACTIVITY 3.11

Name: Make It, Take It   **Type:** Game

About the Game: *Make It, Take It* engages students in practicing making a whole in a variety of ways. The goal of the game is to be the first player to take away all 10 counters. This game works for both decimals and fractions and can also be adapted to a center activity.

Decimal Version

Materials: *Make It, Take It* decimal game board, 10 chips or markers for each player, and one 10-sided die for the group

Directions:
1. Players place their 10 chips on their game board at random. They can place more than one chip on any space.

2. Players then take turns rolling the die (representing tenths) to make the targeted whole number.

3. The player figures out what number plus their roll equals the whole number. The player can remove one chip from that stack.

4. If a player rolls a 0, they lose their turn. If a player cannot remove a chip, play goes to the next player.

5. The first player who removes all their chips wins the game.

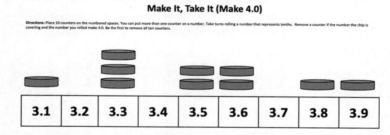

In this example, players are playing *Make It, Take It* to make 4.0. The player has put 10 counters on the game board. On this player's first turn, she rolled a 5 representing 5 tenths. She could remove one chip from 3.5 because 3.5 and 0.5 make 4.0. On her second turn, she rolls an 8 (8 tenths, 0.8) and loses her turn because she has no game piece on 3.2. The game continues until she removes all of her chips.

RESOURCE(S) FOR THIS ACTIVITY

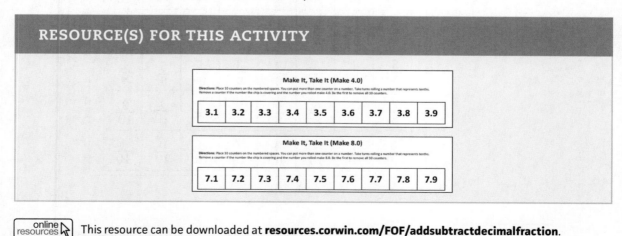

online resources This resource can be downloaded at **resources.corwin.com/FOF/addsubtractdecimalfraction**.

(Continued)

(Continued)

Fraction Version

Materials: *Make It, Take It* fraction game board, 10 chips or markers, and two 10-sided dice

Directions:
1. Players place their 10 chips on the larger *Make It, Take It* fraction game board.

2. Players then take turns generating a fraction by rolling the two dice. If a 2 and a 3 are rolled, the smaller value is the numerator, so the fraction they create is $\frac{2}{3}$. The 0 on the die is translated to be a 10.

3. Players look for a way to make a whole with the roll they have. In this case, they can remove a marker on $\frac{1}{3}$ (if they have one placed there), $\frac{2}{6}$, *or* any other equivalency. If students happen to have chips on two values that would, in fact, make a whole, they can remove two chips.

4. The first player who removes all of their chips wins the game.

Note: After they play this version a few times, students notice what are "good" spaces to occupy (they are more likely) and which ones are not.

RESOURCE(S) FOR THIS ACTIVITY

Make It, Take It (Make a Whole With Fractions)

Directions: Place 10 game pieces on the chart. Take turns rolling two 10-sided dice (0 = 10). Use the two numbers to make a fraction that is less than 1. Remove a game piece from a space that combines with your fraction to make a whole. Be the first to remove all 10 pieces.

$\frac{1}{2}$	$\frac{1}{3}$	$\frac{2}{3}$	$\frac{1}{4}$	$\frac{2}{4}$	$\frac{3}{4}$	$\frac{1}{5}$	$\frac{2}{5}$
$\frac{3}{5}$	$\frac{4}{5}$	$\frac{1}{6}$	$\frac{2}{6}$	$\frac{3}{6}$	$\frac{4}{6}$	$\frac{5}{6}$	$\frac{1}{8}$
$\frac{2}{8}$	$\frac{3}{8}$	$\frac{4}{8}$	$\frac{5}{8}$	$\frac{6}{8}$	$\frac{7}{8}$	$\frac{1}{10}$	$\frac{2}{10}$
$\frac{3}{10}$	$\frac{4}{10}$	$\frac{5}{10}$	$\frac{6}{10}$	$\frac{7}{10}$	$\frac{8}{10}$	$\frac{9}{10}$	$\frac{1}{10}$
$\frac{1}{2}$	$\frac{1}{3}$	$\frac{2}{3}$	$\frac{1}{4}$	$\frac{2}{4}$	$\frac{3}{4}$	$\frac{1}{5}$	$\frac{2}{5}$
$\frac{3}{5}$	$\frac{4}{5}$	$\frac{1}{6}$	$\frac{2}{6}$	$\frac{3}{6}$	$\frac{4}{6}$	$\frac{5}{6}$	$\frac{1}{8}$
$\frac{2}{8}$	$\frac{3}{8}$	$\frac{4}{8}$	$\frac{5}{8}$	$\frac{6}{8}$	$\frac{7}{8}$	$\frac{1}{10}$	$\frac{2}{10}$
$\frac{3}{10}$	$\frac{4}{10}$	$\frac{5}{10}$	$\frac{6}{10}$	$\frac{7}{10}$	$\frac{8}{10}$	$\frac{9}{10}$	$\frac{1}{10}$

This resource can be downloaded at **resources.corwin.com/FOF/addsubtractdecimalfraction**.

ACTIVITY 3.12

Name: A Winning Streak   **Type:** Game

About the Game: *A Winning Streak* has students trying to get three, four, or five in a row (a streak) on a game board as they add numbers. The game boards are set up for using the Make a Whole strategy, although they can easily be modified to other addends that may or may not lend to using the strategy.

Materials: *A Winning Streak* game board per pair; digit cards (0–9), playing cards (queens = 0 and aces = 1; remove tens, kings, and jacks), or a 10-sided die; and counters in two different colors (about 15 of each color)

Directions:

1. Players take turns rolling a number to represent the number of tenths and adding it to 1.9. If a player rolls (draws) a 0 (queen), 1 (ace), or 2, they lose a turn and play goes to their opponent.

2. Players place a counter on the sum. For example, if Player 1 rolls a 7, she adds 0.7 to 1.9 and can choose any available 2.6 to place one of her counters.

3. A player tries to get three, four, or five spaces in a row. Rows can overlap but only by one square. Three-in-a-row is 5 points, four-in-a-row is 10 points, and five-in-a-row is 20 points.

4. The game ends when all the spaces are filled or time is up.

5. Players add up their points and the player with the highest score wins.

Fraction Variation: Rather than applying the Make a Whole strategy to add, this variation has students find the combination that will equal one whole.

1. Players take turns rolling a die two times or drawing two cards to make a fraction less than 1. If they roll/draw the same number, they lose a turn.

2. Players place a counter on their choice of a space that has a fraction that makes a whole with the fraction they rolled. For example, a player rolls 5 and 8, makes the fraction $\frac{5}{8}$, and therefore can take any $\frac{3}{8}$ place on the game board.

3. A player tries to get three, four, or five spaces in a row. Rows can overlap but only by one square. Three-in-a-row is 5 points, four-in-a-row is 10 points, and five-in-a-row is 20 points.

4. The game ends when all the spaces are filled or time is up.

5. Players add up their points and the player with the highest score wins.

RESOURCE(S) FOR THIS ACTIVITY

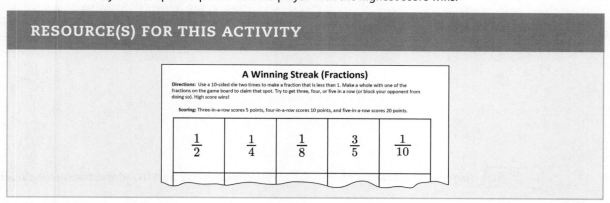

A Winning Streak (Fractions)

Directions: Use a 10-sided die two times to make a fraction that is less than 1. Make a whole with one of the fractions on the game board to claim that spot. Try to get three, four, or five in a row (or block your opponent from doing so). High score wins!

Scoring: Three-in-a-row scores 5 points, four-in-a-row scores 10 points, and five-in-a-row scores 20 points.

$\frac{1}{2}$	$\frac{1}{4}$	$\frac{1}{8}$	$\frac{3}{5}$	$\frac{1}{10}$

online resources — This resource can be downloaded at **resources.corwin.com/FOF/addsubtractdecimalfraction**.

ACTIVITY 3.13

Name: Fraction Track Race   **Type:** Center (or Game)

About the Center: Fraction Track Race can be a single-player card game for students to practice finding ways to make a whole or a game for multiple players. Also see Activity 3.4 ("Build the Fraction and Decimal Track") for a fraction and decimal track teaching activity.

Materials: a deck of fraction cards, fraction track to 2, and five counters for the game board or a pencil for shading

Directions:
1. Students deal themselves five cards face down.

2. Students flip one card at a time and shade the related distance (or move their counter) on their choice of fraction tracks. For example, if a student draws $\frac{1}{2}$, they can mark $\frac{1}{2}$ on the Halves Track, $\frac{2}{4}$ on the Fourths Track, $\frac{3}{6}$ on the Sixths Track, or $\frac{6}{12}$ on the Twelfths Track.

3. Students complete three of the fraction tracks in as few moves as possible. (Each track must be completed exactly; it cannot add to more than 2.)

4. To conclude, students write an addition equation above each track to show how they made it to 2.

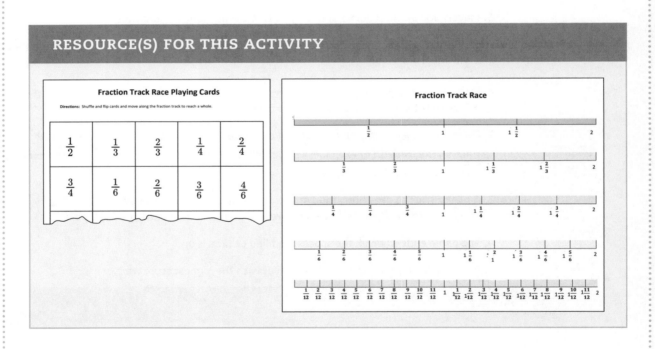

RESOURCE(S) FOR THIS ACTIVITY

online resources   These resources can be downloaded at **resources.corwin.com/FOF/addsubtractdecimalfraction**.

ACTIVITY 3.14

Name: Roll to Make a Whole   **Type:** Center

About the Center: This center activity has students create their own expressions (based on dice rolls) and then apply the Make a Whole strategy to solve. This means students will want to create expressions that lend to the strategy. You can modify this activity by offering different or fewer options on the placemat.

Materials: four 10-sided dice, a Roll to Make a Whole laminated placemat, and a dry-erase marker (optional: number lines or other physical tools to support reasoning)

Directions: 1. Students roll four dice.

2. Students decide which of the four options they want to use to write their expression (A–D on the placemat). *Note*: Students can place the dice right on the placemat and move them around to help select an option.

3. Students use a dry-erase marker to record the expression in the selected box.

4. Students rewrite the expression in a way that shows they applied the Make a Whole strategy.

5. Students solve the problem.

6. They roll the dice again and repeat the process, but this time there are just three options remaining on the placemat.

7. Students try to create four expressions, rewrite them using Make a Whole, and solve.

RESOURCE(S) FOR THIS ACTIVITY

Roll to Make a Whole Placemat

Directions: Roll four 10-sided dice. Use those numbers to create an expression, using your choice of expression templates. Then rewrite the expression to show the Make a Whole strategy.

A.

$$\underline{\quad} . \underline{\quad} + \underline{\quad} . \underline{\quad}$$

Rewritten Expression and Answer:

B.

$$\underline{\quad} . \underline{\quad} + 0.\underline{\quad}\ \underline{\quad}$$

Rewritten Expression and Answer:

C.

$$0.\underline{\quad}\ \underline{\quad} + 0.\underline{\quad}\ \underline{\quad}$$

Rewritten Expression and Answer:

D.

$$\frac{\square}{\square} + \frac{\square}{\square}$$

Rewritten Expression and Answer:

online resources ☞ This resource can be downloaded at **resources.corwin.com/FOF/addsubtractdecimalfraction**.

ACTIVITY 3.15

Name: Create an Expression   **Type:** Center

About the Center: This center focuses students' attention on writing equivalent expressions by changing an original expression into one that has a whole number addend.

Materials: digit cards (0–9) or playing cards (queens = 0 and aces = 1; remove tens, kings, and jacks); *Create an Expression* recording sheet

Directions: 1. Students use four digit cards to make two addends, neither of which can be whole numbers. Students can work only with decimals (with numbers to the tenths place or hundredths place) or only with fractions, whichever form they want.

2. Students record the expression.

3. Students write a new equivalent expression that has a whole number as one of the addends.

Decimal Example: A student pulls 9, 4, 3, and 5. She arranges them to make 3.5 + 4.9. She rewrites the problem as 3.4 + 5.0 and records the sum as 8.4. Then, she reshuffles the digit cards and creates a new problem.

Fraction Example: A student pulls 1, 2, 5, and 6. She arranges them to make $\frac{1}{2}+\frac{5}{6}$. She first rewrites the expression with a common denominator: $\frac{3}{6}+\frac{5}{6}$. Then she decomposes $\frac{5}{6}$. She moves $\frac{3}{6}$ over and writes the equivalent expression of $1+\frac{2}{6}$ and records an answer of $1\frac{2}{6}$.

RESOURCE(S) FOR THIS ACTIVITY

Create an Expression: Decimals

Directions: Use four digit cards to make two addends. Record the problem. Rewrite the problem using the Make a Whole strategy and then record the sum.

My Problem	My New Make a Whole, Tenths, Hundredths Problem	Sum
3.5 + 4.9	3.4 + .1 + 4.9 *or* 3.4 + 5.0	8.4

Create an Expression: Fractions

Directions: Use four digit cards to make two addends. Record the problem. Rewrite the problem using the Make a Whole strategy and then record the sum.

My Problem	My New Make Tens Problem	Sum
$\frac{1}{2}+\frac{5}{6}$	$\frac{3}{6}+\frac{5}{6}=1+\frac{2}{6}$	$1\frac{2}{6}$

online resources These resources can be downloaded at **resources.corwin.com/FOF/addsubtractdecimalfraction**.

NOTES

Think Addition Strategy

STRATEGY OVERVIEW:
Think Addition

What is Think Addition? Think Addition means that subtraction is being thought of as a compare situation (How many more?). Students rethink the subtraction expression as a missing addend equation and then count up or back to find the difference.

	FRACTIONS	DECIMALS
Examples	$7\frac{3}{8} - 5\frac{5}{8}$	8.5 – 6.75
Think Addition translation	$5\frac{5}{8} + ? = 7\frac{3}{8}$	6.75 + ? = 8.5
Related language	How much more to get from [addend] to [answer] *or* What is the difference (distance) between these two numbers?	

HOW DOES THINK ADDITION WORK?

In general, this strategy works by finding the difference between the two numbers. On a number line, students use efficient jumps to find the distance (difference) between the two numbers. There are typically several options, and students can count up or back to find the difference (although counting up is more common).

Fraction Example: $7\frac{3}{8} - 5\frac{5}{8}$

Think: What is the distance (difference) between $5\frac{5}{8}$ and $7\frac{3}{8}$?

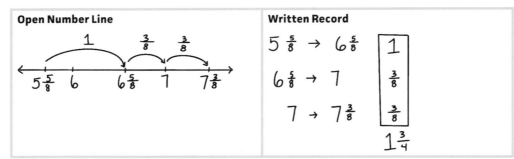

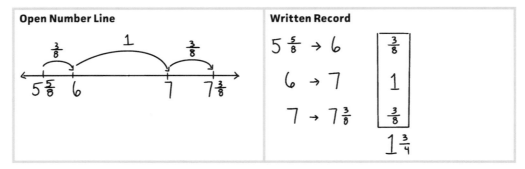

Decimal Example: 8.5 – 6.75

Think: What is the distance (difference) between 6.75 and 8.5?

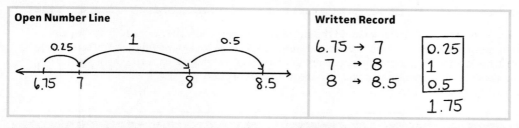

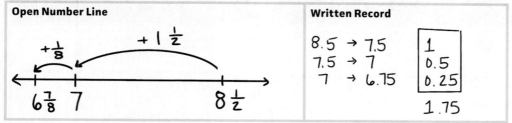

Notice that when you count up to *find the difference*, the answer is *the sum of the jumps*. This is different from when you count back as *take away*, wherein the answer is *where you land* on the number line.

WHEN DO YOU CHOOSE THINK ADDITION?

This is a versatile strategy that can be used in many problems. It is particularly useful when the two numbers being subtracted are close together, like the earlier examples. It is also useful when the two numbers are near whole numbers that are easy to subtract mentally (e.g., 16.2 – 5.8). Think 5.8 to 6 (0.2) to 16 (10) to 16.2 (0.2)—the answer is 10.4. With both fractions and decimals, this strategy is a good option when regrouping would be needed to solve it otherwise. For example, to solve $6\frac{1}{4} - 3\frac{1}{2}$, a student can count up to $5\frac{1}{2}$ (2) and then count up to $6\frac{1}{4}\left(\frac{3}{4}\right)$ to equal $2\frac{3}{4}$.

MODULE 1 Foundations for Reasoning Strategies

MODULE 2 Count On/Count Back Strategy

MODULE 3 Make a Whole Strategy

MODULE 4 Think Addition Strategy

MODULE 5 Compensation Strategy

MODULE 6 Partial Sums and Differences Strategy

MODULE 7 Standard Algorithms

THINK ADDITION:
Strategy Briefs for Families

It is important that families understand the strategies and know how they work so that they can be partners in the pursuit of fluency. These strategy briefs are a tool for doing that. You can include them in newsletters for parents or caregivers, or at a school event like a Back to School Night. They are available for download so that you can adjust them as needed.

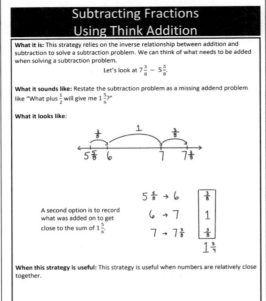

Subtracting Fractions Using Think Addition

What it is: This strategy relies on the inverse relationship between addition and subtraction to solve a subtraction problem. We can think of what needs to be added when solving a subtraction problem.

Let's look at $7\frac{3}{8} - 5\frac{5}{8}$.

What it sounds like: Restate the subtraction problem as a missing addend problem like "What plus $\frac{1}{2}$ will give me $1\frac{5}{6}$?"

What it looks like:

A second option is to record what was added on to get close to the sum of $1\frac{5}{6}$.

When this strategy is useful: This strategy is useful when numbers are relatively close together.

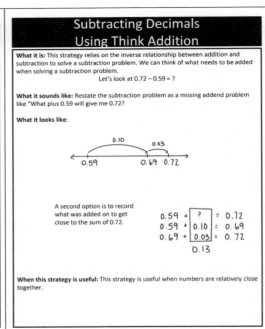

Subtracting Decimals Using Think Addition

What it is: This strategy relies on the inverse relationship between addition and subtraction to solve a subtraction problem. We can think of what needs to be added when solving a subtraction problem.

Let's look at $0.72 - 0.59 = ?$

What it sounds like: Restate the subtraction problem as a missing addend problem like "What plus 0.59 will give me 0.72?"

What it looks like:

A second option is to record what was added on to get close to the sum of 0.72.

When this strategy is useful: This strategy is useful when numbers are relatively close together.

 This resource can be downloaded at **resources.corwin.com/FOF/ addsubtractdecimalfraction.**

NOTES

TEACHING ACTIVITIES for Think Addition

Before students are able to choose strategies, which is a key to fluency, they first must be able to understand and use relevant strategies. These activities focus specifically on Think Addition. While students may employ other methods to subtract, which is appropriate, they also must learn this important strategy that leverages and strengthens their understanding of the relationship between addition and subtraction.

ACTIVITY 4.1
START WITH, GET TO (WITH DECIMAL CHARTS)

Students first learn about the inverse relationship between addition and subtraction in primary grades when they work with single-digit numbers. Students who show understanding of the concept with single-digit numbers may be challenged to transfer the understanding to two- and three-digit numbers. In this instructional activity, students advance their understanding of Think Addition by employing an idea of "start with, get to." First, students are shown a subtraction problem like 0.84 – 0.39. Then, students identify the potential Think Addition equation (0.39 + ? = 0.84). Students use this equation to establish the idea of "starting with one" number and counting on to "get to" the other. The decimal chart can be leveraged to support their thinking as needed.

0.91	0.92	0.93	0.94	0.95	0.96	0.97	0.98	0.99	1.00
0.81	0.82	0.83	0.84	0.85	0.86	0.87	0.88	0.89	0.90
0.71	0.72	0.73	0.74	0.75	0.76	0.77	0.78	0.79	0.80
0.61	0.62	0.63	0.64	0.65	0.66	0.67	0.68	0.69	0.70
0.51	0.52	0.53	0.54	0.55	0.56	0.57	0.58	0.59	0.60
0.41	0.42	0.43	0.44	0.45	0.46	0.47	0.48	0.49	0.50
0.31	0.32	0.33	0.34	0.35	0.36	0.37	0.38	0.39	0.40
0.21	0.22	0.23	0.24	0.25	0.26	0.27	0.28	0.29	0.30
0.11	0.12	0.13	0.14	0.15	0.16	0.17	0.18	0.19	0.20
0.01	0.02	0.03	0.04	0.05	0.06	0.07	0.08	0.09	0.10

0.84 – 0.39

Start With

0.39 + ? = 0.84

0.39 + 0.40 = 0.79

0.79 + 0.01 = 0.80
0.80 + 0.04 = 0.84

0.39 + 0.45 = 0.84
0.84 – 0.39 = 0.45

As you facilitate the discussion, be sure to emphasize why one number is the "start with" and the other is the "get to." Keep in mind that these designations are opposite of counting back, so some students may be challenged to explain or represent their thinking.

Some problems to use for this activity include the following:

0.84 – 0.58	0.98 – 0.64	0.83 – 0.36
0.55 – 0.36	0.87 – 0.37	0.61 – 0.48
0.73 – 0.49	0.55 – 0.28	0.71 – 0.55

TEACHING TAKEAWAY

You can provide base-10 blocks or place value disks to support students as they count up if needed.

ACTIVITY 4.2
USING OPEN NUMBER LINES

Open number lines are excellent models for helping students develop understanding of the Think Addition relationship. For this activity, pose a subtraction expression to students such as 0.72 – 0.59. Have students work to create an open number line to represent the expression as a missing addend equation (as seen on the left in the following example). Then, have students determine the related Think Addition equation and count up to solve it (as seen on the right).

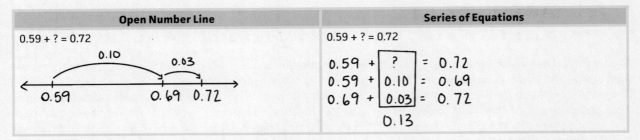

The open number line diagram representations do not have to be proportionate to the numbers they represent. For fractions, the strategy also takes advantage of benchmarks in counting up, as illustrated by the solution to $7\frac{1}{6} - 5\frac{2}{3}$.

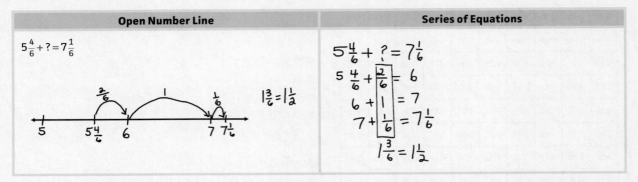

The following problems lend themselves to Think Addition and can be modeled on a number line. When the denominators are halves, fourths, or eighths, rulers (inches) can be used as a context and a visual.

$3\frac{3}{4} - 1\frac{2}{4}$	$3\frac{2}{6} - 1\frac{5}{6}$	$4\frac{1}{8} - 2\frac{7}{8}$
$4\frac{5}{8} - 2\frac{2}{8}$	$4\frac{1}{4} - 3\frac{1}{2}$	$3\frac{1}{12} - 1\frac{10}{12}$
$4\frac{3}{5} - 3\frac{1}{5}$	$5\frac{3}{4} - 2\frac{1}{2}$	$7\frac{1}{6} - 5\frac{2}{3}$

Number lines are good tools for representing subtraction in both interpretations (take away and compare). Using any of the problems shown here, as well as problems from Module 2 (wherein the focus is on counting back using the take-away interpretation), have students solve both on the open number line. Before beginning, ask students if they think they will get the same answer using "take away" as using "find the difference." Have students model both on open number lines to prove that they are the same. Here is a count back (take-away) illustration for the problem solved above as Think Addition, $7\frac{1}{6} - 5\frac{2}{3}$:

$$7\frac{1}{6} - 5\frac{2}{3} = 7\frac{1}{6} - 5\frac{4}{6}$$

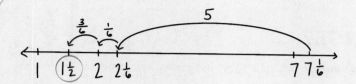

These number line proofs work with both fractions and decimal subtraction problems. And this helps students to see that while some problems may lend to a take-away interpretation and others may lend to a find the difference interpretation, either one will lead to an accurate answer.

ACTIVITY 4.3
UNCOVERED LEGO

In this activity, students lay smaller LEGO® pieces on top of larger (whole) pieces to determine the difference between the quantities (discovering how much of the whole or wholes are uncovered). Thus, the situation is set up as a compare situation where students are figuring out how many more to cover the whole(s). During this discussion, you want to reinforce that addition can be a handy tool for finding differences.

Start with a 2 × 8 LEGO as the whole. Begin by discussing the LEGO's characteristics. For example, its 16 studs are arranged in a 2 × 8 array, so our whole is 16 sixteenths. Now place a 2 × 6 LEGO on top of it; note its 12 studs, which is 12 sixteenths or $\frac{3}{4}$ of the whole.

Ask students what they notice. Then ask, "What part of the whole is uncovered? What equations could be used to find out what fraction is uncovered?"

As a subtraction equation: $1 - \frac{6}{8} = \frac{2}{8}$ or $1 - \frac{3}{4} = \frac{1}{4}$

As a Think Addition problem: $\frac{6}{8} + \frac{2}{8} = 1$ or $\frac{3}{4} + \frac{1}{4} = 1$

LEGO pieces work great for mixed numbers. Let's say we have three 2 × 8 LEGO pieces (three wholes) and we place two 2 × 6 LEGO pieces (or $\frac{12}{16}$ and another $\frac{12}{16}$) on top of them. This is 24 studs, which is 24 sixteenths $\left(\frac{24}{16}\right)$ or $1\frac{1}{2}$. *Note*: The LEGO pieces can be positioned several ways, as shown next, such as placing the 2 × 6 piece over each whole piece or end to end. Students will love trying different ways! The question is, "What's uncovered?"

Record subtraction and Think Addition equations that could be used to find what's uncovered.

Continue the process with additional LEGO situations and ask, "What's fraction is uncovered?":

- You have a 3 × 4 LEGO (one whole) and you place a 3 × 2 LEGO on top of it.

- You have two 3 × 2 LEGO pieces (one 3 × 2 represents one whole) and you place a 4 × 2 LEGO on top of it.

- You have three 2 × 6 LEGO pieces (one 2 × 6 represents one whole) and you place four 1 × 4 LEGO pieces on top of them.

- You have two 4 × 4 LEGO pieces (one 4 × 4 represents one whole) and you place five 2 × 2 LEGO pieces on top of it.

ACTIVITY 4.4
WHAT'S THE CHANGE?

Many cashiers or bank tellers count up to give back change. In this activity, we use money as a context to explore the Think Addition strategy.

Pose this problem to students:

> You buy school supplies that cost $18.72. You pay with a $20 bill. The cashier counts up from $18.72, $19.72, $19.82, and $19.92 then $20. What coins did she give back as change? What was the exact change? What equations represent this situation?

After discussing the initial task, pose the following scenarios. Encourage students to use a decimal chart or coins to support their reasoning and find the change.

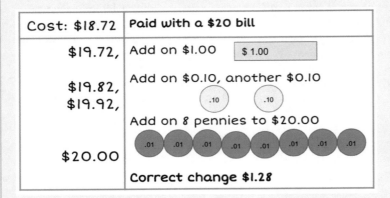

> Ms. Diego spends $7.89 and pays using a $10 bill. Use Think Addition as a strategy to count up the change she should be receiving. What coins did she give back as change? What was the exact change?

> Your mom buys dog food that costs $15.67 with tax. She pays with a $20 bill. Use Think Addition as a strategy to be sure you get the correct change.

After exploring the scenarios, post problems such as 14.50 – 9.75 and ask students to find the difference. Invite them to think of it as a change-finding situation so they can solve it mentally.

ACTIVITY 4.5
PROMPTS FOR TEACHING THINK ADDITION

Use the following prompts as opportunities to develop understanding of and reasoning with the Think Addition strategy and/or as assessments to determine whether students understand the strategy. You can require that students use representations and tools to justify their thinking, including open number lines, money, LEGO pieces, dot patterns, and so on, or you can focus on mental math. If you are using these prompts for whole class discourse, first provide individual think time, then small-group (e.g., triads) talk time, and finally whole-group time. Any prompt can be easily modified to feature different decimals and fractions.

Decimal Prompts

- Jerome says that 2.61 – 1.37 can be solved by thinking 1.37 + 2.61. Do you agree or disagree with Jerome? Explain your thinking.

- Use a number line to show how 5.81 – 2.55 = ? is related to 2.55 + ? = 5.81.

- Allison uses Think Addition to solve 9.91 – 9.4. Tell why you agree or disagree with her thinking.

Fraction Prompts

- Julio is making a quilt and it is already $4\frac{1}{3}$ feet long. The quilt needs to be 7 feet long. Julio says he needs to add 3 more feet. What would you say Julio?

- Do you prefer counting back or counting up to solve subtraction problems? Tell how they are the same and different. Use a problem like $3\frac{2}{5} - 1\frac{4}{5}$ to show your thinking.

General Prompts

- Tell how you can use addition to solve a subtraction problem. Use examples to show your thinking.

- Tell how counting back and counting up (for Think Addition) are the same and how they are different.

- How would you explain Think Addition to someone new to your math class? Use situations (real-life examples) and illustrations to provide a strong explanation.

PRACTICE ACTIVITIES for Think Addition

Fluency is realized through quality practice that is focused, varied, processed, and connected. The activities in this section focus students' attention on how this strategy works and when to use it. The activities are a collection of varied engagements. Game boards, recording sheets, digit cards, and other required materials are available as online resources for you to download, possibly modify, and use.

As students practice, look for how well they are using the new strategy and assimilating it into their collection of strategies. Post-activity discussions help students reflect on *how* they reasoned and *when* that strategy was useful (and when it was not). Discussions can also help students reflect on how that strategy connects to recent instruction and to other strategies they have learned.

FLUENCY COMPONENT	WHAT TO LOOK FOR AS STUDENTS PRACTICE THIS STRATEGY
Efficiency	• Do students choose the Think Addition strategy when it is a good fit for the problem? • Are students using the strategy adeptly (not getting hung up)? • Do students overuse the strategy (i.e., try to use it when it is not a good fit, such as 7.3 – 0.45)? • Are students using the strategy efficiently? (e.g., Do they count up in chunks?)
Flexibility	• Are students using the Think Addition strategy or are they reverting to previously learned and/or possibly less appropriate strategies? • Are students carrying out Think Addition in flexible ways? (e.g., Do they count up in different ways or do they count up in the same way each time?) • Do they change their approach to Think Addition when another becomes overly complicated? (e.g., Do they begin to use partial differences for 3.17 – 2.98 and then switch to counting up? Do they abandon Think Addition when it isn't working well?)
Accuracy	• Are students using the strategy accurately? • Are students finding accurate solutions? • Are they considering the reasonableness of their solution? • Are students estimating before finding solutions?

ACTIVITY 4.6
THINK ADDITION WORKED EXAMPLES

Worked examples can be used as a warmup, as a focus of a lesson, at a learning center, or on an assessment. Here we share examples and ideas for preparing worked examples to support student understanding of the Think Addition strategy. There are different ways to pose worked examples, and they each serve a different fluency purpose:

TYPE OF WORKED EXAMPLE	PURPOSES: COMPONENT (FLUENCY ACTIONS)	QUESTIONS FOR DISCUSSIONS OR FOR WRITING RESPONSES
Correctly Worked Example	Efficiency (selects an appropriate strategy) and flexibility (applies a strategy to a new problem type)	What did _____ do? Why does it work? Is this a good method for this problem?
Partially Worked Example (Implement the Strategy Accurately)	Efficiency (selects an appropriate strategy; solves in a reasonable amount of time) and accuracy (completes steps accurately; gets correct answer)	Why did _____ start the problem this way? What does _____ need to do to finish the problem?
Incorrectly Worked Example (Highlight Common Errors)	Accuracy (completes steps accurately; gets correct answer)	What did _____ do? What mistake does _____ make? How can this mistake be fixed?

Also ask students to *compare* two correctly worked examples. For Think Addition, students can compare examples to determine if they are better off thinking of the problem as a *take-away* or *compare* situation. Partially worked examples can focus on common obstacles students encounter when working through the strategy. Incorrectly worked examples can focus on the common counting challenges students may have. For example, one student might count up to friendly decimal benchmark numbers but struggle with keeping track, whereas another student might make an error combining the parts while counting up or back. The instructional prompts from Activity 4.5 can also be used for collecting worked examples. Throughout the module are various worked examples that you can use as fictional worked examples.

(Continued)

(*Continued*)

CORRECTLY WORKED EXAMPLES FOR THINK ADDITION	
Fraction example: $8\frac{1}{2}-6\frac{7}{8}$ Compare these two ways: 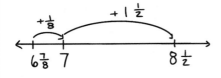	Decimal example: $0.82 - 0.53 = ?$ Compare these two ways: 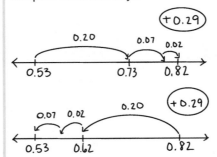

PARTIALLY WORKED EXAMPLES FOR THINK ADDITION	
Jeremy's start for $2\frac{1}{4}-\frac{7}{8}$: 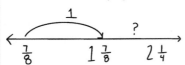 Highlight the importance of finding common denominators to count up.	Lauren's start for $1.57 - 0.82$: 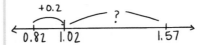 Lauren started to use Think Addition and added 0.2 to get to 1.02. What is her next move?

INCORRECTLY WORKED EXAMPLES FOR THINK ADDITION	
Jessica's work for $3\frac{5}{8}-1\frac{7}{8}$: 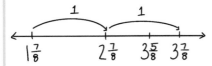 What has Jessica done correctly and what does she need to fix?	Jonah's work for $0.72 - 0.48$: 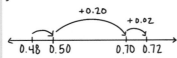 What has Jonah done correctly and what does he need to fix?

ACTIVITY 4.7

Name: "Two Lies and a Truth"   **Type:** Routine

About the Routine: Students may seem to understand Think Addition situations by connecting addition and subtraction equations. However, they may not truly or fully understand the relationship between addition and subtraction. "Two Lies and a Truth" has students compare related equations to see if they, in fact, are correctly representing the inverse relationship.

Materials: This routine does not require any materials.

Directions: 1. Pose three pairs of equations to students.

2. Give students individual think time to determine which two are lies and which one is a truth.

3. Have students discuss if the two equations are related through the Think Addition strategy.

4. After students discuss with partners, bring the group together to share ideas. When students identify equations that aren't true, have them determine a new equation that would be true.

The following tables share three pairs for fractions and three pairs for decimals.

1	$\frac{1}{2} - ? = \frac{1}{8}$	$\frac{1}{2} + ? = \frac{1}{8}$	**Lie.** Students might believe these are related through Think Addition because both equations have the same numbers and are in the same order.
2	$\frac{3}{4} - \frac{1}{2} = ?$	$? + \frac{1}{2} = \frac{3}{4}$	**True.** These two equations are inverses of each other.
3	$\frac{1}{2} + \frac{5}{6} = \frac{6}{8}$	$\frac{6}{8} - \frac{1}{2} = \frac{5}{6}$	**Lie.** Students might think this is true because they add or subtract the numerator and denominator across without attending to common denominators.

1	72.4 – ? = 6.14	72.4 + ? = 6.14	**Lie.** Students might believe these are related through Think Addition because both equations have the same numbers and are in the same order.
2	23.7 + 78.9 = ?	78.9 – 23.7 = ?	**Lie.** Similar to the first example, these equations have the same numbers. Also note that the subtraction equation has a larger minuend, which some students may rely on to determine correct subtraction expressions.
3	68.9 – ? = 6.45	6.45 + ? = 6.89	**True.** These two equations are inverses of each other.

An extension of this routine is to give students card strips like the following and ask them to create some more true statements to add to the pile (or they can create their own two lies and a truth, or two truths and a lie).

	Subtraction Problem Create a missing-value subtraction equation.	**Think Addition Problem** Create a missing-value addition equation that matches your subtraction equation (the missing value will be the same number).
#		

ACTIVITY 4.8

Name: "Close But Not Too Much" **Type:** Routine

About the Routine: In "Close But Not Too Much," the teacher posts a subtraction problem and students figure out the biggest jump they can make between the two numbers, without going over (as they seek to find the difference). (Going over and coming back is a good method, as discussed for compensation. This routine, however, just focuses on jumping between the two numbers.) This routine also involves estimation because seeking the biggest jump is also a good estimate for the difference.

Materials: This routine does not require any materials.

Directions:
1. Pose a subtraction problem recorded on the board (e.g., $4\frac{2}{5} - 1\frac{4}{5}$).

2. Ask students to estimate the answer, write it on a piece of paper, and put it away.

3. Ask students to then write or state a Think Addition equation that reflects the equation posted (e.g., $1\frac{4}{5} + ? = 4\frac{2}{5}$). Record this equation on the board and mark the two numbers on a number line.

4. Explain that their goal is to use jumps to get as close as possible without going over to find the difference between the two numbers.

5. Ask students to think about the first jump they would make.

6. Students share their thinking with a partner. Ask the whole group and mark the jump on the number line.

7. Repeat steps 3 and 4 until students reach their destination (in this case, $4\frac{2}{5}$).

8. Ask students for the answer. Ask students to explain what the answer represents in the original problem and how it compares to their estimate.

For example, 26.1 – 14.6 is posted. Students estimate the difference at about 12. Then, they record the addition sentence: 14.6 + ? = 26.1. Students discuss the largest jump. They realize that a jump of 12 overshoots their goal. So, they report back that they will first jump 11 (to 25.6). Students disagree on the next jump. Some say 0.4 to get to 26, and some say 0.5 to get to the total (both ideas are good ones). The answer is 11.5, and it means that the difference between the two given numbers is 11.5.

ACTIVITY 4.9

Name: The Smallest Difference   **Type:** Game

About the Game: Reasoning about results supports the accuracy component of fluency. *The Smallest Difference* helps students practice reasoning by having them determine what numbers will generate the smallest difference. You can enrich the experience by having students estimate differences before finding exact solutions.

Materials: prepared deck of *Smallest Difference* number cards (decimals or fractions)

Directions:

1. The deck of number cards is shuffled and players are dealt three cards.

2. Players choose two of the three cards to make a subtraction problem.

3. Players use Think Addition to find the difference between the two cards they kept.

4. The player with the smallest difference gets a point.

5. All cards are returned to the deck, the deck is shuffled, and players are dealt three cards again.

6. Play continues until a player earns 5 points.

Any numbers can be used for this game. Cards can be easily made with index cards or number cards can be printed on cardstock. Cards with hundredths and larger whole numbers are also available.

> **TEACHING TAKEAWAY**
>
> Have students record their work in their math journals or on a recording sheet. The work could also be used for student reflection and formative assessment.

RESOURCE(S) FOR THIS ACTIVITY

$\frac{1}{2}$	$\frac{1}{4}$	$\frac{3}{4}$	1
$\frac{1}{8}$	$\frac{3}{8}$	$\frac{5}{8}$	$\frac{7}{8}$
$1\frac{1}{2}$	$1\frac{3}{4}$	$1\frac{3}{8}$	2
$2\frac{1}{2}$	$2\frac{3}{4}$	3	$3\frac{1}{8}$
$3\frac{1}{2}$	$3\frac{3}{4}$	$3\frac{5}{8}$	$3\frac{7}{8}$

9.7	4.5	6.3	8.1
7.8	9.1	8.4	5.4
2.8	1.7	4.4	7.4
1.9	6.6	7.7	3.1
9.0	3.6	1.9	2.8

 This resource can be downloaded at **resources.corwin.com/FOF/addsubtractdecimalfraction.**

ACTIVITY 4.10

Name: Empty the Money Bag   **Type:** Game

About the Game: In this game, players act as store keepers and count up change, a context that supports Think Addition reasoning. The object of the game is to empty the money bag the fastest.

Materials: *Empty the Money Bag* recording sheet, two 10-sided dice, and play money (optional)

Directions: 1. Players have $10.

2. Players take turns rolling two dice to form an amount of change. They subtract that much money from their money bag. For fun and to give the activity a more authentic feel, players can make change for each other in each round.

3. Players record an equation to represent the money spent, show how much money is left in their money bag, and then record the correct change in column 3.

4. Play continues until someone empties their money bag.

For example, Player 1 rolled a 7 and a 9 and made the amount $0.97. Player 1 records the related addition expression ($0.97 + ? = $10.00). Player 1 records their remaining money in the third column ($9.03). Player 2 (the cashier) makes sure that player 1 has the correct bills and coins showing in their money bag.

RESOURCE(S) FOR THIS ACTIVITY

Empty the Money Bag [MONEY BAG]

Directions: Players start with $10. They take turns rolling two dice and subtracting the money in the money bag. They record the money spent and mark the correct change in their money bag. They play until someone empties their money bag or until they play 10 rounds.

Purchase	Change in My Money Bag	? =
Example: Player 1 rolls a 7 and 9 and makes the amount $0.97. $10.00 − 0.97 = ?	0.97 + ? = 10.00 $5 .01 .01 .01 $1 $1 $1 $1	? = $9.03
$10.00 − 0._ _ = ?	_____	

Empty the Money Bag

Directions: Players start with $10. They take turns rolling two dice and subtracting the money in the money bag. They record the money spent and mark the correct change in their money bag. They play until someone empties their money bag or until they play 10 rounds.

Purchase	Change in My Money Bag	? =
_____		? =
_____		? =

[online resources] This resource can be downloaded at **resources.corwin.com/FOF/addsubtractdecimalfraction**.

ACTIVITY 4.11

Name: Think Addition Math Libs   **Type:** Game

About the Game: *Math Libs* is a relatively simplistic and enjoyable game of chance. Students draw cards and try to fill in missing values in order to be first to complete the *Math Lib* card.

Materials: *Think Addition Math Libs* game board and digit cards (0–9) or playing cards (queens = 0 and aces = 1; remove tens, kings, and jacks)

Directions: 1. Players take turns pulling a digit card. They use the number to fill a space on their board, if they can.

2. Once a player fully completes a problem, they use Think Addition to find the unknown. Their opponent also finds the unknown to confirm they are correct (but cannot record it on their game board).

3. A player loses their turn if a digit they pull can't be used for any space on their board.

4. The first player to find all of the unknowns and solve the problems correctly wins.

For example, Lindy draws a 3. She uses it to complete 3.4 + ? = 5.2. On her next turn she draws an 8. It can't be used so she loses her turn. On her third turn she draws a 3 and uses it to complete 2.7 + ? = 6.3.

Fraction Mad Libs is almost the same, with one important change: equivalent fractions can be used to fill in missing values. For example, the mixed number in the first row might be $12\frac{1}{2}$, $12\frac{2}{4}$, or $12\frac{3}{6}$.

Think Addition Math Libs – Decimals

Directions: Take turns choosing a digit card. Use the digit to fill a number in the Think Addition column. Once a number is completely filled in, find the value of the question mark (?). Be the first to find all the ? values.

$5.2 - 3.4 = ?$	$\underline{3}.4 + ? = 5.2$	$? = 1.8$
$6.3 - 2.7 = ?$	$2.7 + ? = 6.\underline{3}$	$? = 3.6$

Think Addition Math Libs

Directions: Take turns choosing a digit card. Use the digit to fill in the missing numerators that will give you the equivalent fractions to help with the think addition strategy. Once a number is completely filled in find the ?. Be the first to find all of the ?.

$12\frac{1}{2} - 6\frac{1}{4} = ?$	$6\frac{1}{4} + ? = 12\frac{\underline{2}}{4}$	$? = 6\frac{1}{4}$
$8\frac{6}{10} - 3\frac{1}{2} = ?$	$3\frac{\underline{5}}{10} + ? = 8\frac{6}{10}$	$? = 5\frac{1}{10}$

online resources ↖ Blank *Think Addition Math Libs* game boards can be downloaded at **resources.corwin.com/FOF/ addsubtractdecimalfraction.**

ACTIVITY 4.12

Name: Triangle Cards   **Type:** Center

About the Center: You can use triangle cards to help students learn their basic facts. Triangle cards help students see the relationship between addition and subtraction, so they are also an excellent tool for Think Addition.

Materials: prepared triangle cards and Triangle Cards recording sheet

Directions: 1. Students select a triangle card.

2. On their recording sheet, students record two addition equations and two subtraction equations using the numbers on the triangle card.

For example, a student picks the card on the left. They record 5.9 + 1.8 = 7.7, 1.8 + 5.9 = 7.7, 7.7 – 5.9 = 1.8, and 7.7 – 1.8 = 5.9.

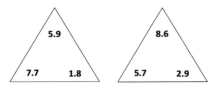

To extend this activity to missing values, you can do one of two things. First, you can have students simply place their thumb over one of the numbers and have a partner reason to identify the missing number. Second, you can create triangle cards with a question mark in one of the corners, as illustrated here (notice the total is circled to clarify the starting value).

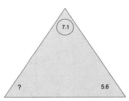

RESOURCE(S) FOR THIS ACTIVITY

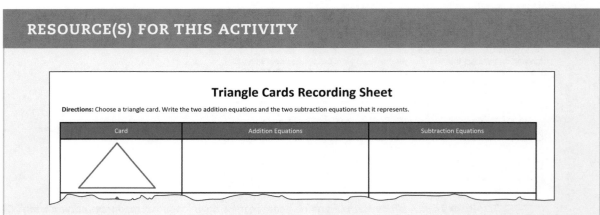

Triangle Cards Recording Sheet

Directions: Choose a triangle card. Write the two addition equations and the two subtraction equations that it represents.

Card	Addition Equations	Subtraction Equations

  This recording sheet and the triangle cards can be downloaded at **resources.corwin.com/FOF/ addsubtractdecimalfraction.**

ACTIVITY 4.13

Name: Make the Difference   **Type:** Center

About the Center: This center challenges students to create different expressions that have the same difference.

Materials: digit cards (0–9) or playing cards (queens = 0 and aces = 1; remove tens, kings, and jacks), and Make the Difference recording sheet

Directions: 1. For fractions, students draw three cards and form a mixed number. For decimals, students draw three cards and make a decimal number. (The number of cards drawn can be increased to make different decimal numbers with a variety of digits.)

2. Students create two different subtraction equations that have a difference equal to the number they made with the cards.

3. Students rewrite their subtraction equations as addition equations and confirm that their equations are correct.

For example, Amy uses 3, 4, and 8 to make $4\frac{3}{8}$ and creates two problems with that difference:
$7\frac{6}{8} - 3\frac{3}{8} = 4\frac{3}{8}$ and $4\frac{7}{8} - \frac{1}{2} = 4\frac{3}{8}$.

Giovanni draws 3, 4, and 8 and makes the decimal 34.8. He writes two subtraction equations: 44.8 – 10 = 34.8 and 65.8 – 31 = 34.8. He records addition equations and adds to see if the answer is correct. Notice that Giovanni's first problem (44.8 – 10 = 34.8) is straightforward. To push students to think more deeply about decimal differences, you can insert restrictions on the type of numbers they have to use. For example, you might say that students cannot use whole numbers.

RESOURCE(S) FOR THIS ACTIVITY

Make the Difference

Directions: Select digit cards to make a number. Create two problems that have that number as the difference. Use Think Addition to prove your thinking.

My Number	Subtraction Problems With My Number as a Difference	Think Addition Problems and Adding Up
	Problem 1	
	Problem 2	
	Problem 1	
	Problem 2	
	Problem 1	
	Problem 2	

online resources   This resource can be downloaded at **resources.corwin.com/FOF/addsubtractdecimalfraction.**

Compensation Strategy

STRATEGY OVERVIEW:
Compensation

What is Compensation? This strategy involves *adjusting* the expression to make it easier to add or subtract, and then *compensating* to preserve equivalence. The quantities tend to be *rounded up* to a convenient number (a benchmark).

HOW DOES COMPENSATION WORK FOR ADDITION?

This strategy is the zero property in action. If 0.3 is added to an addend, then 0.3 must also be subtracted. While this is true for both addition and subtraction, they look different in action and are explained separately in this overview.

Here is an example: 5.8 + 2.6. Think, "How can I adjust this expression to make it easier to add?"

One Option: Adjust One Addend	Another Option: Adjust Both
Adjust: 5.8 + 2.6 → 6 + 2.6 [I added 0.2]	Adjust: 5.8 + 2.6 → 6 + 3 [I added 0.6]
Add: 6 + 2.6 = 8.6	Add: 6 + 3 = 9
Compensate: [I need to subtract 0.2]	Compensate: [I need to subtract 0.6]
8.6 − 0.2 = 8.4	9 − 0.6 = 8.4

This strategy can also be modeled on a number line. Here is an example with $2\frac{1}{2} + 5\frac{7}{8}$, adjusting $5\frac{7}{8}$ to 6.

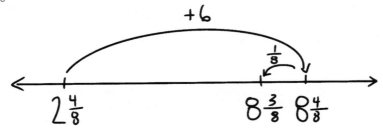

HOW DOES COMPENSATION WORK FOR SUBTRACTION?

Compensation when subtracting "behaves" differently than when adding, and attention must be given to *which* number is being changed. Let's explore how to change just one of the numbers using a subtraction example: $8\frac{1}{2} - 3\frac{7}{8}$.

1. First, think of the problem with eighths: $8\frac{4}{8} - 3\frac{7}{8}$.

2. Then adjust the minuend by adding 3 eighths: $8\frac{7}{8} - 3\frac{7}{8}$. Subtract. The difference is 5.

   Compensate: Three-eighths *too much* was added to the problem. To compensate, it must be subtracted: $5 - \frac{3}{8} = 4\frac{5}{8}$.

   Generalization: If you add to the minuend, you must compensate by removing that extra from the answer.

3a. Adjust the subtrahend by adding 1 eighth: $8\frac{4}{8} - 4$. Subtract. The difference is $4\frac{4}{8}$

  Compensate: You subtracted an extra eighth and must add it back in: $4\frac{4}{8} + \frac{1}{8} = 4\frac{5}{8}$.

  Generalization: If you add to the subtrahend, you are taking too much away and you must compensate by adding that quantity back.

Subtraction is not only take away but also compare (find the difference). The difference between $3\frac{3}{4}$ and $6\frac{1}{2}$ is the same as the difference between 4 and $6\frac{3}{4}$. Thus, it is a *constant difference*. It is a slide on the number line that makes subtraction easier.

TEACHING TAKEAWAY

Think of a slide on the number line to write an equivalent, but easier to solve, subtraction problem.

3b. Adjust both numbers in the problem by sliding up one-eighth: $8\frac{5}{8} - 4$.

  (The idea is to round the subtrahend to a whole and increase the minuend the same.)

These options can also be illustrated on number lines, as illustrated with the decimal example 0.63 – 0.38.

OPTION 1: ADJUST THE MINUEND (START NUMBER)

Adjust: 0.63 to 0.68 [Add 0.05 too much]

Subtract: 0.68 – 0.38 = 0.30

Compensate: [Subtract the 0.05]

0.30 – 0.05 = 0.25

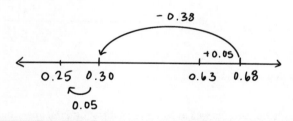

OPTION 2: ADJUST THE SUBTRAHEND (SECOND NUMBER)

Adjust: 0.38 to 0.40 [*Subtract* 0.02 too much]

Subtract: 0.63 – 0.40 = 0.23

Compensate: [*Add* 0.02 back]

0.23 + 0.02 = 0.25

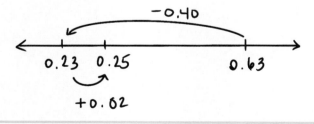

(Continued)

MODULE 1 Foundations for Reasoning Strategies

MODULE 2 Count On/Count Back Strategy

MODULE 3 Make a Whole Strategy

MODULE 4 Think Addition Strategy

MODULE 5 Compensation Strategy

MODULE 6 Partial Sums and Differences Strategy

MODULE 7 Standard Algorithms

(Continued)

OPTION 3: ADJUST BOTH (COMMON DIFFERENCE)

Adjust: 0.63 − 0.38 → 0.65 to 0.40 [sliding up 0.02 on the number line]

Solve: 0.65 − 0.40 = 0.25

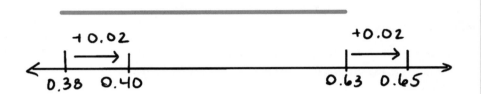

TEACHING TAKEAWAY

Compensation as a common difference works great for mixed number problems.

Compensation is very efficient for mixed number problems, especially with common denominators. Slide the subtrahend up to the nearest whole number, creating a problem where only the whole numbers are subtracted. Let's use the example $6\frac{4}{12} - 3\frac{9}{12}$.

$$6\frac{4}{12} + \frac{3}{12} = 6\frac{7}{12}$$
$$-3\frac{9}{12} + \frac{3}{12} = 4$$
$$\overline{\qquad\qquad\qquad}$$
$$2\frac{7}{12}$$

WHEN DO YOU CHOOSE COMPENSATION?

Compensation is very versatile, so it works well in adding or subtracting decimals and fractions, in particular when one or both numbers are near a benchmark. It is particularly useful in subtraction situations that involve regrouping because it is an efficient way to get an answer and avoid the common pitfalls of regrouping.

COMPENSATION:
Strategy Briefs for Families

It is important that families understand the strategies and know how they work so that they can be partners in the pursuit of fluency. These strategy briefs are a tool for doing that. You can include them in newsletters for parents or caregivers, or at a school event like a Back to School Night. They are available for download so that you can adjust them as needed.

Compensation Strategy for Fraction Addition

What it is: This strategy involves *adjusting* the expression to make it easier to add or subtract, and then *compensating* (or undoing) to preserve equivalence. The quantities tend to be **rounded up** to a convenient number.

Let's look at $3\frac{7}{8} + 2\frac{6}{8}$.

What it sounds like: 2 options	How it looks
I can **adjust** one number to make it easier to add. If I pretend $3\frac{7}{8}$ is 4, then $4 + 2\frac{6}{8} = 6\frac{6}{8}$. However, to adjust the start number to 4, I had to add $\frac{1}{8}$ too much. To **compensate** for that I need to subtract $\frac{1}{8}$ from $6\frac{6}{8}$, so $6\frac{6}{8} - \frac{1}{8} = 6\frac{5}{8}$.	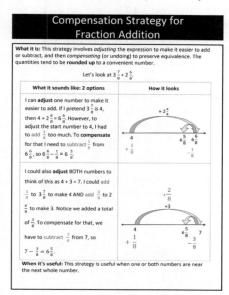
I could also **adjust** BOTH numbers to think of this as $4 + 3 = 7$. I could add $\frac{1}{8}$ to $3\frac{7}{8}$ to make 4 AND add $\frac{2}{8}$ to 2 $\frac{6}{8}$ to make 3. Notice we added a total of $\frac{3}{8}$. To compensate for that, we have to subtract $\frac{3}{8}$ from 7, so $7 - \frac{3}{8} = 6\frac{5}{8}$.	

When it's useful: This strategy is useful when one or both numbers are near the next whole number.

Compensation Strategy for Fraction Subtraction

What it is: This strategy involves *adjusting* the expression to make it easier to add or subtract, and then *compensating* (or undoing) to preserve equivalence. The quantities tend to be **rounded up** to a convenient number. Let's look at $6\frac{4}{12} - 3\frac{9}{12}$.

What it sounds like	How it looks
I can **adjust** the first number (the minuend) to make it easier to subtract. I add $\frac{3}{12}$ to $6\frac{9}{12}$ so it should be $6\frac{9}{12} - 3\frac{9}{12} = 3$. But adding to the first number made the difference $\frac{3}{12}$ too much. To **compensate**, I subtract $\frac{3}{12}$: $3 - \frac{3}{12} = 2\frac{9}{12}$.	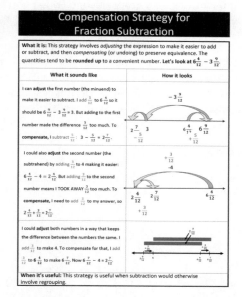
I could also **adjust** the second number (the subtrahend) by adding $\frac{4}{12}$ to 4 making it easier: $6\frac{4}{12} - 4 = 2\frac{4}{12}$. But adding $\frac{3}{12}$ to the second number means I TOOK AWAY $\frac{3}{12}$ too much. To **compensate**, I need to add $\frac{3}{12}$ to my answer, so $2\frac{4}{12} + \frac{3}{12} = 2\frac{7}{12}$.	
I could adjust both numbers in a way that keeps the difference between the numbers the same. I add $\frac{3}{12}$ to $3\frac{9}{12}$ to make 4. To compensate for that, I add $\frac{3}{12}$ to $6\frac{4}{12}$ to make $6\frac{7}{12}$. Now $6\frac{7}{12} - 4 = 2\frac{7}{12}$.	

When it's useful: This strategy is useful when subtraction would otherwise involve regrouping.

Compensation Strategy for Decimal Addition

What it is: This strategy involves *adjusting* the expression to make it easier to add or subtract, and then *compensating* (or undoing) to preserve equivalence. The quantities tend to be **rounded up** to a convenient number.

Let's look at $3.8 + 4.9$.

What it sounds like: 2 options	How it looks
I can **adjust** one number to make it easier to add. If I pretend that 4.9 is 5, then $3.8 + 5 = 8.8$. However, to adjust the start number from 4.9 to 5 I had to add 0.1. That means my answer is 0.1 too much. To **compensate** for that, I need to subtract 0.1 from 8.8: $8.8 - 0.1 = 8.7$.	3.8 8.7 8.8
I can **adjust** BOTH numbers to think of this as $4 + 5 = 9$. I could add 0.2 to 3.8 to make it 4 AND add 0.1 to 4.9 to make it 5. I added 0.3 too much (0.1 and 0.2). To compensate for that, I subtract 0.3 from 9: $9 - 0.3 = 8.7$.	3.8 4 8.7 9

When it's useful: This strategy is useful when one or both numbers are near the next whole number.

Compensation Strategy for Decimal Subtraction

What it is: This strategy involves *adjusting* the expression to make it easier to add or subtract, and then *compensating* (or undoing) to preserve equivalence. The quantities tend to be **rounded up** to a convenient number.

Let's look at $0.63 - 0.38$.

What it sounds like: 3 options	How it looks
I can **adjust** the first number (the minuend) to make it easier to subtract. I add 0.05 to 0.63 the first number (the minuend), so no regrouping is needed: $0.68 - 0.38 = 0.30$. But adding 0.05 to the first number made the difference 0.05 too much. To **compensate**, I subtract 0.05: $0.30 - 0.05 = 0.25$.	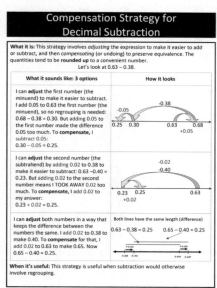
I can **adjust** the second number (the subtrahend) by adding 0.02 to 0.38 to make it easier to subtract: $0.63 - 0.40 = 0.23$. But adding 0.02 to the second number means I TOOK AWAY 0.02 too much. To **compensate**, I add 0.02 to my answer: $0.23 + 0.02 = 0.25$.	
I can **adjust** both numbers in a way that keeps the difference between the numbers the same. I add 0.02 to 0.38 to make 0.40. To **compensate** for that, I add 0.02 to 0.63 to make 0.65. Now $0.65 - 0.40 = 0.25$.	Both lines have the same length (difference) $0.63 - 0.38 = 0.25$ $0.65 - 0.40 = 0.25$

When it's useful: This strategy is useful when subtraction would otherwise involve regrouping.

online resources ↖ This resource can be downloaded at **resources.corwin.com/FOF/ addsubtractdecimalfraction**.

MODULE 1 Foundations for Reasoning Strategies

MODULE 2 Count On/Count Back Strategy

MODULE 3 Make a Whole Strategy

MODULE 4 Think Addition Strategy

MODULE 5 Compensation Strategy

MODULE 6 Partial Sums and Differences Strategy

MODULE 7 Standard Algorithms

TEACHING ACTIVITIES for Compensation

Before students are able to choose strategies, a key to fluency, they first must be able to understand and use relevant strategies. These activities focus on using compensation to add and subtract. While students may employ other methods, which is appropriate, they must understand how this strategy works, be able to implement it mentally, and become familiar with examples of problems in which they will want to use it.

ACTIVITY 5.1
QUICK LOOKS WITH VISUAL IMAGES

Physical models and visuals help students see how compensation works. The Compensation strategy involves adjusting quantities, so a groupable model is a good fit because students can actually add some in and take the same amount back out again.

"Quick Looks" is a short routine, typically used with basic facts, wherein students get two quick looks at a visual representation of a number (usually in ten-frames) and then a third and final look to discuss the answer to these questions: "How many dots?" and "How do you know?" This activity extends this idea to different visual images. Quantities are chosen that are close to the next benchmark so the idea of adjusting to that benchmark is a good way to figure out how many.

Fraction Quick Looks: Fill the Pie

Circle fractions make it easier to see the whole. To add a context, ask, "How much pie is on two tables?"

Table 1

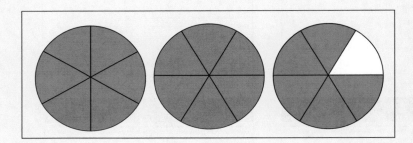

Table 2

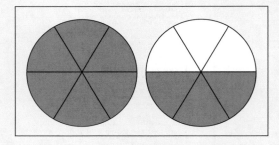

A student may reason, "I thought of 3 pies on Table 1 and $1\frac{1}{2}$ more on Table 2, so $4\frac{3}{6}$ pies. Take away the piece of pie I added and the answer is $4\frac{2}{6}$."

Decimal Quick Looks: How Many Hundredths?

Decimal squares (10 × 10 grid representing one whole) help students see tenths and hundredths and can support compensation reasoning. This pair of shaded decimal squares shows 0.57 + 0.39.

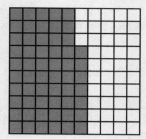 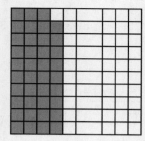

Because both numbers are close to the next tenth, students are likely to think of compensation: "I saw 6 tenths and 4 tenths. That is one whole. And then I subtracted 4 hundredths. That's 96 hundredths." Or they may just adjust the second decimal square: "I added 4 tenths to 57 hundredths. That is 97 hundredths. And then subtracted 1 hundredth to get 96 hundredths."

Several fraction and decimal quick look cards are available for download, but these are also easy to make using virtual manipulative sites (e.g., Brainingcamp, Math Learning Center, and others). To create cards that "fit" compensation, one or both of the tables of pies should include a nearly filled pie (fraction or decimal close to a whole number).

RESOURCE(S) FOR THIS ACTIVITY

This resource can be downloaded at **resources.corwin.com/FOF/addsubtractdecimalfraction**.

ACTIVITY 5.2
THE JUMPS HAVE IT

A Decimal Chart is a good tool for proving if the Compensation strategy yields the same result if applied correctly. In this activity, students mark the jumps to show how they adjust the addend or subtrahend to make addition or subtraction easier. For the problem 0.37 + 0.58, a student starts at 0.37 and sees that 0.58 is the same as adding 6 tenths (0.6) and subtracting 2 hundredths (0.02).

0.91	0.92	0.93	0.94	0.95	0.96	0.97	0.98	0.99	1.00
0.81	0.82	0.83	0.84	0.85	0.86	0.87	0.88	0.89	0.90
0.71	0.72	0.73	0.74	0.75	0.76	0.77	0.78	0.79	0.80
0.61	0.62	0.63	0.64	0.65	0.66	0.67	0.68	0.69	0.70
0.51	0.52	0.53	0.54	0.55	0.56	0.57	0.58	0.59	0.60
0.41	0.42	0.43	0.44	0.45	0.46	0.47	0.48	0.49	0.50
0.31	0.32	0.33	0.34	0.35	0.36	0.37	0.38	0.39	0.40
0.21	0.22	0.23	0.24	0.25	0.26	0.27	0.28	0.29	0.30
0.11	0.12	0.13	0.14	0.15	0.16	0.17	0.18	0.19	0.20
0.01	0.02	0.03	0.04	0.05	0.06	0.07	0.08	0.09	0.10

0.37 + 0.58 is the same as

0.37 + 0.60 – 0.02

0.37 + 0.60 – 0.02

0.97 – 0.02 = 0.95

Sentence frames can help students describe their thinking. Here is an example:

_____ is the same as _____.
       Original expression   *Revised, equivalent expression*

In this case, a student might say, "0.37 + 0.58 is the same as 0.37 + 0.60 – 0.02 because 60 hundredths minus 2 hundredths equals 58 hundredths." Teachers can record the process using equations, as illustrated next to the Decimal Chart.

Students can overapply addition compensation when subtracting. The Decimal Chart can help students notice the difference when they adjust the subtrahend. For 0.83 – 0.37, a student might adjust the problem to 0.83 – 0.40 (adding 0.03 to the subtrahend). As the Decimal Chart nicely shows, *too much was taken away* and must be compensated by adding back 0.03. Recording the related expressions can also help students make sense of compensation when changing the subtrahend.

0.91	0.92	0.93	0.94	0.95	0.96	0.97	0.98	0.99	1.00
0.81	0.82	0.83	0.84	0.85	0.86	0.87	0.88	0.89	0.90
0.71	0.72	0.73	0.74	0.75	0.76	0.77	0.78	0.79	0.80
0.61	0.62	0.63	0.64	0.65	0.66	0.67	0.68	0.69	0.70
0.51	0.52	0.53	0.54	0.55	0.56	0.57	0.58	0.59	0.60
0.41	0.42	0.43	0.44	0.45	0.46	0.47	0.48	0.49	0.50
0.31	0.32	0.33	0.34	0.35	0.36	0.37	0.38	0.39	0.40
0.21	0.22	0.23	0.24	0.25	0.26	0.27	0.28	0.29	0.30
0.11	0.12	0.13	0.14	0.15	0.16	0.17	0.18	0.19	0.20
0.01	0.02	0.03	0.04	0.05	0.06	0.07	0.08	0.09	0.10

0.83 – 0.37 is the same as

0.83 – 0.40 + 0.03

0.83 – 0.40 + 0.03

0.43 + 0.03 = 0.46

ACTIVITY 5.3
MEASUREMENT COMPENSATION (CONSTANT DIFFERENCE)

Meter sticks and yardsticks make excellent number lines for decimals and fractions, respectively. Meter sticks show tenths (decimeters), hundredths (centimeters), and thousandths (millimeters) and you can put multiple meter sticks together to show numbers greater than 1. In this activity, students measure objects by placing them in different places on the meter stick to show that the length (difference between two numbers) remains constant. Give each small group of students a meter stick and objects for which they can measure length (e.g., crayons, pencils, recorder instruments, erasers). An alternative to handing out things to measure is to have students cut out a paper strip the length of their shoe and measure the paper strip. Or they can simply cut strips of colored construction paper to different lengths. Students choose an item and place it on the meter stick anywhere *except starting at 0*. They determine the length of their object at that location, recording the end points and the length (difference). Then students slide the object to a new location on the meter stick (still not using 0 as an endpoint) and find the difference, recording the endpoints and the length. On the third slide, they move the object to start at 0 and find the length. Repeat the three-measure process with a new object and a different student measuring. Ask students what they are noticing from sliding their object on the meter stick.

Next, have students place new objects anywhere on the meter stick (except with 0 as an endpoint). Ask one member of the group to record the expression (e.g., 65 – 48). Have the team discuss how far to slide the object to most easily find its length. In this case, a student might suggest "up 2" or "down 5." Have them record the new endpoints and find the length. Here is one group's illustration of what they did to measure a color strip that was first placed between 0.27 and 0.35.

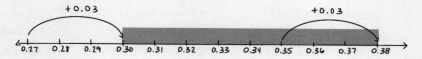

They slid it up by adding 0.03 to both numbers. Now, it is easy to see that the color tape has a length of 0.08 meters. Here is the students' answer:

Meter Stick Compensation: 0.35 – 0.27 has the same difference as 0.38 – 0.30 = 0.08

Help students make the connection to abstract reasoning by recording (and having them record) the process symbolically:

$$0.35 \quad - \quad 0.27$$
$$+0.03 \downarrow \qquad \downarrow +0.03$$
$$0.38 \quad - \quad 0.30 = 0.08$$

Students should record each measurement showing how they adjusted the measurement. After students engage in the exploration, you highlight a discussion about how expressions such as 0.65 – 0.58 are the same as 0.67 – 0.60.

For fractions, common differences can be explored with an inch ruler or yardstick. You can frame the task as a broken ruler (so students can't place the object on 0 to measure). For example, a student measures a plastic butterfly. He says, "The seashell spans from $\frac{3}{4}$ to $3\frac{1}{4}$ inches." He then explains how he figured out the difference: "I slid the shell up so that it added $\frac{1}{4}$ to both measurements. Then the difference was from 1 to $3\frac{2}{4}$, which is a length of $2\frac{2}{4}$ or $2\frac{1}{2}$."

Broken Ruler: I want to measure the length of the shell but only have a broken ruler. How long is it? Explain how you know.	
$3\frac{1}{4} \quad - \quad \frac{3}{4}$ $+\frac{1}{4} \downarrow \qquad \downarrow +\frac{1}{4}$ $3\frac{2}{4} \quad - \quad 1 = 2\frac{2}{4}$	

ACTIVITY 5.4
COMPENSATION CORNERS

With compensation, students can adjust one or more addends to make the adding more convenient. The decision of whether to change one or to change both addends is dependent on the numbers and the person. Help students consider the options and decide how they want to add For this activity, pose a problem such as 0.37 + 0.38. Provide think time and have students determine which addend they would adjust or if they would adjust both. Ask them to work on their plan and record their method. Assign each option to one of three corners of the room (change first, change second, change both). Have students take their work and go to the corner that corresponds with the method they chose and discuss with this "same option" group how they carried out the process. Next, organize a "lineup" from each corner in order to form triads with one student from each corner. The first person in each line forms the first triad, the second in each line forms the second triad, and so on. In these triads, students each share their way and at the end they discuss which option(s) they liked. If there are not many people in one of the corners and therefore that corner is not represented in the group, the pair of students can discuss how to solve the problem that way.

TEACHING TAKEAWAY

Help students consider the options and decide on which they prefer for the particular situation.

ORIGINAL PROBLEM	ADJUST FIRST NUMBER THEN COMPENSATE	ADJUST SECOND THEN COMPENSATE	ADJUST BOTH THEN COMPENSATE
0.37 + 0.38	0.37 + 0.38 Adjust: 0.40 + 0.38 = 0.78 Compensate: 0.78 − 0.03 = 0.75	0.37 + 0.38 Adjust: 0.37 + 0.40 = 0.77 Compensate: 0.77 − 0.02 = 0.75	0.37 + 0.38 Adjust both: 0.4 + 0.4 = 0.8 Compensate: 0.80 − 0.05 = 0.75

This activity also works for fractions, including mixed numbers.

ORIGINAL PROBLEM	ADJUST FIRST NUMBER THEN COMPENSATE	ADJUST SECOND NUMBER THEN COMPENSATE	ADJUST BOTH THEN COMPENSATE
$\frac{7}{8}+\frac{6}{8}$	$\frac{7}{8}+\frac{6}{8}$ Adjust: $1+\frac{6}{8}=1\frac{6}{8}$ Compensate: $1\frac{6}{8}-\frac{1}{8}=1\frac{5}{8}$	$\frac{7}{8}+\frac{6}{8}$ Adjust: $\frac{7}{8}+1=1\frac{7}{8}$ Compensate: $1\frac{7}{8}-\frac{2}{8}=1\frac{5}{8}$	$\frac{7}{8}+\frac{6}{8}$ Adjust both: $1+1$ Compensate: $2-\frac{3}{8}=1\frac{5}{8}$

You can create more problems. The key is to select problems in which at least one number is close to a benchmark. Here are some to consider.

DECIMAL ADDITION		FRACTION ADDITION	
1.7 + 3.8	1.6 + 0.9	$3\frac{2}{3}+2\frac{2}{3}$	$3\frac{3}{4}+4\frac{2}{4}$
10.9 + 7.3	2.8 + 4.8	$1\frac{3}{8}+2\frac{7}{8}$	$1\frac{6}{8}+3\frac{5}{8}$
1.74 + 1.69	6.8 + 0.7	$5\frac{2}{5}+2\frac{7}{10}$	$2\frac{3}{6}+\frac{5}{6}$

DECIMAL SUBTRACTION		FRACTION SUBTRACTION	
3.52 – 1.19	6.1 – 2.8	$4\frac{2}{5}-2\frac{4}{5}$	$9\frac{11}{12}-4\frac{3}{4}$
5.74 – 2.49	9.3 – 7.8	$3\frac{2}{6}-1\frac{1}{2}$	$7\frac{1}{2}-2\frac{5}{6}$
6.46 – 0.27	7.9 – 3.8	$2\frac{1}{4}-\frac{7}{8}$	$12\frac{7}{10}-5\frac{9}{10}$

 This resource can be downloaded at **resources.corwin.com/FOF/addsubtractdecimalfraction**.

ACTIVITY 5.5
PROMPTS FOR TEACHING COMPENSATION

Use the following prompts as opportunities to develop understanding of and reasoning with the strategy. Have students use representations and tools to justify their thinking, including base-10 models, number lines, number charts, and so on. After students work with the prompt(s), bring the class together to exchange ideas. These could be useful for collecting evidence of student understanding. Any prompt can be easily modified to feature different numbers (e.g., mixed fractions or decimals of different lengths) and any prompt can be offered more than once if modified.

Decimal Prompts

- Marlo changed 2.37 + 3.58 into 2.40 + 3.60. What does he have to do next to find the sum of the original problem?

- Yanzi thought to add 6.27 + 3.28 as 6.3 + 3.3 and then took 0.05 away. Fazio added 6.30 + 3.28 and then took 0.03 away. Did Yanzi and Fazio have the same sum?

- Brea solved 7.44 – 3.88 by thinking 7.44 – 4. What do you think she did next?

- Mr. Delrosa found three different ways students were solving 12.43 + 8.38:

  ○ Ramone solved it 12.43 + 8.38 → 12.40 + 8.40 = 20.80 → 20.80 + 0.01 = 20.81.

  ○ Talia solved it 12.40 + 8.38 = 20.78 → 20.78 + 0.03 = 20.81.

  ○ Celine solved it 12.43 + 8.40 = 20.83 → 20.83 – 0.02 = 20.81.

  How are the students' strategies the same? How are they different?

Fraction Prompts

- Share two ways one might compensate when adding $3\frac{3}{5}+4\frac{4}{5}$.

- Explain how you know that $3\frac{3}{8}-1\frac{1}{2}$ is the same as $3\frac{7}{8}-2$.

- Use a number line to show how one might use compensation for a fraction problem like $6\frac{2}{5}-3\frac{4}{5}$.

- Mrs. Norris found three different ways students were solving $5\frac{1}{5}-2\frac{4}{5}$.

  ○ Daniel solved it $5\frac{1}{5}-3=2\frac{1}{5}\to2\frac{1}{5}+\frac{1}{5}=2\frac{2}{5}$.

  ○ Loraine solved it $5\frac{4}{5}-2\frac{4}{5}=3\to3-\frac{3}{5}=2\frac{2}{5}$.

  ○ Mia solved it $5\frac{2}{5}-3=2\frac{2}{5}$.

  What strategy is each student using and how are they using compensation?

- Lance said for subtraction, he changed the minuend (first number) to make it easier to subtract and then compensated. Ernestina says she changed the subtrahend (second number) to make it easier to subtract and then compensated. Roxie said she changed both to slide to a friendly number. What do they all mean? Use $2\frac{1}{2}-\frac{7}{8}$ to show what they mean.

PRACTICE ACTIVITIES for Compensation

Fluency is realized through quality practice that is focused, varied, processed, and connected. The activities in this section focus students' attention on how this strategy works and when to use it. The activities are a collection of varied engagements. Game boards, recording sheets, digit cards, and other required materials are available as online resources for you to download, possibly modify, and use.

As students practice, look for how well they are using the new strategy and assimilating it into their collection of strategies. Post-activity discussions help students reflect on *how* they reasoned and *when* that strategy was useful (and when it was not). Discussions can also help students reflect on how that strategy connects to recent instruction and to other strategies they have learned.

FLUENCY COMPONENT	WHAT TO LOOK FOR AS STUDENTS PRACTICE THIS STRATEGY
Efficiency	• Do students choose Compensation when it is a good fit for the problem? • Are students using the strategy efficiently (not getting bogged down in selecting what to adjust and how to compensate)? • Do students overuse the strategy? (Compensation likely isn't efficient for problems like $3\frac{1}{4}+2\frac{3}{8}$ or $5.61-4.6$.)
Flexibility	• Are students carrying out Compensation in flexible ways (e.g., using it with addends such as 0.8 or 0.9, using it with both operations, etc.)? • Do they change their approach to or from Compensation as it proves inappropriate or overly complicated for the problem? (e.g., Do students change to Compensation as they start to decompose 4.06 + 7.99 for finding partial sums?) • Are they seeing how to apply this strategy in "new" situations (e.g., extending to tenths)?
Accuracy	• Are students compensating accurately when adding (if adjusting by adding, then compensating by subtracting)? • Are students compensating accurately when subtracting (attending to whether the compensation involves adding or subtracting the change)? • Are students estimating before solving the problems? • Are students considering the reasonableness of their solutions? • Are students finding accurate solutions?

ACTIVITY 5.6
COMPENSATION WORKED EXAMPLES

Worked examples are problems that have been solved. As you have read throughout this module, compensation has *options*. And compensation *works differently* for addition and subtraction. Hence, worked examples are important for helping students make sense of compensation and implement it accurately. Correctly worked examples can help students make sense of a strategy, and incorrectly worked examples attend to errors. Common challenges or errors when using compensation include the following:

1. The student applies an idea that works in addition to a subtraction problem.
    * $5.58 - 4.29$: changes problem to $5.57 - 4.30$ by "moving one over" (using the idea that $5.58 + 4.29 = 5.57 + 4.30$).

2. The student changes the problem but does not compensate for that change.
    * $0.78 + 0.44$: changes problem to $0.80 + 0.44$, adds to get 1.24, then stops.
    * $4.79 - 3.8$: changes problem to $4.8 - 3.8$, subtracts to get 1, then stops.

3. The student goes the opposite direction in adjusting the answer.
    * $2.49 - 1.98$: changes problem to $2.49 - 2$, subtracts to get 1.49, then subtracts 0.02 instead of adding 0.02.

There are different ways to pose worked examples, and they each serve a different fluency purpose.

TYPE OF WORKED EXAMPLE	PURPOSES: COMPONENT (FLUENCY ACTIONS)	QUESTIONS FOR DISCUSSIONS OR FOR WRITING RESPONSES
Correctly Worked Example	Efficiency (selects an appropriate strategy) and flexibility (applies a strategy to a new problem type)	What did _____ do? Why does it work? Is this a good method for this problem?
Partially Worked Example (Implement the Strategy Accurately)	Efficiency (selects an appropriate strategy; solves in a reasonable amount of time) and accuracy (completes steps accurately; gets correct answer)	Why did _____ start the problem this way? What does _____ need to do to finish the problem?
Incorrectly Worked Example (Highlight Common Errors)	Accuracy (completes steps accurately; gets correct answer)	What did _____ do? What mistake does _____ make? How can this mistake be fixed?

The prompts from Activity 5.5 can be used for collecting examples. Throughout the module are various worked examples that you can use as fictional worked examples. A sampling of additional ideas is provided in the following table.

(Continued)

(*Continued*)

CORRECTLY WORKED EXAMPLES FOR COMPENSATION WITH FRACTIONS	
ADDITION	**SUBTRACTION**

ADDITION

$$4\tfrac{7}{8} + \tfrac{1}{8} \rightarrow 5$$
$$+7\tfrac{3}{4} + \tfrac{1}{4} \rightarrow \underline{\tfrac{8}{}}$$
$$13$$
$$13 - \tfrac{3}{8} = 12\tfrac{5}{8}$$

SUBTRACTION

$$6\tfrac{4}{12} \;\boxed{+\tfrac{3}{12}}\; \rightarrow 6\tfrac{7}{12}$$
$$-3\tfrac{9}{12} \;\boxed{+\tfrac{3}{12}}\; \rightarrow \underline{-4}$$
$$2\tfrac{7}{12}$$

PARTIALLY WORKED EXAMPLES FOR COMPENSATION WITH FRACTIONS	

$3\tfrac{3}{4} + 2\tfrac{3}{4} = ?$

Kendra says, "I will add $\tfrac{1}{4}$ to both numbers and add $4 + 3$." What should she do next?

$$3\tfrac{3}{4} + 2\tfrac{3}{4} = ?$$
$$\downarrow \qquad \downarrow$$
$$4 + 3$$

$5\tfrac{1}{6} - 1\tfrac{5}{6} = ?$

Jamal says, "I can change $1\tfrac{5}{6}$ to 2 to make it easier to subtract." What should he do next?

$$5\tfrac{1}{6} - 1\tfrac{5}{6} = ?$$
$$\qquad \downarrow$$
$$5\tfrac{1}{6} - 2$$

INCORRECTLY WORKED EXAMPLES FOR COMPENSATION WITH FRACTIONS	

$2\tfrac{3}{4} + 5\tfrac{7}{8} = ?$

$$3 + 6 = 9$$
$$9 - \tfrac{2}{8} = 8\tfrac{6}{8}$$

$4\tfrac{1}{8} - 2\tfrac{6}{8} = ?$

$$\overset{+\tfrac{2}{8}}{4\tfrac{1}{8}} - 3 = 1\tfrac{1}{8}$$
$$1\tfrac{1}{8} - \tfrac{2}{8} = \tfrac{7}{8}$$

CORRECTLY WORKED EXAMPLES FOR COMPENSATION WITH DECIMALS	
ADDITION	**SUBTRACTION**

ADDITION

$1.7 + 3.8 = ?$

$$1.7 + 3.8$$
$$+ .2$$
$$1.7 + 4.0 = 5.7$$
$$5.7 - .2 = 5.5$$

SUBTRACTION

$3.52 - 1.19 = ?$

$$3.52 - 1.19$$
$$+.01 \qquad +.01$$
$$3.53 - 1.20 = 2.33$$

PARTIALLY WORKED EXAMPLES FOR COMPENSATION WITH DECIMALS	

$10.9 + 7.3 = ?$

Kristen says, "I will adjust the first addend by adding 0.1 to 10.9 to round up to 11." What should she do next?

$5.74 - 2.49 = ?$

Ian says, "I can adjust 2.49 as 2.5 by adding 0.01 to make it easier to subtract." What should he do next?

INCORRECTLY WORKED EXAMPLES FOR COMPENSATION WITH DECIMALS	

$1.74 + 1.69 = ?$

Samir says, "I added 0.01 to both addends to make it easier to add. 1.75 + 1.7 = 3.45." What would you tell Samir?

$7.3 - 3.8 = ?$

Mackenzie adds to the second number to make it easier to subtract and gets 7.3 − 4.0 = 3.3. What would you tell Mackenzie?

ACTIVITY 5.7

Name: "Or You Could . . ."   **Type:** Routine

About the Routine: This routine helps students think about different ways they might solve a problem. Although this activity will hopefully elicit compensation thinking, other strategies will emerge. Avoid inadvertently suggesting that there is a certain way to solve the problems and focus the discussion on efficiency and flexibility.

Materials: "Or You Could . . ." recording sheet, additional problems with prepared expressions for students to adjust into friendlier problems

Directions:
1. Pose a few expressions to students. To encourage discussion, include some expressions for which the Compensation strategy is *not* useful.

2. Have partners discuss other ways they could think about the problem.

3. Bring the group together to discuss and record the different ways an expression might be thought about. Keep in mind that the point of the routine is not to find the sum or difference but to simply rethink (rewrite) the problem.

4. After recording different ideas, ask students which rewrites make the problem easier to solve. Have them pick one and solve the problem.

For the problem 5.9 + 9.8, students might round up then compensate as 6 + 10 − 0.3. Or they could move 0.1 from one addend to another, like 6 + 9.7. They could even break apart and add 5 + 9 + 0.9 + 0.8. Here is a way students or teachers might record their compensation thinking.

5.9 [+0.1] → (6.0) ⟶ (16.0) [−0.3] = (15.7) + 9.8 [+0.2] → (10.0)	You could compensate by rounding up then adjusting.
Or you could . . . 5.9 [+0.1] → (6.0) ⟶ (15.7) + 9.8 [−0.1] → (9.7)	You could Make a Whole by adding/taking from one addend to another.

The same compensation methods used in decimals apply to fraction problems. Let's take a look at the example $5\frac{6}{8}+2\frac{5}{8}=8\frac{3}{8}$.

$5\frac{6}{8}$ $[+\frac{2}{8}]$ (6) ⟶ ($8\frac{3}{8}$) $+2\frac{5}{8}$ $[-\frac{2}{8}]$ ($2\frac{3}{8}$)	You could Make a Whole by adding/subtracting from one addend to another.
$5\frac{6}{8}$ $[+\frac{2}{8}]$ (6) ⟶ (9) ⟶ ($8\frac{3}{8}$) $+2\frac{5}{8}$ $[+\frac{3}{8}]$ (3) $[-\frac{5}{8}]$	You could compensate by rounding up and then adjusting.

(Continued)

(*Continued*)

This routine works great with subtracting and using the Compensation strategy because there are (at least) three ways to compensate and solve.

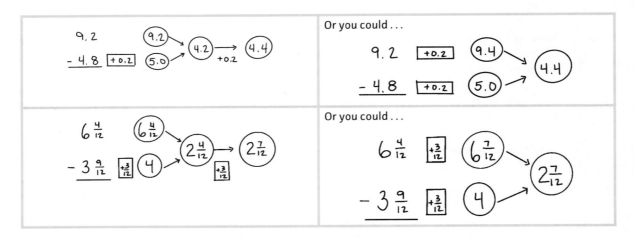

RESOURCE(S) FOR THIS ACTIVITY

Or You Could . . .

Directions: In the first column, make the subtraction problem easier by solve using Compensation. Compare your strategy with a classmate or find your own second possible way to create an easier problem to solve.

You could solve $6\frac{1}{3} - 3\frac{3}{4} = ?$ this way:	Or you could . . .
You could solve _____ this way:	Or you could . . .
You could solve _____ this way:	Or you could . . .

More Problems for the Routine
Or You Could . . .

Fraction Addition and Subtraction

Like denominators	Unlike denominators
$3\frac{1}{6} + 4\frac{2}{6}$	$3\frac{1}{4} + 4\frac{2}{3}$
$1\frac{5}{8} + 3\frac{3}{8}$	$2\frac{1}{4} + \frac{2}{3}$
$2\frac{1}{5} + \frac{3}{5}$	$4\frac{5}{8} + \frac{3}{4}$
$4\frac{3}{9} + 2\frac{4}{9}$	$2\frac{5}{6} + 1\frac{1}{3}$
$5\frac{4}{9} + 1\frac{5}{9}$	$1\frac{5}{8} + \frac{1}{4}$
$2\frac{4}{5} + \frac{3}{5}$	$4\frac{3}{4} + 1\frac{1}{3}$

Like denominators	Unlike denominators
$7\frac{1}{6} - 4\frac{2}{6}$	$3\frac{1}{4} - 1\frac{3}{4}$
$5\frac{4}{9} - 3\frac{7}{9}$	$2\frac{5}{6} - \frac{6}{7}$
$2\frac{3}{6} - \frac{5}{6}$	$4\frac{1}{2} - \frac{2}{4}$
$4\frac{1}{3} - 2\frac{2}{3}$	$3\frac{5}{8} - 1\frac{1}{2}$
$5\frac{4}{9} - 1\frac{8}{9}$	$1\frac{4}{5} - \frac{1}{3}$
$5\frac{3}{8} - 1\frac{4}{8}$	$4\frac{5}{8} - \frac{2}{3}$

online resources ▶ This resource can be downloaded at **resources.corwin.com/FOF/addsubtractdecimalfraction**.

ACTIVITY 5.8

Name: "Same Difference" **Type:** Routine

About the Routine: This routine practices using the Compensation strategy for subtraction where both numbers are adjusted, as though the numbers were slid on a number line. Students explore how changing both numbers the same amount results in the same answer.

Materials: prepared expressions (examples follow)

Directions: 1. Post an expression.

2. Have students visually locate the two values on a ruler, meter stick, or number line. For example, they put their pointer fingers on both numbers.

3. Ask students to find another expression (difference or distance) that is the same.

4. Collect several students' ideas, recording the related expressions on the board.

5. Ask which option makes it easiest to find the difference.

Possible Expressions for the "Same Difference" Routine

$3\frac{3}{8}-1\frac{5}{8}$	$4\frac{1}{2}-\frac{7}{8}$	$0.72 - 0.46$	$7.5 - 1.75$
$3\frac{1}{8}-1\frac{2}{8}$	$5\frac{3}{5}-2\frac{4}{5}$	$1.84 - 0.28$	$3.23 - 1.95$
$4\frac{1}{6}-1\frac{10}{12}$	$3\frac{1}{4}-\frac{7}{8}$	$4.84 - 1.89$	$4.7 - 2.8$

Ways to Represent Common Differences

$$0.72 - 0.46$$
$$+0.04 \downarrow \qquad \downarrow +0.04$$
$$0.76 - 0.50 = 0.26$$

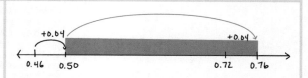

For example, 0.72 – 0.46 has the same difference as 0.76 – 0.50. The difference is 0.26.

$$3\frac{3}{8} - 1\frac{5}{8}$$
$$+\frac{3}{8} \downarrow \qquad \downarrow +\frac{3}{8}$$
$$3\frac{6}{8} - 2 = 1\frac{6}{8}$$

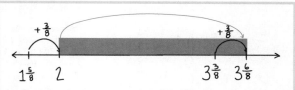

For example, $3\frac{3}{8}-1\frac{5}{8}$ has the same difference as $3\frac{6}{8}-2$. The difference is $1\frac{6}{8}$.

ACTIVITY 5.9

Name: Compensation Concentration   **Type:** Game

About the Game: The matching cards in *Compensation Concentration* focus students' attention on how to rethink expressions using the Compensation strategy. After the game, you can have students create their own matching cards.

Materials: *Compensation Concentration* cards (one set per pair of students)

Directions:

1. Players mix up the cards and then put them face down in rows.

2. Player 1 turns over two cards. If they don't match, the player turns them back over. If two cards match, the player keeps the cards and explains how they know it is a match.

3. Player 2 does the same.

4. Like the classic game of *Concentration*, players watch and remember where each card was.

5. The player with the most cards matched at the end is the winner.

Compensation Concentration cards can be downloaded or you can use index cards to create your own.

> **TEACHING TAKEAWAY**
>
> Have students record their matches on a recording sheet so they can look for patterns across the cards and create their own pairs.

RESOURCE(S) FOR THIS ACTIVITY

$3.9 + 7.8$	You can think $4.0 + 8.0$ then subtract 0.3 $4.0 + 8.0 = 12.0$ $12.0 - 0.3 = 11.7$
$8.6 + 1.8$	You can think $9.0 + 2.0$ then subtract 0.6 $9.0 + 2.0 = 11.0$ $11.0 - 0.6 = 10.4$
$6.8 + 1.7$	You can think $6.8 + 2.0$ then subtract 0.3 $6.8 + 2.0 = 8.8$ $8.8 - 0.3 = 8.5$
$3.69 + 7.17$	You can think $3.70 + 7.20$ then subtract 0.04 $3.70 + 7.20 = 10.90$ $10.90 - 0.04 = 10.86$
$0.28 + 0.75$	You can think $0.30 + 0.75$ then subtract 0.02 $0.30 + 0.75 = 1.05$ $1.05 - 0.02 = 1.03$

$2\frac{1}{6} - \frac{5}{6}$	You can think $2\frac{1}{6} - 1$ then add $\frac{1}{6}$ $2\frac{1}{6} - 1 = 1\frac{1}{6}$ $1\frac{1}{6} + \frac{1}{6} = 1\frac{2}{6} = 1\frac{1}{3}$
$3\frac{1}{4} - 1\frac{3}{4}$	You can think give $\frac{1}{4}$ to each $3\frac{2}{4} - 2 = 1\frac{2}{4} = 1\frac{1}{2}$
$8\frac{5}{12} - 2\frac{10}{12}$	You can think $8\frac{5}{12} - 3$ then add $\frac{2}{12}$ $8\frac{5}{12} - 3 = 5\frac{5}{12}$ $5\frac{5}{12} + \frac{2}{12} = 5\frac{7}{12}$
$9\frac{5}{8} - 4\frac{7}{8}$	You can think give $\frac{1}{8}$ to each $9\frac{6}{8} - 5 = 4\frac{6}{8} = 4\frac{3}{4}$
$5\frac{2}{10} - 2\frac{9}{10}$	You can think $5\frac{2}{10} - 3$ then add $\frac{1}{10}$ $5\frac{2}{10} - 3 = 2\frac{2}{10}$ $2\frac{2}{10} + \frac{1}{10} = 2\frac{3}{10}$

online resources ↘ This resource can be downloaded at **resources.corwin.com/FOF/addsubtractdecimalfraction**.

ACTIVITY 5.10

Name: Adjust and Go! Tic-Tac-Toe   **Type:** Game

About the Game: This game helps students practice thinking about how they would adjust a problem and what compensation would look like after they have adjusted it.

Materials: *Adjust and Go! Tic-Tac-Toe* game board for players to share; expression cards

Directions:
1. Players place the stack of expression cards face down.

2. Players take turns flipping over a problem and deciding how they would adjust the problem (the first number, the second number, or both numbers). Then they follow that plan to find the sum or difference.

3. Players put a counter on a space that matches their thinking for the problem.

4. The first player to get a Tic-Tac-Toe wins.

RESOURCE(S) FOR THIS ACTIVITY

Addition Adjust and Go!
Tic-Tac-Toe

Directions: Players take turns choosing addition cards. A player chooses a card and decides if they would **adjust** the first addend, **adjust** the second addend, or **adjust** both addends. The player tells their partner their choice and how they would **compensate** after adjusting the problem. The player puts a counter on a space that matches their thinking. The first player to get a tic-tac-toe wins.

adjust **first** addend	adjust **second** addend	adjust **BOTH** addends
adjust **second** addend	adjust **BOTH** addends	adjust **first** addend
adjust **BOTH** addends	adjust **first** addend	adjust **second** addend

This resource can be downloaded at **resources.corwin.com/FOF/addsubtractdecimalfraction**.

ACTIVITY 5.11

Name: Compensation Lane   **Type:** Center

About the Center: The purpose of this center is for students to record their compensation thinking. The Compensation Lane helps them avoid missing the last step where they have to compensate for the change that they made to the problem in order to get the correct sum or difference.

Materials: expression cards, Compensation Lane recording sheet

Directions: 1. Students select an expression.

2. Students work through the compensation lane to solve the expression.

3. Students record the adjustments they make to solve the problem.

4. Students then compensate for their adjustment (as shown in the example).

For the problem 0.57 + 0.19, they might adjust by adding 0.01 to the second addend to solve for 0.57 + 0.20 = 0.77. Then to compensate for adding 0.01, they would subtract 0.01, resulting in 0.77 − 0.01= 0.76.

For the problem $4\frac{2}{5} - 1\frac{4}{5}$, you can add $\frac{1}{5}$ to the subtrahend and solve for $4\frac{2}{5} - 2 = 2\frac{2}{5}$. Since we added more to the subtrahend, we can compensate by adding back to the difference: $2\frac{2}{5} + \frac{1}{5} = 2\frac{3}{5}$.

RESOURCE(S) FOR THIS ACTIVITY

2.6 + 8.3	3.9 + 1.5
9.2 + 2.3	6.8 + 6.7
5.5 + 8.8	8.7 + 1.3
0.59 + 0.25	0.26 + 0.25
0.22 + 0.48	0.37 + 0.44

Compensation Lane

Example   +0.1   compensate by −0.1

| 2.6 + 6.9 | → | 2.6 + 7 = 9.6 | → | 9.6 − 0.1 = 9.5 |

	→		→	
	→		→	
	→		→	
	→		→	
	→		→	

online resources ↘ This resource can be downloaded at **resources.corwin.com/FOF/addsubtractdecimalfraction**.

ACTIVITY 5.12

Name: Prove It   **Type:** Center

About the Center: Students can confuse how compensation works with addition and how it works with subtraction. Even within subtraction, how you compensate depends on what initial change was made. Prove It gives students an opportunity to reason about adjusting and compensating. As an alternative to a center, the cards can be posted on walls or desks around the classroom in a gallery-walk fashion. Students can work with a partner or small group and rotate from poster to poster, recording their ideas on their recording page as they go.

Materials: Compensation Prove It cards and recording sheet

Directions: 1. Students select a Compensation Prove It card and record the label for the card on the recording sheet.

2. Students use words, equations, or number lines to justify whether the card is true or false.

For example, a student pulls a card that says 7.5 + 2.8 is the same as 7.4 + 2.7. The student then determines that the statement is false and explains that both addends in the second problem are less, so the answer cannot be the same. A different student pulling this card might use base-10 pieces to show that 0.5 + 0.8 ≠ 0.4 + 0.7.

> **TEACHING TAKEAWAY**
>
> It is useful to label the cards with a letter so that it is easy to determine the situations that students were working with.

RESOURCE(S) FOR THIS ACTIVITY

8.1 + 8.7 is the same as 8.0 + 8.8 **A**	7.5 + 2.8 is the same as 7.4 + 2.7 **B**
3.9 + 4.3 is the same as 4.0 + 4.0 and then take away 0.4 **C**	6.5 + 5.5 is the same as 7.7 + 4.4 **D**
39.0 + 41.4 is the same as 40.0 + 40.4 **E**	40.6 + 72.1 is the same as 40.6 + 72.0 and 1 more **F**
2.29 + 8.94 is the same as 2.29 + 9.00 and take 0.6 away **G**	5.4 + 6.4 is the same as 5.5 + 6.3 **H**

Prove It – Decimals

Directions: Pull a Prove It card. Prove if it is true or false.

Card I Pulled	Proof That It's TRUE or FALSE
A	True! 8.1 + 8.7 is the same as 8.0 + 8.8 because you can take 0.1 from the first addend and add it to the second addend and the sum is the same: 8.1 + 8.7 = 16.8 is the same as 8.0 + 8.8 = 16.8

online resources 🔎 This resource can be downloaded at **resources.corwin.com/FOF/addsubtractdecimalfraction**.

ACTIVITY 5.13

Name: One and the Other   **Type:** Center

About the Center: There are often several appropriate ways to adjust numbers in order to use the Compensation strategy. To develop proficiency with this strategy, students need to explore and practice different approaches and consider when and why they are useful.

Materials: addition or subtraction expression cards, One and the Other recording sheet

Directions: 1. Students select an addition or subtraction problem.

2. Students solve the problem by adjusting *one* of the numbers in the problem.

3. Students solve the problem by adjusting *both* numbers in the problem.

4. Students mark the approach that they prefer with a star.

For example, a student selects 3.4 – 1.5. She adjusts one number by adding 0.1 to 3.4, making 3.5 – 1.5 = 2. To compensate, she takes the 1 tenth away from 2.0; thus, 3.4 – 1.5 = 1.9. Next, she adjusts both numbers, adding 0.5 and making 3.9 – 2, which she subtracts to get 1.9. She marks the first option with a star because she thinks it's easier to think about that way.

> **TEACHING TAKEAWAY**
>
> Instead of making cards, you could provide a list of problems for students to choose from.

This strategy would work with fraction addition and subtraction problems as well. For the problem $3\frac{2}{3}+2\frac{2}{3}$, a student adjusts by adding $\frac{1}{3}$ to the first number, adds $4+2\frac{2}{3}$, and gets $6\frac{2}{3}$. To compensate, she subtracts $\frac{1}{3}$ and gets the answer $6\frac{1}{3}$. Then she changes both addends, add $4 + 3$, and compensates by subtracting $\frac{2}{3}$. She likes the second option better and stars that work.

List of Problems for *One and the Other*

DECIMAL ADDITION		FRACTION ADDITION	
1.7 + 3.8	1.6 + 0.9	$3\frac{2}{3}+2\frac{2}{3}$	$3\frac{3}{4}+4\frac{3}{4}$
10.9 + 7.3	2.8 + 4.7	$1\frac{3}{8}+2\frac{7}{8}$	$1\frac{6}{8}+3\frac{5}{8}$
1.74 + 1.69	6.8 + 0.7	$5\frac{2}{5}+2\frac{7}{10}$	$2\frac{3}{6}+\frac{5}{6}$
DECIMAL SUBTRACTION		**FRACTION SUBTRACTION**	
3.4 – 1.5	6.1 – 2.8	$4\frac{2}{5}-2\frac{4}{5}$	$9\frac{11}{12}-4\frac{3}{4}$
5.74 – 2.49	9.2 – 7.9	$3\frac{2}{6}-1\frac{1}{2}$	$7\frac{1}{2}-2\frac{5}{6}$
6.46 – 0.27	7.3 – 3.8	$2\frac{1}{4}-\frac{7}{8}$	$12\frac{7}{10}-5\frac{9}{10}$

One and the Other

Directions: Pull a card. Show how you can solve it by adjusting one number, then compensate. Then show how you can solve it adjusting both numbers, then compensate. Put a star on the way you think is better.

Original Problem	Adjust One Number	Adjust Both Numbers
2.9 + 3.8	I added 0.2 to 3.8 to make 4. Then, 2.9 + 4 = 6.9. That was 0.2 too much, so the answer is 6.7.	I added 0.1 to 2.9 and 0.2 to 3.8. Then I had 3 + 4 = 7. That was 0.3 too much, so the answer is 6.7. ★

Partial Sums and Differences Strategy

STRATEGY OVERVIEW:
Partial Sums and Differences

What is Partial Sums and Differences? This strategy refers to a process of adding or subtracting place values, starting with the *largest* place value and moving to the smallest (the reverse of standard algorithms). Using the Partials strategy with decimals encourages students to think of the place value of the digits in the number by adding the parts of the number according to their place value. When no regrouping is involved, the Partials strategy is straightforward—just add or subtract each place value. In other cases, the regrouping is captured when combining the partial sums or differences.

HOW DO PARTIAL SUMS AND DIFFERENCES WORK?

This strategy works by breaking apart the numbers into parts, working with the larger parts first, and then combining the partials. The following examples use a horizontal written record.

PARTIAL SUMS: DECIMALS	PARTIAL SUMS: DECIMALS	PARTIAL SUMS: FRACTIONS
$3.7 + 3.8$ $3 + 3 = 6$ $0.7 + 0.8 = 1.5$ $6 + 1.5 = 7.5$	$7.7 + 12.58$ $7 + 12 = 19$ $0.7 + 0.5 = 1.2$ $0 + 0.08 = 0.08$ $19 + 1.2 + 0.08 = 20.28$	$13\frac{4}{5} + 2\frac{1}{10}$ $13 + 2 = 15$ $\frac{4}{5} + \frac{1}{10} = \frac{9}{10}$ $15 + \frac{9}{10} = 15\frac{9}{10}$

Partial sums for decimal addition are often recorded in a vertical form, with each partial sum written in its own row:

$$
\begin{array}{r}
3.7 \\
+\ 3.8 \\
\hline
6.0 \\
+\ 1.5 \\
\hline
7.5
\end{array}
\qquad
\begin{array}{r}
7.7 \\
+\ 12.58 \\
\hline
19.00 \\
1.20 \\
+\ 6.08 \\
\hline
20.28
\end{array}
$$

Partial differences work in a similar fashion when the minuend in each place value is larger than the subtrahend, as shown by the following examples. This may also be done mentally.

PARTIAL DIFFERENCES: DECIMAL	PARTIAL DIFFERENCES: DECIMAL	PARTIAL DIFFERENCES: FRACTION
Using place value $87.55 - 12.03$ $80 - 10 = 70$ $7 - 2 = 5$ $0.5 - 0 = 0.5$ $0.05 - 0.03 = 0.02$ $70 + 5 + 0.5 + 0.02 = 75.52$	Using more efficient chunks $87.55 - 12.03$ $87 - 12 = 75$ $0.55 - 0.03 = 0.52$ $75 + 0.52 = 75.52$	$12\frac{5}{6} - 7\frac{1}{2}$ $12 - 7 = 5$ $\frac{5}{6} - \frac{1}{2} = \frac{2}{6}$ $5 + \frac{2}{6} = 5\frac{2}{6} = 5\frac{1}{3}$

Consider, however, when the minuend in a particular place value is smaller than the subtrahend (i.e., when regrouping would be needed in the standard algorithm). In such circumstances, a partial difference will result in a negative number, which typically has not been introduced when students are learning to subtract fractions or decimals. To illustrate how partial differences work in this case, the partials are given a sign telling students whether to add or to subtract the partials. It looks like this for fractions:

$12\frac{5}{12}$ $-\ 4\frac{11}{12}$ 8 $\frac{-6}{12}$ $7\frac{6}{12} = 7\frac{1}{2}$	Subtract the whole numbers 12 – 4 = 8 Think, "I am supposed to take away 11 twelfths. I can take away 5 twelfths, but that means I still need to take away 6 twelfths." $8 - \frac{6}{12} = 7\frac{1}{2}$

For the decimal example 6.2 – 1.57, the process might be notated and described in two ways: one using integer language (left) and the other using the zero properties with no reference to negative numbers (right).

USING INTEGER LANGUAGE	USING ALTERNATIVE LANGUAGE AND NOTATION
6.20 –1.57 5.00 ← Ones –0.3 ← Subtract 3 tenths (to 4.70) –0.07 ← Subtract 7 hundredths (to 4.63) 4.63 ← Combine	Subtract ones: **5**
	Subtract tenths: 0.2 – 0.5
	Break apart: 0.2 – 0.2 **– 0.3 [still need to subtract 0.3]**
	Subtract hundredths: 0.00 – 0.07
	Break apart: **– 0.07 [still need to subtract 0.07]**
	Combine: 5 – 0.3 – 0.07 = **4.63**

WHEN DO YOU CHOOSE PARTIAL SUMS AND DIFFERENCES?

Unlike some other strategies wherein the numbers "lend" themselves to the strategy, Partial Sums and Differences is almost always applicable (like the standard algorithm) but perhaps not most efficient (e.g., 2.9 + 13.45 is solved more efficiently with Make a Whole or Compensation). The front-end, left-to-right approach makes it more conceptual and less error-prone than the standard algorithms. In the special case of partial differences that would involve regrouping with the standard algorithm, this strategy may not be more efficient than the related standard algorithm, but it does require and reinforce students' understanding of the whole and of place value.

MODULE 1 Foundations for Reasoning Strategies

MODULE 2 Count On/Count Back Strategy

MODULE 3 Make a Whole Strategy

MODULE 4 Think Addition Strategy

MODULE 5 Compensation Strategy

MODULE 6 Partial Sums and Differences Strategy

MODULE 7 Standard Algorithms

PARTIAL SUMS AND DIFFERENCES:
Strategy Briefs for Families

It is important that families understand the strategies and know how they work so that they can be partners in the pursuit of fluency. These strategy briefs are a tool for doing that. You can include them in newsletters for parents or caregivers, or at a school event like a Back to School Night. They are available for download so that you can adjust them as needed.

Partial Sums Strategy: Fraction Addition

What it is: This strategy involves breaking apart each of the addends (the numbers being added), usually by wholes and fractional parts. We add the parts to find "partial sums" (parts of the total). Then, we can add the partial sums together to find the answer.

Let's look at $4\frac{2}{5} + 5\frac{2}{5}$.

What it sounds like: I will break apart the mixed numbers so I have whole number and fractional parts $4 + \frac{2}{5} + 5 + \frac{2}{5}$. Then I will add the whole number parts together and the fraction parts together $(4 + 5 + \frac{2}{5} + \frac{2}{5} = 9\frac{4}{5})$. If the fraction is greater than 1, I will simplify by creating another whole (for example, if the partial sums are 5 and $\frac{9}{8}$, my answer will be $6\frac{1}{8}$).

What it looks like: The strategy can be recorded horizontally (across) as shown above or it can be recorded vertically in a way that allows the parts to be "lined up" with each other.

$$4\tfrac{2}{5} + 5\tfrac{2}{5}$$

Whole number part → $4 + 5 = 9$ ⟵ Partial sums
Fraction part → $\frac{2}{5} + \frac{2}{5} = \frac{4}{5}$

$9 + \frac{4}{5} = 9\frac{4}{5}$ ⟵ Sum

When it's useful: This strategy is useful unless another strategy can be applied more efficiently.

Partial Differences Strategy: Fraction Subtraction

What it is: This strategy involves breaking apart the minuend and subtrahend (the numbers being subtracted), usually by wholes and fractional parts. The parts are subtracted to find partial differences. Then, the partial differences are combined to find the answer.

Let's look at $9\frac{3}{5} - 4\frac{2}{5}$.

What it sounds like: I will break apart the mixed numbers so I have whole number parts $(9 - 4)$ and fractional parts $(\frac{3}{5} - \frac{2}{5})$. Then I add the partial differences together to get $5\frac{1}{5}$.

What it looks like: The strategy can be recorded horizontally (across) as shown above or it can be recorded vertically in a way that allows the parts to be "lined up" with each other.

$$9\tfrac{3}{5} - 4\tfrac{2}{5}$$

Whole number part → $9 - 4 = 5$ ⟵ Partial Differences
Fraction part → $\frac{3}{5} - \frac{2}{5} = \frac{1}{5}$

$5 + \frac{1}{5} = 5\frac{1}{5}$ ⟵ Difference

When it's useful: This strategy is useful but sometimes not used because of possibility of encountering negative numbers. But, in these cases, subtraction language can be used, as illustrated here:

Example: $7\frac{1}{8} - 4\frac{5}{8}$

$7 - 4 = 3$ ⟵ Subtract the whole numbers

$\frac{1}{8} - \frac{5}{8} = -\frac{4}{8}$ ⟵ Subtract the fractional parts (you can only remove $\frac{1}{8}$, so will still need to subtract $\frac{4}{8}$)

$3 - \frac{4}{8} = 2\frac{4}{8} = 2\frac{1}{2}$ ⟵ Take away the $\frac{4}{8}$ from the whole number

---

Partial Sums Strategy: Decimal Addition

What it is: This strategy involves breaking apart each of the addends (the numbers being added), usually by wholes and decimal parts. We add the parts to find "partial sums" (parts of the total). Then, we can add the partial sums together to find the answer.

Let's look at 4.37 + 2.85.

What it sounds like: I will break apart the numbers based on their place value. So 4.37 will be 4 + 0.3 + 0.07 and 2.85 will be 2 + 0.8 + 0.05. I will add the ones digits together (4 + 2), the tenths digits together (0.3 + 0.8), and the hundredths digits together (0.07 + 0.05). Then, I combine each of these partial sums to find the answer to the original problem.

You don't have to break the addends apart by place value—sometimes it makes sense to do it another way. The example on the right is such an example. The student noticed 0.42 and 0.58 make a whole number and so the tenths and hundredths were combined together.

Addend Addend
$4.37 + 2.85$ ⟵ Partial sums
$4 + 2 = 6$
$0.3 + 0.8 = 1.1$
$0.07 + 0.05 = 0.12$
Sum → 7.22

Addend Addend
$2.42 + 6.58$ ⟵ Partial sums
$2 + 6 = 8$
$0.42 + 0.58 = 1$
Sum → 9

When it's useful: This strategy is useful unless another strategy can be applied more efficiently.

Partial Differences Strategy: Decimal Subtraction

What it is: This strategy involves breaking apart the minuend and subtrahend (the numbers being subtracted), usually by wholes and fractional parts. Each part is subtracted to find partial difference. Then, the partial differences are combined to find the answer.

Let's look at 5.47 − 2.36.

What it sounds like: First I see that 5.47 − 2.36 can be broken apart by place value. I will subtract the digits in the ones place (5 − 2), then subtract the digits in the tenths place (0.4 − 0.3), and finally subtract the digits in the hundredths place (0.07 − 0.06). Then, I will add each of those partial differences to find the answer to the original problem. The example to the right shows how this thinking would be recorded.

Minuend Subtrahend
$5.47 - 2.36$
$5 - 2 = 3$ ⟵ Partial Differences
$0.4 - 0.3 = 0.1$
$0.07 - 0.06 = 0.01$
Difference → 3.11

When it's useful: This strategy is useful but sometimes not used because of possibility of encountering negative numbers. But, in these cases, subtraction language can be used, as illustrated here:

You subtract the ones, 5 − 1 is 4. But when you subtract the tenths, the result is a negative number (−0.1), meaning you will need to subtract that partial (not add it) when combining the partial differences. The same thing occurs in the hundredths place.

Minuend Subtrahend
$5.24 - 1.37$
$5 - 1 = 4$ ⟵ Partial Differences
$0.2 - 0.3 = -0.1$
$0.04 - 0.07 = -0.03$ ⟵ Subtract the negative amounts
$4 - 0.1 = 3.9$
$3.9 - 0.03 = 3.87$ ⟵ Difference

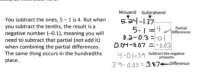

This resource can be downloaded at **resources.corwin.com/FOF/addsubtractdecimalfraction**.

TEACHING ACTIVITIES for Partial Sums and Differences

Before students are able to choose strategies, which is a key to fluency, they first must be able to understand and use relevant strategies. These activities focus on the strategy of Partial Sums and Differences. While students may employ other methods, which is appropriate, they must understand how this strategy works, be able to implement it mentally, and become familiar with examples of problems in which they will want to use it.

ACTIVITY 6.1
BAGS OF DISKS

Unlike place value blocks, place value disks are a nonproportional representation—meaning that the size of the ones, tenths, hundredths, and thousandths is not proportional for the quantity they represent. Determine the place value appropriate for the students. Begin by putting place value disks in small paper bags. Label the bags with letters A and B. Students empty each bag and record the amount in each bag. Then students find the total amount of disks in both bags by using the Partial Sums strategy. Students record their thinking on the Bags of Disks recording sheet or in their math journals.

This activity can be a partner activity and students can rotate from station to station, each station having two different bags of disks. The activity can also become a center, with two bags (you can change out what is in the bags) and a Bags of Disks recording sheet.

RESOURCE(S) FOR THIS ACTIVITY

Bags of Disks

Directions: Empty both bags of disks. Record the number in each bag. Find the sum of the disks using the Partial Sums strategy.

Bag	Bag	Sum (showing partial sums)
3.55	1.67	$3 + 1 = 4$ $0.5 + 0.6 = 1.1$ $0.05 + 0.07 = 0.12$ $4 + 1.1 + 0.12 = 5.22$

ACTIVITY 6.2
PARTIAL SUMS WITH DECIMAL EXPANDER CARDS

Decimal expander cards are foldables that allow students to see a number through place value, which is critical when considering place value to the right of the decimal point. Oftentimes students will mistakenly think that there are 2 "ones" places. This activity also provides an opportunity to emphasize the *ths* on the end of tenths, hundredths, and thousandths to differentiate them from the whole number place values and to connect them to fraction names. The lead place value in these expander cards is the ones place. Each place is followed by the name of that place value, as shown here. To begin, have students fold the light-gray section back so it is behind the white place value column and then fold the dark-gray section so it matches up with the light gray. This will essentially hide all the gray sections. Then give students a number, such as 3.519. With the labels folded back, have students record the digits (one in each box). Have students open the expandable and notice each part.

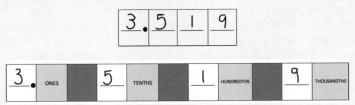

This process is repeated for each of the place value labels. The expander strip can be downloaded on the companion website. Next, provide the students with two folded expander strips and give them an expression to complete, such as 4.21 + 5.168. Students record the expressions with one on each strip.

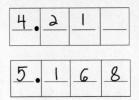

Then students open the expandable and find and record the partial sums.

9 ones, 3 tenths, 7 hundredths, and 8 thousandths = 9 + 0.3 + 0.07 + 0.008 = 9.378

Students should record both the original expression and the set of expanded expressions. Discuss with students how the two sets are similar and different. Connect this work to base-10 models or number lines as needed, particularly in cases where regrouping may be necessary. Subtraction expressions can be incorporated as well.

ACTIVITY 6.3
STRATEGY SHOW AND TELL

Solid conceptual understanding of any strategy is evidenced through a variety of representations and being able to make connections among them. In this activity, students show how to use partial sums with three different representations, including a concrete representation (place value disks, base-10 blocks, fraction circles, etc.), a number line, and expressions. Additionally, students are asked to reflect on whether they think the Partial Sums strategy is the best way to solve that particular problem.

Exploring multiple representations deepens understanding of a strategy, but it can be overdone. As students demonstrate understanding, adapt this activity to have them *choose* a representation. One choice can be "I did it mentally," in which case they can simply write the answer in the oval and complete the "Strategy Reflection" box. The following example shows how to use a graphic organizer to represent Partial Sums addition with decimals, but this organizer is useful across strategies and operations.

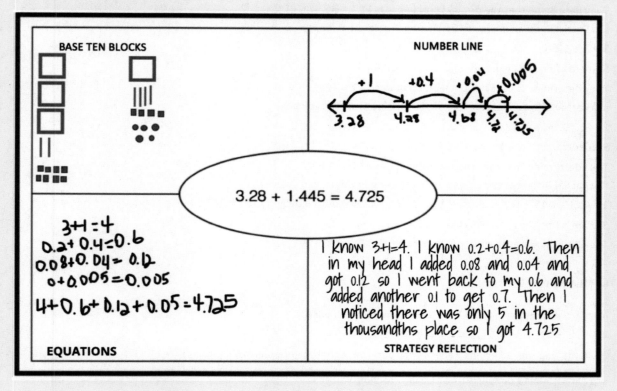

This resource can be downloaded at **resources.corwin.com/FOF/addsubtractdecimalfraction**.

ACTIVITY 6.4
THE MISSING PROBLEM

This problem-based activity is an opportunity to extend or enrich instruction with Partial Sums and Differences. You pose a set of equations with unknowns that represent the partial sums, and students find the unknowns and put the equations back together to determine the original problem. For each, they validate their thinking by solving the problem they created, using the Partial Sums and Differences strategy.

The Missing Problem: Decimals

In a Partial Sums example of The Missing Problem, you pose
$11 + \underline{\hspace{1cm}} = 17$ $0.7 + \underline{\hspace{1cm}} = 1.2$
Students find the unknowns 6 and 0.5.
They determine that the original problem was $11.7 + 6.5$.
In a Partial Sums example of The Missing Problem, you pose
$3 + \underline{\hspace{1cm}} = 10$ $0.4 + \underline{\hspace{1cm}} = 0.6$ $0.07 + \underline{\hspace{1cm}} = 0.11$
Students find the unknowns and 7, 0.2, and 0.04.
They determine that the original problem was $3.47 + 7.24$.
In a Partial Differences example of The Missing Problem, you pose
$23 - \underline{\hspace{1cm}} = 16$ $0.7 - \underline{\hspace{1cm}} = 0.1$ $0.05 - \underline{\hspace{1cm}} = 0.02$
Students find the unknowns 7, 0.6, and 0.03.
They determine that the original problem was $23.75 - 7.63$.
In a Partial Differences example of The Missing Problem, you pose
$15 - \underline{\hspace{1cm}} = 15$ $0.3 - \underline{\hspace{1cm}} = -0.1$ $0.07 - \underline{\hspace{1cm}} = 0.04$ $0.005 - \underline{\hspace{1cm}} = -0.001$
Students find the unknowns to be 0, 0.4, 0.03, and 0.006
They determine the original problem to be $15.375 - 0.436$.

The Missing Problem: Fractions

In a Partial Sums example of The Missing Problem, you pose
$8 + \underline{\hspace{1cm}} = 17$ $\frac{1}{4} + \underline{\hspace{1cm}} = \frac{3}{4}$
Students find the unknowns 9 and $\frac{1}{2}$. They determine that the original problem was $8\frac{1}{4} + 9\frac{1}{2}$.
In a Partial Sums example of The Missing Problem, you pose
$7 + \underline{\hspace{1cm}} = 10$ $\frac{1}{5} + \underline{\hspace{1cm}} = \frac{9}{10}$
Students find the unknowns 3 and $\frac{7}{10}$. They determine that the original problem was $7\frac{1}{5} + 3\frac{7}{10}$.
In a Partial Differences example of The Missing Problem, you pose
$23 - \underline{\hspace{1cm}} = 16$ $\frac{7}{8} - \underline{\hspace{1cm}} = \frac{1}{8}$
Students find the unknowns 7 and $\frac{6}{8}$ or $\frac{3}{4}$. They determine that the original problem was $23\frac{7}{8} - 7\frac{3}{4}$.
In a Partial Differences example of The Missing Problem, you pose
$15 - \underline{\hspace{1cm}} = 6$ $\frac{1}{6} - \underline{\hspace{1cm}} = -\frac{1}{6}$
Students find the unknowns to be 9 and $\frac{2}{6}$. They determine the original problem to be $15\frac{1}{6} - 9\frac{1}{3}$.

ACTIVITY 6.5
PROMPTS FOR TEACHING PARTIAL SUMS AND DIFFERENCES

Use the following prompts as opportunities to develop understanding of and reasoning with the strategy and/or as assessments to determine whether students understand and can use Partial Sums and Differences. You can require that students use representations and tools to justify their thinking including base-10 pieces, place value disks, number lines, and so on, or you can focus on mental math. If you are using these prompts for whole-class discourse, first provide individual think time, then small-group (e.g., triads) talk time, and finally whole-group time. Any prompt can be easily modified to feature different decimals and fractions.

Decimal Prompts

- Davida solved a problem using the Partial Sums strategy seen here. Tell how you know what the original expression might have been.

$$4 + 6 = 10$$
$$0.2 + 0.3 = 0.5$$
$$0.08 + 0.07 = 0.15$$

$$10 + 0.5 + 0.15 = 10.65$$

- Joe used Partial Differences to solve 3.42 – 1.7. See her work shown here. What does she have to do next? Why does she have –0.3 as part of her work?

$$3.42 - 1.7$$

$$3 - 1 = 2$$
$$0.4 - 0.7 = {}^-0.3$$
$$0.02 - 0 = 0.02$$

- Kai used Partial Differences to subtract 5.16 – 2.74. Do you agree or disagree with Kai's work? Explain your thinking.

$$5.16 - 2.74$$

$$5 - 2 = 3$$
$$0.7 - 0.1 = 0.6$$
$$\underline{0.06 - 0.04 = 0.02}$$

$$3.62$$

(Continued)

- Timothy used Partial Sums to solve the problem shown here. Juan said there is an error in Timothy's work. Can you find the mistake that Timothy made?

$$
\begin{array}{r}
7.41 \\
+\ 0.29 \\
\hline
7.00 \\
0.60 \\
0.010 \\
\hline
7.61
\end{array}
$$

- Tell how Partial Differences works when the subtrahend has a bigger value in one of its places (like 4.15 − 1.78). You can use this example to explain the process.

Fraction Prompts

- Julio solved $4\frac{1}{5}+2\frac{2}{5}$ as shown here. Do you agree with Julio? Tell why you agree or disagree with Julio.

$$4\tfrac{1}{5} + 2\tfrac{2}{5}$$

$$4 + 2 = 6$$
$$\tfrac{1}{5} + \tfrac{2}{5} = \tfrac{3}{5}$$

$$6 + \tfrac{3}{5} = 6\tfrac{3}{5}$$

- The class was working on solving $5\frac{1}{3}-3\frac{1}{2}$. Jameel solved the problem as shown here. Do you agree with Jameel? Explain your thinking.

$$5\tfrac{1}{3} - 3\tfrac{1}{2}$$

$$5 - 3 = 2$$
$$\tfrac{1}{3} - \tfrac{1}{2} = \tfrac{2}{6} - \tfrac{3}{6} = \tfrac{1}{6}$$

$$2 + \tfrac{1}{6} = 2\tfrac{1}{6}$$

- Kha'Mario used Partial Differences to subtract $7\frac{1}{2}-3\frac{1}{6}$. Do you agree or disagree with Kha'Mario's work? Explain your thinking.

$$7\tfrac{1}{2} - 3\tfrac{1}{6}$$

$$7 - 3 = 4$$
$$\tfrac{1}{2} - \tfrac{1}{6} = \tfrac{3}{6} - \tfrac{1}{6} = \tfrac{2}{6}$$

$$4 - \tfrac{2}{6} = 3\tfrac{4}{6} \text{ or } 3\tfrac{2}{3}$$

- Create two different problems that would *not* be a good fit for solving with the Partial Sums strategy. Explain why.

PRACTICE ACTIVITIES for Partial Sums and Differences

Fluency is realized through quality practice that is focused, varied, processed, and connected. The activities in this section focus students' attention on how this strategy works and when to use it. The activities are a collection of varied engagements. Game boards, recording sheets, digit cards, and other required materials are available as online resources for you to download, possibly modify, and use.

As students practice, look for how well they are using the new strategy and assimilating it into their collection of strategies. Post-activity discussions help students reflect on *how* they reasoned and *when* that strategy was useful (and when it was not). Discussions can also help students reflect on how that strategy connects to recent instruction and to other strategies they have learned.

FLUENCY COMPONENT	WHAT TO LOOK FOR AS STUDENTS PRACTICE THIS STRATEGY
Efficiency	• Do students choose Partial Sums and Differences when it is a good fit for the problem? • Do students overuse the strategy (i.e., try to use it when it is not a good fit, such as 4.9 + 1.5)? • Are students using Partial Sums and Differences adeptly (not getting hung up)?
Flexibility	• Are students carrying out the strategy in flexible ways (e.g., sometimes decomposing by place value, sometimes using friendly numbers, sometimes decomposing just one number)? • Do they change their approach to or from the strategy as it proves inappropriate or overly complicated for the problem? • Are they seeing how to apply this strategy in "new" situations (e.g., applying to longer decimal values or to problems with different denominators)?
Accuracy	• Are students using the Partial Sums and Differences strategy accurately? • Are students finding accurate solutions? • Are they considering the reasonableness of their solution? • Are students estimating before finding solutions?

ACTIVITY 6.6
PARTIAL SUMS AND DIFFERENCES
WORKED EXAMPLES

Worked examples are problems that have been solved. As you have read, Partial Sums and Differences can become rote. Worked examples can help introduce other ways to make use of this strategy. Incorrectly worked examples can highlight common challenges or errors when using partial sums or differences. Here are some examples:

1. The student subtracts when the subtrahend place value is larger than the digit in the minuend.
   - 5.28 − 2.55: subtracts 0.2 − 0.5 and gets 0.3 as a partial difference.
   - $12\frac{1}{5} - 6\frac{4}{5}$: subtracts $\frac{1}{5} - \frac{4}{5}$ and gets $\frac{3}{5}$ as a partial difference.

2. The student makes errors when adding the partials together.
   - 2.37 + 5.46: adds 2 + 5 to equal 7, 0.3 + 0.7 to equal 1, and 0.07 + 0.06 to equal 0.13, but records the answer as 7.23.
   - 4.6 + 7.8: adds 4 + 7 = 11, adds 0.6 + 0.8, and puts more than one digit in a column, resulting in 0.14 rather than 1.4.
   - $5\frac{3}{4} + 4\frac{3}{4}$: adds 5 + 4 to equal 9, adds $\frac{3}{4} + \frac{3}{4}$ to equal $\frac{6}{4}$, and records the answer as $9\frac{6}{4}$ rather than regroup and give the simplified answer of $10\frac{1}{2}$. (This example is not an error, but in not completing the problem, the student may not understand the regrouping to make another whole number.)

There are different ways to pose worked examples, and they each serve a different fluency purpose.

TYPE OF WORKED EXAMPLE	PURPOSES: COMPONENT (FLUENCY ACTIONS)	QUESTIONS FOR DISCUSSIONS OR FOR WRITING RESPONSES
Correctly Worked Example	Efficiency (selects an appropriate strategy) and flexibility (applies a strategy to a new problem type)	What did _____ do? Why does it work? Is this a good method for this problem?
Partially Worked Example (Implement the Strategy Accurately)	Efficiency (selects an appropriate strategy; solves in a reasonable amount of time) and accuracy (completes steps accurately; gets correct answer)	Why did _____ start the problem this way? What does _____ need to do to finish the problem?
Incorrectly Worked Example (Highlight Common Errors)	Accuracy (completes steps accurately; gets correct answer)	What did _____ do? What mistake does _____ make? How can this mistake be fixed?

The instructional prompts from Activity 6.5 provide numerous worked examples. Throughout the module are more worked examples that you can use. A sampling of additional ideas is provided in the following table.

CORRECTLY WORKED EXAMPLES	
Jamal's work for $5\frac{3}{4}+1\frac{1}{2}=$?	David's work for $5.75 + 1.389 =$?
$5 + 1 = 6$ $\frac{3}{4} + \frac{1}{4} + \frac{1}{4} = 1\frac{1}{4}$ $\overline{7\frac{1}{4}}$	$5 + 1 = 6$ $0.7 + 0.3 = 1.0$ $0.05 + 0.089 = \underline{0.139}$ 7.139

PARTIALLY WORKED EXAMPLES	
Lucy's start for $12\frac{3}{8}-8\frac{3}{4}=$?	Michael's start for $3.48 - 1.839 =$?
$12 - 8 = 4$ $\frac{3}{8} - \frac{6}{8} =$	$3.4 - 1.4 = 2$

INCORRECTLY WORKED EXAMPLES	
Laila's work for $12\frac{1}{5}-6\frac{4}{5}=$?	Ryan's work for $3.19 - 1.56 =$?
$12 - 6 = 6$ $\frac{1}{5} - \frac{4}{5} = \frac{3}{5}$ $6 + \frac{3}{5} = 6\frac{3}{5}$	$2 + 0.4 + 0.03 = 2.43$

ACTIVITY 6.7

Name: "The Parts"   **Type:** Routine

About the Routine: "The Parts" is a routine for reasoning that reinforces place value concepts and the Partial Sums and Differences strategy. Students think backward to try to figure out the original problem, based on clues they are given about the partial sums. Students discover that different problems can end up having the same partial sums.

Materials: prepared Partial Sums equations; whiteboards or sticky notes for students (optional)

Directions:
1. Write each partial sum on the board, starting with the largest place value. These are clues to figure out the teacher's hidden addition problem.

2. Students use the clues to create partials of an addition or subtraction problem.

3. Based on their partials, students write what they think the original addition problem is and solve it.

4. Students compare their expressions and answers with a partner.

5. The teacher reveals the hidden problem. As time allows, have students compare their expressions with the teacher's expression.

THE PARTS: PARTIAL SUMS DECIMAL EXAMPLE

Teacher writes on the board: **9**
Teacher poses: The sum of the ones is 9. What might the ones of each addend be?
Students determine a possibility. For example, Ashley records 3 + 6.

Teacher writes on the board: **0.7**
Teacher says: The sum of the tenths is 0.7. What might the tenths of each addend be?
Students write down a possibility. For example, Ashley records 0.2 + 0.5.

Teacher writes on the board: **0.14**
Teacher says: The sum of the hundredths is 0.14. What might the hundredths of each addend be?
Students determine a possibility. For example, Ashley records 0.7 + 0.7.

The teacher asks students to write their full equation. Ashley writes 3.27 + 6.57 = 9.84 and compares her equation with a partner.

The teacher solicits different student solutions and then reveals her equation: 4.23 + 5.61.

THE PARTS: PARTIAL DIFFERENCES DECIMAL EXAMPLE

Teacher writes on the board: **14**
Teacher says: The difference of the whole numbers is 14. What might each addend be?
Students determine a possibility. For example, Reese thinks 24 − 10.

Teacher writes on the board: **−0.5**
Teacher says: The difference of the tenths is −0.5. What might the tenths of each addend be?
Students determine a possibility. For example, Reese thinks 0.2 − 0.7.

Teacher writes on the board: **0.03**
Teacher says: The difference of the hundredths is 0.03. What might the hundredths of each addend be?
Students determine a possibility. For example, Reese thinks 0.05 − 0.02.

The teacher asks students to write their full equation. Reese records 24.25 − 10.72 = 13.53 and compares her equation with a partner.

The teacher solicits different student solutions and then reveals his equation: 16.15 − 2.62.

THE PARTS: PARTIAL SUMS FRACTION EXAMPLE

Teacher writes on the board: **7**
Teacher says: The sum of the whole numbers is 7. What might each addend be?
Students determine a possibility. For example, Tao thinks 3 + 4.

Teacher writes on the board: $\frac{7}{10}$
Teacher says: The sum of the fractional part is $\frac{7}{10}$. What might the tenths of each addend be?
Students determine a possibility. For example, Tao thinks $\frac{2}{10} + \frac{5}{10}$.

The teacher asks students to write their full equation. Tao writes $3\frac{2}{10} + 4\frac{5}{10}$ and compares his equation with a partner.

The teacher solicits different student solutions and then reveals her equation: $2\frac{3}{10} + 5\frac{4}{10}$.

THE PARTS: PARTIAL DIFFERENCES FRACTIONS EXAMPLE

Teacher writes on the board: **4**
Teacher says: The difference of the whole numbers is 4. What might each addend be?
Students determine a possibility and share their thinking. For example, Alisa thinks 9 − 5.

Teacher writes on the board: $-\frac{3}{8}$
Teacher says: The difference of the fractional part is $-\frac{3}{8}$. What might the fractional part of each addend be?
Students determine a possibility and share their thinking. For example, Alisa thinks $\frac{2}{8} - \frac{5}{8}$.

The teacher asks students to write their full equation. Alisa writes $9\frac{2}{8} - 5\frac{5}{8}$ and compares her equation with a partner.

The teacher solicits different student solutions and then reveals his equation: $6\frac{4}{8} - 2\frac{7}{8}$.

ACTIVITY 6.8

Name: "Decimal Number Strings"   **Type:** Routine

About the Routine: Students benefit from opportunities to practice adding tenths, hundredths, and thousandths in ways that relate back to their basic facts. This routine helps students see patterns in problems with related addends while also reinforcing connections to basic facts.

Materials: series of related expressions

Directions:

1. Provide a matrix of related number strings with one known sum.

2. Students use the known sum to work across the rows and down the columns.

3. After students signal that they know the sums of each, you hold a class discussion about how the first known relates to the others. You want to draw students' attention to how adding the ones relates to the number of tenths, hundredths, and thousandths. Use appropriate language and help students make sense of the relative size of these numbers.

TEACHING TAKEAWAY

Use the language of tenths, hundredths, or thousandths and help students makes sense of the relative size of these values.

9 + 7 = 16	0.9 + 0.7 =	0.09 + 0.07 =	0.009 + 0.007 =
9 + 6 =	0.9 + 0.6 =	0.09 + 0.06 =	0.009 + 0.006 =
9 + 3 =	0.9 + 0.3 =	0.09 + 0.03 =	0.009 + 0.003 =
9 + 2 =	0.9 + 0.2 =	0.09 + 0.02 =	0.009 + 0.002 =
9 + 0.2 =	0.9 + 0.02 =	0.09 + 0.002 =	0.009 + 0.0002 =

Try making your own number string matrix. While the table may look a bit overwhelming to create, the problems stem from a basic fact (e.g., 9 + 7 = 16). Create a row of related problems with decreasing place values (0.09 + 0.07, 0.009 + 0.007, etc.). Then create some problems just below the basic fact that is related in some way (an addend is one more or one less, half, and so on). Then create rows for each of the new basic facts in a similar way for the original basic fact.

ACTIVITY 6.9

Name: "Fraction Number Strings"   **Type:** Routine

About the Routine: Students benefit from opportunities to practice adding fractions and mixed numbers that are related. This routine helps students see patterns in problems with related addends and encourages focus on partial sums (or differences).

Materials: Series of related expressions

Directions: 1. This routine can be implemented in (at least) two different ways.
- Provide students with a complete matrix of related problems. (See first matrix.)
- Post the first addition expression. Have students carry the sum over to the next column and continue to use the same second addend. (See second matrix.)

2. Students use the known sum to work across the rows and down the columns.

3. As a class, have a discussion about patterns that they notice and strategies they find useful.

$\frac{1}{2}+\frac{1}{4}=$	$\frac{3}{4}+\frac{1}{4}=$	$1+\frac{1}{4}=$	$1\frac{1}{4}+\frac{1}{4}=$
$\frac{3}{4}+\frac{3}{4}=$	$1\frac{1}{2}+\frac{3}{4}=$	$2\frac{1}{4}+\frac{3}{4}=$	$3+\frac{3}{4}=$
$1\frac{3}{4}+1\frac{3}{4}=$	$3\frac{1}{2}+1\frac{3}{4}=$	$5\frac{1}{4}+1\frac{3}{4}=$	$7+1\frac{3}{4}=$
$1\frac{3}{5}+1\frac{3}{10}=$	$2\frac{9}{10}+1\frac{3}{10}=$	$4\frac{1}{5}+1\frac{3}{10}=$	$5\frac{4}{5}+1\frac{3}{10}=$

$\frac{1}{2}+\frac{1}{4}=$	$\rule{2em}{0.4pt}+\frac{1}{4}=$	$\rule{2em}{0.4pt}+\frac{1}{4}=$	$\rule{2em}{0.4pt}+\frac{1}{4}=$
$\frac{3}{4}+\frac{3}{4}=$	$\rule{2em}{0.4pt}+\frac{3}{4}=$	$\rule{2em}{0.4pt}+\frac{3}{4}=$	$\rule{2em}{0.4pt}+\frac{3}{4}=$
$1\frac{3}{4}+1\frac{3}{4}=$	$\rule{2em}{0.4pt}+1\frac{3}{4}=$	$\rule{2em}{0.4pt}+1\frac{3}{4}=$	$\rule{2em}{0.4pt}+1\frac{3}{4}=$
$1\frac{3}{5}+1\frac{3}{10}=$	$\rule{2em}{0.4pt}+1\frac{3}{10}=$	$\rule{2em}{0.4pt}+1\frac{3}{10}=$	$\rule{2em}{0.4pt}+1\frac{3}{10}=$

ACTIVITY 6.10

Name: "Too Much Taken???" **Type:** Routine

About the Routine: Using Partial Differences can be challenging because there are situations where we encounter a negative amount. When using a standard algorithm, one would regroup from the ones so that the negative is avoided. Understanding the negative result, why it occurs, and how it is used is essential for this strategy. Students *can* do this. In this routine, students practice taking away too much. It is first described as a decimal activity, and then as a fraction activity.

Materials: This routine does not require any materials.

Directions: 1. Pose a few related equations.

2. Have students determine if they think the equations are true or false.

3. Conclude the routine by asking students, "How do you know when there will be 'too much taken?'"

"Too Much Taken?" With Decimals

Example 1 →	5 − 7 = −2	0.5 − 0.7 = −0.2	0.05 − 0.07 = −0.02
Example 2 →	9 − 6 = 3	0.9 − 0.6 = 0.3	0.09 − 0.06 = 0.03
Example 3 →	3 − 8 = −5	0.3 − 0.8 = −0.5	0.03 − 0.08 = −0.05
Example 4 →	7 − 3 = 4	0.7 − 0.3 = −0.4	0.07 − 0.03 = 0.04

TEACHING TIP

To incorporate active movement, have students choose one side of the room if they think "true" and the other side if they think "false." They can discuss with those that agree and then debate with those that do not.

Note the relationship of the numbers across each row. This helps students make sense of place value and apply their whole number knowledge to decimals. Each row intentionally does not take too much away so that students must attend to the numbers in the problem to decide.

"Too Much Taken?" With Fractions

With fractions, the relationship across each row culminates with the result in the last column where the "too much taken" is reconciled. Ask students, "What do you notice?" and "Why does that work?"

Example 1 →	5 − 3 = 2	$\frac{1}{5} - \frac{2}{5} = -\frac{1}{5}$	$5\frac{1}{5} - 3\frac{2}{5} = 1\frac{4}{5}$
Example 2 →	9 − 6 = 3	$\frac{3}{4} - \frac{1}{2} = \frac{1}{4}$	$9\frac{3}{4} - 6\frac{1}{2} = 3\frac{1}{4}$
Example 3 →	8 − 3 = 5	$\frac{3}{8} - \frac{3}{4} = -\frac{3}{8}$	$8\frac{3}{8} - 3\frac{3}{4} = 4\frac{5}{8}$
Example 4 →	7 − 3 = 4	$\frac{5}{6} - \frac{1}{6} = \frac{4}{6}$	$7\frac{5}{6} - 3\frac{1}{6} = 4\frac{2}{3}$

ACTIVITY 6.11

Name: For Keeps   **Type:** Game

About the Game: *For Keeps* is an opportunity to practice adding or subtracting in an engaging way that also helps students develop reasoning about numbers. The goal is to keep two sums that will have a sum greater than an opponent's sum of sums. This is a game to be played with partners.

Materials: *For Keeps* game board; digit cards (0–9), playing cards (queens equal 0 and aces equal 1; remove tens, kings, and jacks), or a 10-sided die

Directions:

1. By drawing cards or rolling the die, players generate four numbers and make 2 two-digit addends using tenths and hundredths places.

2. Players find the sum of the two addends and decide whether they want to keep the sum as the score for the round. Once they decide (before the next problem), the decision is final and the sum can't be moved later.

3. Players play a total of four rounds yet can only keep two of those rounds. At the end of the fourth round, each player adds the two scores that they kept.

4. The player with the higher score wins.

In the following example, players are using hundredths. This player first makes 0.62 + 0.41 for a sum of 1.03 and chooses not to keep it. The second sum of 1.25 was kept, as it was a relatively high sum. The player chooses not to keep the third sum, so they must keep the sum in the fourth round. The sum of the two kept scores (1.25 and the fourth round) will be the player's score.

For Keeps

Directions: Make two addends. Find the sum and decide if you want to keep the sum as a score or not keep it. You can only keep two of the four rounds. After the fourth round, add the two scores you kept. The player with the higher score wins.

Round	Numbers Created		Sum For Keeps	Sum and NOT Kept
1	0.62	0.41		1.03
2	0.40	0.85	1.25	
3	0.21	0.32		0.53
4				
	Sum of Keeps			

 A blank *For Keeps* game board can be downloaded at **resources.corwin.com/FOF/ addsubtractdecimalfraction**.

ACTIVITY 6.12

Name: Sum Duel   **Type:** Game

About the Game: *Sum Duel* is a unique way to practice adding with partials. Players make sums or differences and earn points for each condition their sum matches. This is a game to be played with partners and can be played with fractions and with decimals.

Materials: one *Sum Duel* game board per player; *Sum Duel* condition cards; two different-colored counters (four of each color for each player)

Directions:

1. Player 1 puts four chips (white chips in the example) on the board to show a decomposed four-digit number and records the number.

2. The player then puts four chips (gray chips in the example) on the board to show another decomposed four-digit number and the player records the number.

3. The player adds the two recorded numbers using the Partial Sums strategy. Other players also add to confirm the solution.

4. This process is repeated for the other player(s).

5. The players then turn over *Sum Duel* cards and get a point for each condition their sum matches.

6. The first player to earn 5 points wins the game.

Here is a fraction example: $5\frac{3}{4}$ (white chips) + $7\frac{7}{8}$ (gray chips)

Sum Duel

Directions: Place 2 counters on the board (1 whole number and 1 fraction) to make a mixed number. Have your opponent place 2 counters on the board to make another mixed number. Find the sum of the two numbers. Then, flip Sum War cards. If your sum matches the Sum War condition you get a point. The first player with 5 points wins.

Whole Numbers		Fractions			
9	(5)	$\frac{1}{2}$	$\frac{5}{8}$	$\frac{1}{4}$	$\frac{1}{5}$
8	4	$\frac{1}{8}$	$\frac{1}{10}$	$(\frac{3}{4})$	$\frac{3}{10}$
(7)	3	$\frac{2}{5}$	$\frac{1}{6}$	$\frac{5}{6}$	$\frac{2}{3}$
6	2	$\frac{3}{5}$	$\frac{3}{8}$	$\frac{1}{3}$	$(\frac{7}{8})$

Here is a decimal example: 86.67 (white chips) + 37.58 (gray chips)

Sum Duel

Directions: Place 4 counters on the board to make a 4-digit decimal number. Have your opponent place 4 counters on the board to make another 4-digit number. Find the sum of the two numbers. Then, flip Sum War cards. If your sum matches the Sum War condition you get a point. The first player with 5 points wins.

Tens		Ones		Tenths		Hundredths	
90	50	9	5	.9	(.5)	.09	.05
(80)	40	8	4	.8	.4	(.08)	.04
70	(30)	(7)	3	.7	.3	(.07)	.03
60	20	(6)	2	(.6)	.2	.06	.02

Largest sum	Smallest sum	Sum closest to 5
Sum closest to 10	Sum greater than 18 (1 extra bonus point for this condition!)	Sum with largest fractional part
Sum with smallest fractional part	Sum with fractional part equivalent to $\frac{1}{2}$	Sum with fractional part that required regrouping

online resources ▶ This resource can be downloaded at **resources.corwin.com/FOF/addsubtractdecimalfraction**.

ACTIVITY 6.13

Name: Decimals Target 10 or 0   **Type:** Game

About the Game: In this partner game, students practice both adding and subtracting decimals. The goal of each round is to get as close to the target as possible (10 if adding, 0 if subtracting). You can change the addition target to 1 for adding addends with hundredths or 0.1 for adding thousandths. To play with more than two players, use two sets of digit cards.

Materials: two decks of digit cards (0–9), playing cards (queens equal 0 and aces equal 1; remove tens, kings, and jacks), or a 10-sided die; *Decimals Target 10 or 0* recording sheet; 1 two-sided counter or a coin

Directions:
1. Players each get four digit cards (or roll the die four times) to create 2 two-digit decimal numbers.

2. A player flips the two-sided counter to see if they will add or subtract (e.g., yellow means add, red means subtract).

3. Players arrange their cards to make expressions that get close to 10 (if adding) or to 0 (if subtracting).

4. The player closest to 10 or 0 gets a point. The first to earn 5 points wins. *Optional*: Players score a bonus point if they can make a sum or difference that is exactly 10 or 0.

TEACHING TAKEAWAY
Games can be modified to be used as centers, and centers can be adjusted to be played as games.

The recording sheet provides an example of how the game is played. The player pulls digit cards of 1, 5, 7, and 5. They flip to determine that they will be adding for a target of 10. Then the player makes 5.1 + 5.7 for a sum of 10.8, showing their work with Partial Sums. While this was a great hand for this player, the player was not closest to 10 (their opponent has 9.4; not shown).

RESOURCE(S) FOR THIS ACTIVITY

10 or 0

Directions: Pull four cards. Flip a counter or coin to see if you will add or subtract. Use your 4 cards to make two, two-digit numbers that are close to 10 (if adding) or close to 0 (if subtracting). The player closest to 10 or 0 wins a point. The first player to 5 points wins the game.

My Numbers	+ or -	My problem	Closest to 10 or 0
1, 5, 7, 5	+	5.1 + 5.7 so 5.1 + 5.7 = 10.8 5 + 5 = 10 0.1 + 0.7 = 0.8	No

online resources — This resource can be downloaded at **resources.corwin.com/FOF/addsubtractdecimalfraction**.

ACTIVITY 6.14

Name: Decimal Partial Concentration   **Type:** Game

About the Game: This partner game helps students think about how partial sums and differences are used to solve expressions. Students work to match problems with Partial Sum recordings of the problem. This game is played like the traditional game of *Memory* or *Concentration*.

Materials: one deck of *Partial Concentration* cards

Directions:
1. Players place cards mixed up and face down in an array.

2. Players take turns flipping over cards and attempting to match an expression with a card that shows how to solve the problem with Partial Sums and Differences. When students find a match, they must tell their partner how they know it is a match.

3. The player who finds the most matches wins the game.

Partial concentration cards are available for download. Note that you can also create a set of partial concentration cards with index cards.

RESOURCE(S) FOR THIS ACTIVITY

$9.41 + 3.7$	$9 + 3 = 12$ $0.4 + 0.7 = 1.1$ $0.01 + 0 = 0.01$ 13.11	$58.94 - 12.3$	$50 - 10 = 40$ $8 - 2 = 6$ $0.9 - 0.3 = 0.6$ $0.04 - 0 = 0.04$ $40 + 6 + 0.6 + 0.04 = 46.64$
$56.5 + 4.4$	$50 + 0 = 50$ $6 + 4 = 10$ $0.5 + 0.4 = 0.9$ $50 + 10 + 0.9 = 60.9$	$8.94 - 3.727$	$8 - 3 = 5$ $0.9 - 0.7 = 0.2$ $0.04 - 0.02 = 0.02$ $0 - 0.007 = -0.007$ $5 + 0.2 + 0.02 - 0.007 = 5.213$
$7.1 + 7.89$	$7 + 7 = 14$ $0.1 + 0.8 = 0.9$ $0 + 0.09 = 0.09$ $14 + 0.9 + 0.09 = 14.99$	$5.87 - 3.04$	$5 - 3 = 2$ $0.8 - 0 = 0.8$ $0.07 - 0.04 = 0.03$ $2 + 0.8 + 0.03 = 2.83$
$66 + 8.5$	$60 + 0 = 60$ $6 + 8 = 14$ $0 + 0.5$ $60 + 14 + 0.5 = 74.5$	$39.17 - 4.5$	$30 - 0 = 30$ $9 - 4 = 5$ $0.1 - 0.5 = -0.4$ $0.07 - 0 = 0.07$ $30 + 5 - 0.4 + 0.07 = 34.67$
$3.4 + 19.43$	$0 + 10 = 10$ $3 + 9 = 12$ $0.4 + 0.4 = 0.8$ $0 + 0.03$ $10 + 12 + 0.8 + 0.03 = 22.83$	$89.41 - 7.16$	$80 - 0 = 80$ $9 - 7 = 2$ $0.4 - 0.1 = 0.3$ $0.01 - 0.06 = -0.05$ $80 + 2 + 0.3 - 0.05 = 82.25$

online resources This resource can be downloaded at **resources.corwin.com/FOF/addsubtractdecimalfraction**.

ACTIVITY 6.15

Name: Adding With Ten-Frames and Place Value Disks

Type: Center

About the Center: This center activity can be done individually or with a partner. Students practice decomposing a number by place value and then adding to find partials with place value disks. This center helps students see partial sums with different representations.

Materials: Ten-Frame Place Value mats (two per student); place value disks (about two handfuls per student); Adding With Ten-Frames and Place Value Disks recording sheet

Directions:
1. Students scoop a pile of place value disks.

2. Students sort the pile and place the disks on the place value ten-frame mat.

3. Students record the number on a recording sheet or in their journal.

4. Students scoop a second pile of place value disks and then sort and arrange them on a second mat.

5. Students record the second number.

6. Students find the sum of the two numbers using the Partial Sums strategy.

A Ten-Frame Place Value mat is available for download. Students may not grab a place value disk for every column and this is represented with a zero. They may also grab place value disks so that when added together they require regrouping (0.09 + 0.04 = 0.13). To model this more explicitly, they can add the place value disks from the second mat to the first mat.

Student collects and sorts her place value disks.   Student puts her place value disks on the Ten-Frame Place Value mat.   Student records the number she made (4.296).

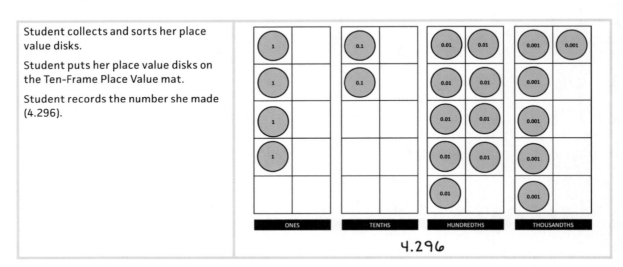

4.296

Student collects and sorts her place value disks. Student puts her place value disks on the Ten-Frame Place Value mat. Student records the second number she made (3.042).	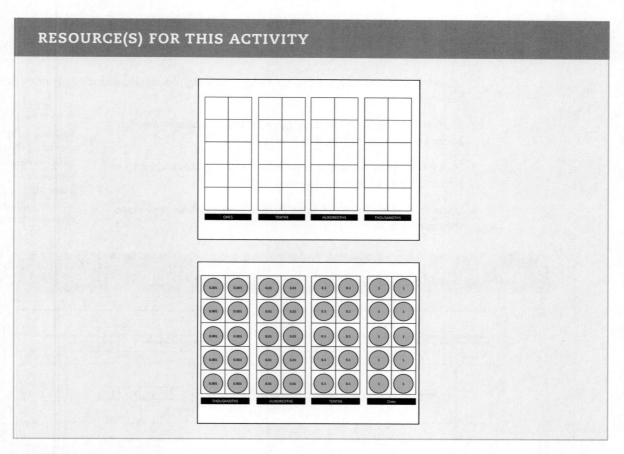 3.042
The student then finds the sum of these two numbers using Partial Sums.	4 + 3 = 7 0.2 + 0 = 0.2 0.09 + 0.04 = 0.13 0.006 + 0.002 = 0.008 7 + 0.2 + 0.13 + 0.008 = 7.338

RESOURCE(S) FOR THIS ACTIVITY

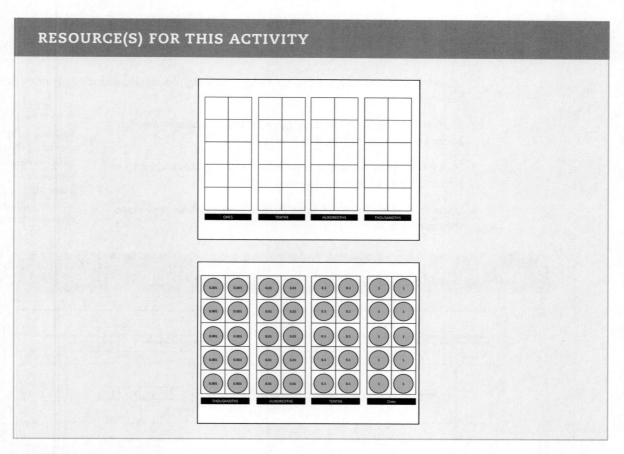

online resources — This resource can be downloaded at **resources.corwin.com/FOF/addsubtractdecimalfraction**.

ACTIVITY 6.16

Name: Target 10   **Type:** Center

About the Center: Target 10 is a center that works well as a partner activity or with a group of three. Target sums and differences games are dynamic opportunities for practice. In the mixed fraction version of this game, students create two mixed numbers with a sum as close to 10 as possible. In the decimal version of this center, students create three-digit addends with a sum as close to 10 as possible. Alternatively, students can subtract and a target can be set, such as 3.

Materials: two decks of digit cards (1–9) or playing cards (aces equal 1; remove tens and face cards); Target 10 recording sheet (either fraction or decimal version)

Fraction Directions:

1. Students pull three cards to make a mixed number.

2. Students pull three more cards to make another mixed number.

3. Students arrange the digits in each to create two addends with a sum as close to 10 as possible.

4. Students add the numbers with Partial Sums to show how close their sum is to 10.

Decimal Directions:

1. Students pull three digit cards to make a two-digit decimal addend (with ones, tenths, and hundredths).

2. Students pull three more digit cards to make another two-digit addend (with ones, tenths, and hundredths).

3. Students arrange the digits in each to create two addends with a sum as close to 10 as possible.

4. Students add the numbers with Partial Sums to show how close their sum is to 10.

> **TEACHING TAKEAWAY**
>
> To save paper, print recording sheets and put them in plastic sleeves or laminate them and have students use dry-erase markers.

RESOURCE(S) FOR THIS ACTIVITY

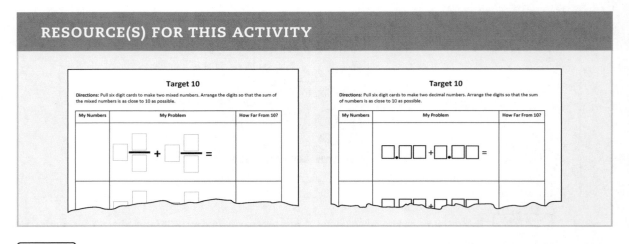

online resources 🔖 This resource can be downloaded at **resources.corwin.com/FOF/addsubtractdecimalfraction**.

NOTES

Standard Algorithms

STRATEGY OVERVIEW:
Standard Algorithms

What is a Standard Algorithm? An algorithm is a step-by-step process for solving a problem. Algorithms have been around for centuries. Ancient Greeks used algorithms to calculate prime numbers, find the greatest common divisors, and approximate pi. Today, we use algorithms when we follow a recipe. Computation algorithms vary from country to country. In the United States, most operations have one particular algorithm named as the "standard" method. The algorithm for decimal addition and subtraction means adding each place value separately, beginning with the smallest place value (farthest to the right) and working to the larger place values. Notations do not define an algorithm (Fuson & Beckmann, 2012–2013). That means that all three of these examples, which all add from right to left, are ways to enact the U.S. standard algorithm for addition. While the first one is more common, it can be the hardest for students to use.

TICK MARKS NOTATED ABOVE	TICK MARKS NOTATED BELOW	NO TICK MARKS, PARTIALS RECORDED
$$\begin{array}{r} {\scriptstyle 1\ \ 1} \\ 7.48 \\ +1.76 \\ \hline 9.24 \end{array}$$	$$\begin{array}{r} 7.48 \\ +1.76 \\ \hline {\scriptstyle 1\ 1} \\ 9.24 \end{array}$$	$$\begin{array}{r} 7.48 \\ +1.76 \\ \hline .14 \\ 1.1 \\ 8. \\ \hline 9.24 \end{array}$$

HOW DO U.S. STANDARD ALGORITHMS WORK?

Standard algorithms, like all of the strategies, involve adding or subtracting *like-sized parts* (tens with tens, ones with ones, eighths with eighths, etc.).

FRACTIONS

The first step with fractions is to find the common denominator. This is also the first step in nearly every strategy, so here we focus on what happens *after* that change. Starting with mixed numbers helps students connect to their whole number knowledge. Students may add the fractions, leave the sum as a fraction or write it as a mixed number, or then combine it with the whole.

$$\begin{array}{r} 9\frac{4}{6} \\ +6\frac{5}{6} \\ \hline 13\frac{3}{6} \\ 15 \\ \hline 16\frac{1}{2} \end{array}$$

To subtract, regrouping must attend to the denominator. One whole is equivalent to 12 twelfths:

$$11 \frac{\cancel{8}^{20}}{\cancel{12}}$$

$$- 4 \frac{11}{12}$$

$$7 \frac{9}{12}$$

DECIMALS

To be sure like parts are being added, the decimal point is lined up. When decimals are different lengths, students can put a zero in "empty" place values to the right of the decimal point. Regrouping is applied the same as it is with whole numbers.

WHEN DO YOU CHOOSE A STANDARD ALGORITHM?

While standard algorithms always work, they are not always the best choice as described earlier. A standard algorithm is needed in these situations:

1. Numbers in the problem do not lend themselves to a mental method.

2. Numbers in the problem do not lend themselves to a convenient written option (e.g., Compensation).

3. You don't know an alternate method.

4. You want to check an answer using a different method.

Sadly, when it comes to fractions and decimals, far too many people "need" the standard algorithm because of point 3. In our hurry to get to standard algorithms, other reasoning strategies are cut short if they are taught at all. This is a mistake that undermines students' confidence and fluency. "Fluently subtract" does *not* mean "use the standard algorithm adeptly." It means "use the standard algorithm adeptly *when it is the most efficient option*." Thus, to ensure that students develop fluency with adding and subtracting decimals and fractions, the algorithms must be presented after reasoning strategies and students must understand when algorithms make sense and when the other options are more efficient.

MODULE 1 Foundations for Reasoning Strategies

MODULE 2 Count On/Count Back Strategy

MODULE 3 Make a Whole Strategy

MODULE 4 Think Addition Strategy

MODULE 5 Compensation Strategy

MODULE 6 Partial Sums and Differences Strategy

MODULE 7 Standard Algorithms

STANDARD ALGORITHMS:
Strategy Briefs for Families

It is important that families understand the strategies and know how they work so that they can be partners in the pursuit of fluency. These strategy briefs are a tool for doing that. You can include them in newsletters for parents or caregivers, or at a school event like a Back to School Night. They are available for download so that you can adjust them as needed.

Standard Algorithm for Decimal Addition

What it is: The algorithm for addition with decimals involves aligning the addends vertically by place value. Each place value is added from right to left. When a sum is more than 10, it is regrouped. Regrouping can be recorded above the addends or below them.

Let's look at 6.35 + 3.8.

What it sounds like: I will start by writing the addends vertically, lining up the decimal point and the corresponding place value columns. I will start by adding the hundredths place. I can rewrite 3.8 as 3.80 to show there is nothing in the hundredths place or I can leave the column empty. I will record 5 in the hundredths place. I will then add the digits in the tenths place. The sum of 3 tenths and 8 tenths is 11 tenths. I will regroup 10 tenths to make 1 whole and add it to the ones place. I will record the remaining 1 tenth in the tenths place. Finally, I will add the 6 and 3 and 1 for a total of 10 ones, which I can regroup and write as 1 ten.

I will use estimation to check to see if my answer is reasonable. 6.35 rounds to 6 and 3.8 rounds to 4. 6 + 4 = 10, so my answer should be about 10.

What it looks like: The place value columns are vertically aligned. The sum of each column is recorded at the bottom and a tally mark to show the regrouping of 10 tenths as 1 whole is recorded at the top of the ones column.

```
    1
  6.35
+ 3.8
───────
 10.15
```

When this algorithm is useful: Knowing when to use an algorithm is just as important as knowing how to use an algorithm. A problem like 6.1 + 2.3 does not need an algorithm for solving, since it is easy to add the parts together mentally to get 8.4. Problems that use more place value columns, are unequal in length, or require regrouping would benefit from the algorithm.

Standard Algorithm for Decimal Subtraction

What it is: The algorithm for subtraction with decimals involves aligning the numbers vertically by place value. Each place value is subtracted from right to left. Regrouping is necessary when the value in the minuend is smaller than then subtrahend. Regrouping is the process of exchanging 1 whole into 10 tenths or 1 tenth into 10 hundredths.

Let's look at 6.35 – 3.8.

What it sounds like: I will start by writing the numbers vertically, lining up the decimal point and the corresponding place value columns. I will start by subtracting the hundredths place. I can rewrite 3.8 as 3.80 to show there is nothing in the hundredths place or I can leave the column empty. I will record 5 in the hundredths place. I will then subtract the digits in the tenths place. I do not have enough tenths to take 8 tenths away from 3 tenths. I will regroup 1 whole to make 10 tenths so I now have 13 tenths. I will subtract the tenths and record a 5 in the tenths place in my answer. Finally, I will subtract 5 – 3 and record a 2 in the ones place.

I will use estimation to check to see if my answer is reasonable. 6.35 rounds to 6 and 3.8 rounds to 4. 6 – 4 = 2, so my answer should be about 2.

What it looks like: The place value columns are vertically aligned. The 6 in the ones column has been crossed out and replaced with a 5. The 1 has been exchanged for 10 tenths, which is notated by crossing out the 3 and replacing it with 13. The difference of each column is recorded at the bottom.

```
   5 13
  6.35
- 3.80
───────
  2.55
```

When this algorithm is useful: Knowing when to use an algorithm is just as important as knowing how to use an algorithm. A problem like 6.5 + 2.3 does not need an algorithm for solving since it is easy to subtract the parts mentally to get 4.2. Problems that use more place value columns, are unequal in length, or require regrouping would benefit from the algorithm.

Standard Algorithm for Fraction and Mixed Number Addition

What it is: The algorithm for addition with fractions involves (1) making sure the denominators (bottom numbers) are the same, (2) adding the numerators (top numbers), and then (3) simplifying the fraction (if needed). When adding mixed numbers, the process involves adding the whole number parts and then fraction parts. When the sum results in a fraction greater than 1, it is regrouped as illustrated in example 3 below.

Let's look at three examples. The first involves fractions with common denominators. The second involves fractions where one denominator needs to be changed. The third involves fractions where both denominators need to be changed.

What It Looks Like:

Add numerators
$\frac{3}{8} + \frac{3}{8} = \frac{6}{8}$

Common denominators

$\frac{6}{8}$ simplifies to $\frac{3}{4}$

$\frac{1}{2} + \frac{1}{4}$
↓ Rewrite with common denominator
$\frac{2}{4} + \frac{1}{4} = \frac{3}{4}$

$\frac{2}{3} + \frac{3}{4}$
Rewrite both fractions with common denominators
$\frac{8}{12} + \frac{9}{12} = \frac{17}{12} \rightarrow 1\frac{5}{12}$

What it sounds like: First, I will look to see if the denominators are the same. If they are, I will add the numerators (see first example above). If the denominators are not the same, I will think about what they have in common to see if one or both of the denominators need to be changed. In the second example, the denominators of 2 and 4 both have a multiple of 4 in common so I will use that. I will rewrite $\frac{1}{2}$ as $\frac{2}{4}$ and then add the numerators and keep 4 as my denominator. In the third example, the denominators of 3 and 4 have a multiple of 12 in common. I will rewrite both fractions so they have a denominator of 12, then add the numerators. I notice that $\frac{17}{12}$ contains $\frac{12}{12}$ which I can regroup as the whole number 1 and now I have $1\frac{5}{12}$

When this algorithm is useful: This algorithm is useful unless another strategy can be applied more efficiently.

Standard Algorithm for Fraction and Mixed Number Subtraction

What it is: The algorithm for subtraction with fractions involves (1) making sure the denominators (bottom numbers) are the same, (2) subtracting the numerators (top numbers), and then (3) simplifying the fraction (if needed). When adding mixed numbers, the process involves subtracting the whole number parts and then subtracting the fraction parts. Regrouping is necessary when the fractional value in the minuend is smaller than then subtrahend. Regrouping is the process of exchanging 1 whole number for a fraction equivalent to 1.

Let's look at $5\frac{1}{4} - 2\frac{5}{8}$.

What it looks like:

$$5\frac{1}{4} \rightarrow 5\frac{2}{8} = 4\frac{10}{8}$$
$$- 2\frac{5}{8} \quad -2\frac{5}{8} \quad -2\frac{5}{8}$$
$$\quad\quad\quad\quad\quad 2\frac{5}{8}$$

What it sounds like: I will start by looking to see if the denominators are the same. If the denominators are not the same, which is the case here, I will think about what they have in common to see if one or both of the denominators need to be changed. The denominators of 4 and 8 both have a multiple of 8 in common so I will use that. I will rewrite $\frac{1}{4}$ as $\frac{2}{8}$ and now I have $5\frac{2}{8} - 2\frac{5}{8}$. I notice that I do not have enough to take $\frac{5}{8}$ away from $\frac{2}{8}$ so I have to regroup by taking one away from 5 and exchanging it for a group of $\frac{8}{8}$. Now I have $4\frac{10}{8} - 2\frac{5}{8}$ and I can subtract and my difference is $2\frac{5}{8}$.

When this algorithm is useful: This algorithm is useful unless another strategy can be applied more efficiently.

This resource can be downloaded at **resources.corwin.com/FOF/ addsubtractdecimalfraction**.

TEACHING ACTIVITIES for Standard Algorithms

Explicit strategy instruction for standard algorithms has been a pillar of elementary school. For many years, concerns about teaching algorithms have focused less on whether to teach them and much more on how to balance conceptual understanding and procedural skill. To effectively develop and use fraction computation algorithms, students need both a sense of the size of fraction quantities as well as an understanding of the meaning of operations. There are several factors to consider when deciding when students are ready to explore an algorithm (Curcio & Schwartz, 1998):

1. The extent they have explored place value and equivalence relationships (conceptual foundations)

2. How skilled they are at implementing reasoning strategies (e.g., Make a Whole)

3. Whether the problems they are solving can be solved more efficiently with a standard algorithm

These teaching activities are designed to bridge students from reasoning with strategies to making sense of standard algorithms.

Many students begin addition and subtraction algorithms involving fractions and decimals without really understanding what a fraction is, and they perform procedures without understanding what they are doing. For example, it is not always clear to students what it means to take away $\frac{1}{4}$ from $\frac{7}{8}$ or why they must find a common denominator. Module 1 provides many activities to support these conceptual foundations!

Visual representations help students make sense of algorithms. Research indicates that transitioning from work with concrete models, representations, and contextualized situations to work with symbolic notation in a meaningful way can be challenging for students (Cramer et al., 2008). So it is critical to help students connect the visuals to the steps of the algorithm. With fractions, this includes using area models (e.g., circles and rectangles) and estimating sums and differences on a number line. With decimals, this includes base-10 blocks, 10 × 10 grids, and estimating sums and differences on the number line.

Because standard algorithms are less intuitive and have numerous steps, it is even more important to focus on reasonableness. Estimation is a means for encouraging reasonableness and an important "thinking tool" in developing fraction algorithms (Johanning, 2011). (See Part 1 for more on both reasonableness and estimation.) When the focus is on standard algorithms, students may see opportunities for reasoning strategies (great!). Use these moments to address efficiency. Ask, "How does [a Make a Whole] strategy compare to the standard algorithm?" Engaging the class in such a discussion places fluency as the focus (not just mastering an algorithm). When students see an opportunity to use a more efficient method, they must be congratulated for their noticing (not scolded for not doing the standard method). Finally, continuing to connect to meaningful contexts helps students make sense of the algorithms (Johanning, 2011; Van De Walle et al., 2019).

ACTIVITY 7.1
THEY ARE THE SAME!

Standard algorithms for addition and subtraction are abstract procedures. Many students, even those with early success, can forget how to carry out the algorithm over time. However, proficiency and retention increase if students understand what is happening. Often this occurs by using base-10 models with decimals or by using fraction strips with fractions to demonstrate how to carry out the algorithm. The purpose of this activity is to make explicit connections between models used to represent the concept and abstract notations. In this activity, provide students with a completed problem, a representation, and a completed algorithm. Then ask students to identify what they observe and what they wonder about the three. After sharing, tell students that all three show the same thing and the sums are correct. Then ask students to find exactly how they are related.

PROBLEM	BASE-10 MODEL	ALGORITHM
$2.1 + 1.45 = 3.55$	□□ ┃ □ ┃┃┃┃ ∷	$\begin{array}{r} 2.1 \\ +\ 1.45 \\ \hline 3.55 \end{array}$

For example, students might share that all three examples show the whole number 2 in the first number in each box or that each has the same number of ones, tenths, and hundredths. You might repeat the activity before extending it. This activity could also be done with place value disks in addition to or instead of base-10 blocks (if students are struggling with nonproportional representations, it would be powerful to use both). To extend the activity, give students two of the three examples and have them work with partners to find the missing example. For instance, a teacher gave the problem 5.14 + 2.3 = 7.44 and the algorithm. Students would then have to determine the base-10 model and tell how all three are connected.

PROBLEM	BASE-10 MODEL	ALGORITHM
$5.14 + 2.3 = 7.44$	□□□ ┃ ∷ □ □ □□ ┃┃┃	$\begin{array}{r} 5.14 \\ +\ 2.3 \\ \hline 7.44 \end{array}$

Early work should use situations that don't call for regrouping. You can shift to regrouping soon after students show understanding of non-regrouping situations.

PROBLEM	BASE-10 MODEL	ALGORITHM
$3.6 + 4.57$	□□□ ┃┃┃┃┃ ┃ □□□ ┃┃┃┃┃ ∷	$\begin{array}{r} {\scriptstyle 1} \\ 3.6 \\ +\ 4.57 \\ \hline 8.17 \end{array}$

With subtraction, the take-away situation also can be modeled with base-10 blocks or place value disks and with the algorithm.

PROBLEM	BASE-10 MODEL	ALGORITHM
$3.65 - 1.23 = 2.42$	⊠□□ ┼┼┃ ∷ ┃┃┃	$\begin{array}{r} 3.65 \\ -\ 1.23 \\ \hline 2.42 \end{array}$

Follow non-regrouping situations with regrouping situations.

PROBLEM	BASE-10 MODEL	ALGORITHM
$4.7 - 1.45 =$	← trade	$\begin{array}{r} \overset{6}{4}.\overset{}{7}\,{}^1 0 \\ -\ 1.45 \\ \hline 3.25 \end{array}$

Fraction strips, fraction circles, pattern blocks, Cuisenaire rods, and other manipulatives or visuals can be used with fraction addition and subtraction.

PROBLEM	FRACTION STRIPS	ALGORITHM
$\dfrac{3}{4} + \dfrac{1}{6} = \dfrac{11}{12}$		$\dfrac{3}{4} + \dfrac{1}{6}$ $\dfrac{9}{12} + \dfrac{2}{12} = \dfrac{11}{12}$
$2\dfrac{1}{2} + 2\dfrac{2}{3} = 5\dfrac{1}{6}$		$\begin{array}{r} \overset{1}{}2\dfrac{1}{2}\ \ \dfrac{3}{6} \\ +\,2\dfrac{2}{3}\ \ \dfrac{4}{6} \end{array} \Big\rangle \dfrac{7}{6} = 1\dfrac{1}{6}$ $\underline{\phantom{+2\dfrac{2}{3}}}$ $\qquad 5\dfrac{1}{6}$

Here pattern blocks are used to model a subtraction problem. Write an equation to represent the pattern block model and record it in the "problem" column. Then use the standard algorithm to solve it and record that in the algorithm column. How can you use the blocks to explain the steps of your algorithm?

PROBLEM	PATTERN BLOCKS	ALGORITHM
$4\dfrac{1}{6} - 2\dfrac{1}{3}$		$\begin{array}{r} \overset{3}{\cancel{4}}\dfrac{\overset{7}{1}}{6} \\ -\,2\dfrac{3}{6} \\ \hline 1\dfrac{5}{6} \end{array}$

ACTIVITY 7.2
CONNECTING PARTIALS AND ALGORITHMS

Standards algorithms are very similar to Partial Sums and Differences. You can leverage students' understanding of Partial Sums and Differences to make sense of the algorithms. To do this, provide a completed algorithm and ask students to find the partial sums or differences. Once completed, discuss how the algorithm and the recording of partials is similar and different.

Look at the left column in the following example. Among other things, students are likely to notice that the addends are the same, that there are similar digits in the sum, and that $60 + 7 + 0.4 + 0.06$ is the same as 67.46. The example on the right has a similar feature and highlights regrouping. A common error students make when working with decimals is to try to put too many digits in one column (i.e., incorrectly recording $0.03 + 0.08 = 0.011$). Ask students, "What is the sum of 3 hundredths and 8 hundredths?" Use visuals and examples to make sense of "11 hundredths." They need to see that 11 hundredths consists of 1 tenth and 1 hundredth. The notation in the bottom right makes this more obvious. However, the sum of the partials, 0.8 and 0.11, may lead to another common error students make with decimals of uneven length (sometimes called ragged decimals), which is to line up the digits on the right rather than line up the place value columns (i.e., incorrectly recording $0.8 + 0.11 = 0.19$).

PROBLEM 52.14 + 15.32		PROBLEM 0.532 + 0.384	
$50 + 10 = 60$ $2 + 5 = 7$ $0.1 + 0.3 = 0.4$ $0.04 + 0.02 = 0.06$	$\begin{array}{r} 52.14 \\ +15.32 \\ \hline 67.46 \end{array}$	$0.5 + 0.3 = 0.8$ $0.03 + 0.08 = 0.11$ $0.002 + 0.004 = 0.006$	$\begin{array}{r} \overset{1}{}0.532 \\ +0.384 \\ \hline 0.916 \end{array}$
$50 + 2 + 0.1 + 0.04$ $+ 10 + 5 + 0.3 + 0.02$ $\overline{60 + 7 + 0.4 + 0.06}$	$\begin{array}{r} 52.14 \\ +15.32 \\ \hline 67.46 \end{array}$	$0.5 + 0.03 + 0.002$ $+ 0.3 + 0.08 + 0.004$ $\overline{0.8 + 0.11 + 0.006}$	$\begin{array}{r} \overset{1}{}0.532 \\ +0.384 \\ \hline 0.916 \end{array}$

You can extend the activity to provide algorithms and charge students with creating the partial sum recordings. This activity applies to fraction addition as well (in fact, it is easier to see similarities in partial sums and the standard algorithm for adding fractions). Comparing partials to the standard algorithm for fractions is also a good activity and students will see the pros and cons of adding front-end estimates first.

Making connections between fraction and decimal standard algorithms for subtraction is valuable because it allows students to compare fraction and decimal notation and make sense of the regrouping. Present students with the problems and have them compare and contrast. They should be able to recognize the whole number 5 in the mixed number is rewritten as a 4 and the fraction written as $\frac{11}{10}$ rather than $\frac{1}{10}$. This corresponds to the decimal subtraction version where 5 is crossed out and replaced with a 4 and a tick mark is recorded in front of 1 tenth to indicate there are now 11 tenths. Students should also notice the results are the same. Ask, "Why is this relationship easier to see when working with fractions with a denominator of 10?"

PROBLEM: $5\frac{1}{10} - 2\frac{7}{10}$	PROBLEM: 5.1 – 2.7
$4\frac{11}{10} - 2\frac{7}{10} = 2\frac{4}{10}$	$\begin{array}{r} \overset{4}{\cancel{5}}.1 \\ -2.7 \\ \hline 2.4 \end{array}$

ACTIVITY 7.3
TO ALGORITHM OR NOT TO ALGORITHM

Fluency with standard algorithms includes knowing not only how to use an algorithm but *when* to use an algorithm. It is critical that we empower students to think critically about when they need this tool. This activity aims to do just that. Pose a collection of addition or subtraction problems to small groups of students. Have the students think about which problems call for an algorithm and which don't. Students must show their strategies for problems that don't call for an algorithm. Conversely, students must tell why a certain problem is best suited for the algorithm.

Use Algorithm	Don't use Algorithm
12.67 + 7.68	2.67 + 5
3.19 + 0.987	7.99 + 2.15
9.16 − 2.48	6.25 − 1.25

In this example, the teacher posed a list of six different problems. Students worked with partners to sort and record those problems. They explained (not shown) that 2.67 + 5 was easy to count on by ones and that you could use Compensation to take 1 hundredth away from 2.15 and give it to 7.99 to make a whole number to get a sum of 10.14. Students also said that they could use partials to subtract 6 − 1 and 0.25 − 0.25 to solve the last problem. They determined that these three problems didn't require the use of an algorithm.

ACTIVITY 7.4
RETHINKING SUBTRACTION WITH ZEROS

Zeros need special attention. It can be challenging for students to subtract using a standard algorithm when zeros are in the minuend. With decimals, students can become confused when inserting a zero changes the value of the quantity and when it doesn't. However, problems like 7 − 2.68 do not need to be the stressful hassle they have traditionally been. In fact, many problems involving zeros are solved more efficiently using a different strategy. For example, for 7 − 2.68, students can use Compensation (or Think Addition). This activity focuses specifically on the compensation option of constant difference (see Module 5 for details, in particular Activity 5.3, "Measurement Compensation," p. 113). In fact, you might want to do that activity prior to this one. Pose a problem like 7 − 2.68. Give students time to use the standard algorithm to solve the problem. Then give students time to apply the constant difference idea. For example, they might notice that they can shift down 1 hundredth: 7 − 2.68 is the same as 6.99 − 2.67. No regrouping needed! This is often an exciting finding for students (see the left column in the following example).

$$
\begin{array}{r} 69 \\ 7.\cancel{0}\cancel{0} \\ -\,2.68 \\ \hline 4.32 \end{array}
\qquad
\begin{array}{r} 6.99 \\ -\,2.67 \\ \hline 4.32 \end{array}
\qquad\qquad
\begin{array}{r} 59 \\ 2\cancel{6}.\cancel{0}1 \\ -\,13.89 \\ \hline 12.12 \end{array}
\qquad
\begin{array}{r} 26.12 \\ -\,14.00 \\ \hline 12.12 \end{array}
$$

Help students determine if adjusting to use the standard algorithm always works by examining other problems. For example, 26.01 − 13.89 might be easier to think about by adding 0.11 to both numbers. This creates 26.12 − 14.00, which doesn't need to be regrouped either (see the right example). *Note:* While fractions don't have the zero challenge, this activity of comparing standard algorithms to a Compensation common difference option is just as powerful and useful.

ACTIVITY 7.5
MYSTERY SOLVED! MAKING SENSE OF FRACTION ALGORITHMS

Traditional teaching of algorithms for addition and subtraction with fractions has often been presented in a piecemeal way that leaves students thinking there are about six algorithms rather than one common idea (of adding wholes with wholes and parts with parts, for example). It is also a mistake to "save" mixed numbers until well into adding and subtracting fractions. Why not start with those, as those values actually make more sense to students and can be readily connected to measuring with inches and other contexts? Rather than look at a series of seemingly different algorithms, explore how the algorithm (adding/subtracting like parts) is adapted to different circumstances. Students need a solid understanding of the aspects of the algorithm itself and how it works. To begin, the pieces must be the same size. Sometimes they come that way (common denominator) and sometimes they don't. Values can be written as fractions or as mixed numbers—equivalent ways to express the same quantity.

This activity goes beyond the *what* and *how* of the standard algorithm and explores the *why* and *when*. To begin, give students completed problems and have them prove the statements are true using models.

$\frac{3}{8} + \frac{5}{8} = \frac{8}{8}$	$2\frac{3}{4} - 1\frac{1}{4} = 1\frac{2}{4} = 1\frac{1}{2}$	$\frac{3}{4} - \frac{3}{8} = \frac{3}{8}$
$2\frac{1}{3} + 2\frac{1}{6} = 4\frac{3}{6} = 4\frac{1}{2}$	$\frac{5}{6} + \frac{1}{4} = \frac{13}{12} = 1\frac{1}{12}$	$3\frac{2}{3} - 1\frac{2}{5} = 2\frac{4}{15}$
$1\frac{9}{12} + \frac{2}{3} = 1\frac{17}{12} = 2\frac{5}{12}$	$3\frac{1}{3} - 1\frac{7}{9} = 1\frac{5}{9}$	

Then post each of the following questions on a piece of poster paper (one on each paper).

- Why do we add or subtract the numerators?

- Why do we need to find a common denominator?

- When we use equivalent fractions, why do we multiply the numerator and denominator of a fraction by the same whole number?

- How do we know what to multiply the numerator and denominator by when we find common denominators?

- Why do we *not* add or subtract the denominators?

- When adding or subtracting mixed numbers, why do we add or subtract the whole numbers?

- How does regrouping work when adding or subtracting fractions greater than 1?

Provide students with blank notecards. Reflecting on the preceding questions, ask students to work as a group to discuss each prompt and record ideas (using words, numbers, and/or drawings) on the notecard. When they have responded to each prompt, they can then tape the notecard to the appropriate poster paper. Use these to guide a whole-class discussion.

ACTIVITY 7.6
"LOW STRESS" OR TOO MUCH MESS?

This activity is intended to extend the work from Activity 7.5. Often, when adding and subtracting fractions, less conceptual-based algorithms are used. Ruais (1978) identified and advocated for what he calls a "low-stress algorithm" for fraction addition and subtraction as illustrated here:

$$\frac{a}{b} + \frac{c}{d} = \frac{ad+bc}{bd}$$

Explore with students whether this is, in fact, low stress. Explore sums and differences that (1) already have a common denominator, (2) where only one fraction needs to be changed, and (3) where both fractions need to be changed. Students will see that this idea is a reasonable option *sometimes* but is not efficient or appropriate other times. Consider adding or subtracting fractions with a common denominator; it is simpler to add or subtract the numerators and keep the denominator. For example, $\frac{1}{5} + \frac{2}{5} = \frac{3}{5}$ is more efficient. The "low-stress algorithm," $\frac{1}{5} + \frac{2}{5} = \frac{1 \times 5 + 2 \times 5}{5 \times 5} = \frac{15}{25} = \frac{3}{5}$, is actually too much stress for these fractions. The same is true when only one fraction needs to be changed (e.g., $2\frac{1}{2} + 1\frac{3}{4}$). In the case where a change to both denominators is needed, the low-stress algorithm *might* make sense. For example, $\frac{3}{4} + \frac{2}{3}$ would have a least common denominator of 12. Pose problems in which both denominators do need to be changed but where the low-stress method may still be too much stress, such as $2\frac{1}{6} + 1\frac{3}{8}$.

Choosing an efficient way to find common denominators is a part of fluency. It is based on the numbers in the problems; thus, students must think flexibly. After discussing these approaches, have students fold a paper into thirds and label each third "Like Denominators," "Change One Denominator," and "Change Both Denominators." Provide students with a set of fraction addition or subtraction problems (e.g., cut up a worksheet or post a mixture) and have students work independently to sort the problems into these three categories. After sorting, pair students to discuss how they sorted the problems and then to identify the problems for which the "low stress" idea is *not* too much of a mess.

ACTIVITY 7.7
PROMPTS FOR TEACHING STANDARD ALGORITHMS

Use the following prompts as opportunities to develop understanding of and reasoning with the standard algorithms. Have students use representations and tools to justify their thinking, including base-10 models, fraction strips, number lines, number charts, and so on. After students work with the prompt(s), bring the class together to exchange ideas. These could be useful for collecting evidence of student understanding. Any prompt can be easily modified to feature different numbers and any prompt can be offered more than once if modified.

Decimal Prompts

- Describe how you would estimate the difference between two decimals, such as 4.893 – 2.3.

- What does the 0 mean in this decimal situation: 5.09 – 1.85? Do you recommend using the standard algorithm or some other method (and which one) for this problem?

- To help her in case she made a mistake using the algorithm, Karmen estimated that 5.28 – 2.3 was about 3. Do you agree with her estimate? Why or why not?

- Clara changed 43.01 – 26.8 to 42.99 – 26.78. Can she do this? Will it help her find the difference?

(Continued)

- Tara solved 6.38 + 1.43 as shown. Do you agree with Tara's work? Why or why not?

$$\begin{array}{r} 6.38 \\ +\ 1.43 \\ \hline 7.711 \end{array}$$

- Tina subtracts a three-digit number from a three-digit number and gets a correct answer of 5.48. What might the two numbers be?

- Zahara subtracted 4 – 2.46 by changing the expression to 3.99 – 2.46 and then added 1 more. Deklan said Zahara was incorrect because that would give her an incorrect difference. Is Deklan correct? Why or why not?

- Find and correct the error(s): 6.7 – 1.52 = 5.22.

Fraction Prompts

- Why do you find common denominators to add? Use context to explain why.

- How is adding fractions less than 1 similar to and different from adding mixed numbers?

- How is subtracting fractions less than 1 similar to and different from subtracting mixed numbers?

- Louis estimated that $\frac{3}{7}+\frac{2}{3}$ is about $\frac{1}{2}$. Do you agree with this estimate? Why or why not?

- Will adding $\frac{5}{9}+\frac{3}{8}$ result in a number that is closest to $\frac{1}{2}$, 1, or 2?

- Without calculating, describe how subtracting $\frac{1}{4}$ from $\frac{2}{5}$ compares to subtracting $\frac{1}{10}$ from $\frac{2}{5}$.

- Maddox changed $5\frac{1}{4}-2\frac{3}{5}$ to $4\frac{25}{20}-2\frac{12}{20}$. Can he do this? Will it help him find the difference?

- Find and correct the error(s): $10\frac{1}{5}+7\frac{3}{10}=17\frac{4}{15}$.

PRACTICE ACTIVITIES for Standard Algorithms

Fluency is realized through quality practice that is focused, varied, processed, and connected. The activities in this section focus students' attention on how this strategy works and when to use it. The activities are a collection of varied engagements. Game boards, recording sheets, digit cards, and other required materials are available as online resources for you to download, possibly modify, and use.

As students practice, look for how well they are using the new strategy and assimilating it into their collection of strategies. Post-activity discussions help students reflect on *how* they reasoned and *when* that strategy was useful (and when it was not). Discussions can also help students reflect on how that strategy connects to recent instruction and to other strategies they have learned.

FLUENCY COMPONENT	WHAT TO LOOK FOR AS STUDENTS PRACTICE THE ALGORITHMS
Efficiency	• Are students using the algorithm efficiently? • Do students use the algorithm regardless of its appropriateness for the problem at hand? • Do they change their approach to or from the algorithm as they begin to work the problem and realize the initial approach will be less efficient?
Flexibility	• Are students using the algorithm when it makes sense for the numbers in the problem, or are they using the algorithm when it is unnecessary? • Do students change their approach to or from the algorithm as it proves inappropriate or overly complicated for the problem?
Accuracy	• Are students using the algorithm accurately? • Are students finding accurate solutions when using the algorithm? • Are students considering the reasonableness of their solution? • Are students estimating before they use the algorithm?

ACTIVITY 7.8
STANDARD ALGORITHMS WORKED EXAMPLES

There are different ways to pose worked examples, and they each serve a different fluency purpose.

TYPE OF WORKED EXAMPLE	PURPOSES: COMPONENT (FLUENCY ACTIONS)	QUESTIONS FOR DISCUSSIONS OR FOR WRITING RESPONSES
Correctly Worked Example	Efficiency (selects an appropriate strategy) and flexibility (applies a strategy to a new problem type)	What did _____ do? Why does it work? Is this a good method for this problem?
Partially Worked Example (Implement the Strategy Accurately)	Efficiency (selects an appropriate strategy; solves in a reasonable amount of time) and accuracy (completes steps accurately; gets correct answer)	Why did _____ start the problem this way? What does _____ need to do to finish the problem?
Incorrectly Worked Example (Highlight Common Errors)	Accuracy (completes steps accurately; gets correct answer)	What did _____ do? What mistake does _____ make? How can this mistake be fixed?

The worked examples in this module are organized differently than the previous modules in order to focus more on common errors. While algorithms always work, enacting established steps and notations can lead to mistakes along the way. Many prompts from Activity 7.7 can be used for collecting examples. Throughout the module are various worked examples that you can use as fictional worked examples. The following table shows common errors and worked examples with those errors. Because standard algorithms are error-prone, estimating and checking for reasonableness is very important.

COMMON ERROR	WORKED EXAMPLE
Partial sums are added and not regrouped	$$\begin{array}{r} 4.3 \\ +\,5.9 \\ \hline 9.12 \end{array}$$
Adds numbers from different place values, especially when number lengths vary	$$\begin{array}{r} \overset{1}{}3.24 \\ +\,5.8 \\ \hline 3.82 \end{array}$$
Finds the differences with decimals, not attending to which quantity is being taken away from the other	$$\begin{array}{r} 6.3 \\ -2.7 \\ \hline 4.4 \end{array} \qquad \begin{array}{r} \overset{0\ 16}{7.\cancel{1}\cancel{6}} \\ -1.37 \\ \hline 6.39 \end{array} \qquad \begin{array}{r} 8.9 \\ -1.54 \\ \hline 7.44 \end{array}$$
Finds the differences with fractions, not attending to which quantity is being taken away from the other	$$\begin{array}{r} 5\frac{1}{8} \\ -2\frac{7}{8} \\ \hline 3\frac{6}{8} \end{array}$$

COMMON ERROR	WORKED EXAMPLE
Regroups incorrectly	$\begin{array}{r} 4.\overset{3}{\cancel{0}}2 \\ -2.46 \\ \hline 1.66 \end{array}$ $\begin{array}{r} \overset{8}{\cancel{9}}\overset{12}{\frac{\cancel{1}2}{5}} \\ -3\frac{3}{5} \\ \hline 5\frac{9}{5} \end{array}$
Adds or subtracts both the numerator and denominator	$\dfrac{2}{5}+\dfrac{3}{5}=\dfrac{5}{10}$
Needs to regroup in the final answer	$\begin{array}{r} 7\frac{1}{2} \quad 7\frac{2}{4} \\ +\ 3\frac{3}{4} \quad 3\frac{3}{4} \\ \hline 10\frac{5}{4} \end{array}$

ACTIVITY 7.9

Name: "Between and About"   **Type:** Routine

About the Routine: Students often make mistakes with algorithms and don't realize that their solution is unreasonable. Reasonableness plays a role in fluency. So practicing reasonableness has significant implications, especially for determining accuracy when using algorithms. Additionally, determining reasonableness cannot become an additional procedure. There are a variety of ways to estimate. This routine offers practice with two of them.

Materials: This routine does not require any materials.

Directions: 1. Post a series of expressions to students, one at a time.

2. Have students determine the range for the answer as being between ___ and ___. Record different ideas for the range and discuss as a class which ideas make the most sense.

3. After a "between" is agreed upon by the group, students then look to find an "about" number that is a reasonable estimate (using rounding, front-end estimation, or compatibles, as they like).

4. Reveal the exact answer and compare it to the "between" and "about" ideas.

(Continued)

(*Continued*)

PROBLEM POSED	BETWEEN	ABOUT
34.6 + 51.9	80 and 90 81.9 and 91.9 84.6 and 86.6	80, 90, 85, 81.9, 84.6
7.32 + 8.48	15 and 17 15.48 and 16.48 15.32 and 16.32	15, 16, 15.32
$12\frac{13}{17}+15\frac{2}{19}$	27 and 29 $27\frac{13}{17}$ and $28\frac{13}{17}$ $27\frac{2}{19}$ and $28\frac{2}{19}$	27, 29, 28
$23\frac{13}{15}+31\frac{17}{20}$	54 and 56 $53\frac{13}{15}$ and $55\frac{13}{15}$ $54\frac{17}{20}$ and $55\frac{17}{20}$	54, 55, 56, 55.5

In the example, some students found a range by using friendly numbers for both addends. Other students used a friendly number for just one addend, thinking of 34.6 as 30 and 40 or of $12\frac{13}{17}$ as 12 or 13. Estimates for these sums function in the same way by finding friendly numbers for both addends or only one addend in other cases.

This routine works with any set of problems, including those that incorporate both fractions and decimals. Consider these examples.

TWO-DIGIT DECIMAL ADDITION	THREE-DIGIT DECIMAL ADDITION	MIXED NUMBER ADDITION	FRACTION/DECIMAL ADDITION
3.2 + 5.9	55.3 + 79.7	$3\frac{1}{5}+5\frac{9}{10}$	$3\frac{3}{5}+7.9$
1.6 + 5.4	27.9 + 61.9	$4\frac{5}{6}+5\frac{3}{4}$	$37.9+41\frac{7}{8}$
3.7 + 4.9	60.5 + 3.27	$12\frac{2}{9}+51\frac{3}{10}$	$2.19+10\frac{1}{6}$
4.6 + 2.5	4.28 + 5.65	$34\frac{7}{16}+14\frac{8}{15}$	$33\frac{9}{19}+14.545$
5.6 + 1.6	10.5 + 2.79	$70\frac{35}{100}+13\frac{37}{50}$	$11\frac{2}{7}+25.671$

TWO-DIGIT DECIMAL SUBTRACTION	THREE-DIGIT DECIMAL SUBTRACTION	MIXED NUMBER SUBTRACTION	FRACTION/DECIMAL SUBTRACTION
4.5 – 2.6	45.2 – 23.7	$13\frac{3}{5}-5\frac{1}{10}$	$13\frac{3}{5}-6.9$
6.1 – 3.3	64.2 – 22.6	$24\frac{5}{6}-5\frac{3}{4}$	$87.9-41\frac{7}{8}$
7.4 – 5.8	7.28 – 1.37	$72\frac{2}{9}-51\frac{3}{10}$	$9.19-2\frac{1}{6}$
9.5 – 1.7	55.4 – 3.26	$34\frac{7}{16}-14\frac{8}{15}$	$33\frac{9}{19}-14.545$
8.6 – 4.8	65.9 – 7.87	$70\frac{35}{100}-13\frac{37}{50}$	$11\frac{2}{7}-5.671$

ACTIVITY 7.10

Name: "That One"   **Type:** Routine

About the Routine: This routine helps students consider when to use an algorithm. It is intended as a practice opportunity that follows instruction of the concept in Activity 7.3 ("To Algorithm or Not to Algorithm").

Materials: This routine does not require any materials.

Directions:
1. Pose a few problems to students.

2. Have students discuss with a partner which problems are good candidates for solving with an algorithm and which are not.

3. Have students explain their decisions. Avoid implying that a problem should or must be solved with an algorithm. In the case where students have alternative strategies for all three problems, they say "None" rather than "That one."

THAT ONE		
64.2 – 37.6	51.9 – 30.4	85.6 – 44.8

In the above example, 64.2 – 37.6 is most likely the only problem that students will select, although they may use a different method. Students might suggest that the middle example, 51.9 – 30.4, can be solved by counting back 30. Some students might consider the right example, 85.6 – 44.8, a problem for the algorithm. However, many should suggest that it can be thought of as 85.8 – 45.0 (using Compensation) or it too can be solved by counting back. It is the discussion that matters (helping students to think about when they may want to use a standard algorithm).

This routine also works well with adding and subtracting fractions.

THAT ONE		
$1\frac{3}{4}+3\frac{3}{4}$	$8\frac{1}{2}+3\frac{3}{4}$	$7\frac{3}{8}+2\frac{5}{12}$

ACTIVITY 7.11

Name: *"Over/Under"*   **Type:** Routine

About the Routine: Determining reasonableness when using standard algorithms is critically important. In this routine, students determine if a sum or difference will be over or under (more or less than) a given number. Contexts of muscle weight (fractions) and temperatures are included to encourage sensemaking and add interest, although this routine is also an excellent opportunity to estimate even without the contexts.

Materials: Identify a target sum or difference and prepare a few addition or subtraction expressions that cannot be easily solved.

Directions: 1. Share the Over/Under target number.

2. Pose a context and corresponding expressions.

3. Have students say whether the sum or difference is over or under the target number.

4. Students share their ideas with partners and then discuss their approaches to reasoning with the class.

5. After ideas are shared, the exact answers can be found and compared to the over/under decisions.

Fraction Addition Example

Context: Four friends have a plan to work out over the summer, with a goal to gain 5 pounds of muscle in 3 months. They weigh themselves each month to find the amount of muscle they gained. Estimate if they were over or under their goal.

OVER/UNDER 5	
Morgan: $1\frac{1}{2}+\frac{3}{4}+2\frac{1}{8}$	*Jackson:* $\frac{1}{4}+3\frac{9}{16}+1\frac{1}{2}$
Darnell: $1\frac{1}{8}+2\frac{3}{4}+\frac{15}{16}$	*Ariana:* $1\frac{15}{16}+1\frac{1}{4}+2\frac{1}{8}$

In the first example, students might reason that $1 + 2 = 3$ and that the sum of the fractional parts is less than 2, so the sum of all three addends is under 5.

Decimal Subtraction Example

Context: Tropical fish prefer temperatures between 75°F and 80°F. Joan tries to keep a consistent temperature in her tank, with less than a 2.5°F variation in temperature each day. Joan checks the temperature of the tank twice a day. The temperatures are recorded in the following chart. Estimate whether the change in temperature is over or under her target, 2.5°F.

OVER/UNDER 2.5°F				
79.7 – 77.9°F	80.1 – 76.9°F	78.1 – 76.2°F	78.9 – 76.2°F	79.6 – 77.1°F

For the first problem, a student might say, "Under," and explain that $79.7 - 77.7$ is less than 2.5, so $79.7 - 77.9$ must be as well.

ACTIVITY 7.12

Name: All Lined Up
(Addition or Subtraction)

Type: Game

About the Game: *All Lined Up* is a game of strategy and luck that gives students an opportunity to practice addition and subtraction with (or without) the standard algorithm. The game can be played with addition or subtraction, but the same operation should be used for the entire game.

Materials: *All Lined Up* game board and recording sheet. Use two decks of digit cards (0–9) or playing cards (queens = 0 and aces = 1; remove tens, kings, and jacks) if playing with decimals. Use four regular dice if playing with fractions or six regular dice if playing with mixed numbers.

Directions:
1. Players take turns drawing the stated number of digit cards to make a decimal number. (The number of digit cards is based on the types of numbers you direct students to make. In the example, students would pull eight cards to make 2 four-digit decimal numbers through hundredths.)

2. Players create a sum and decide where to place it within their six boxes, knowing that all the sums must be in order from least to greatest.

3. On subsequent turns, players repeat the process and place the new sum (anywhere to the right of the first sum if it is greater, and anywhere to the left if the new sum is less than the first sum).

4. If a player can't place their sum, the player loses their turn.

5. The first player to fill all six boxes in order from least to greatest wins.

For example, a student drew eight cards, created the expression 23.45 + 39.01, and found the sum of 62.46. He recorded it in the third box. On his second turn, he found the sum of 84.67. On his third turn, he found a sum of 51.34.

All Lined Up

Directions: Use digit cards to make two numbers. Find the sum or difference of the numbers. Place the sum or difference in one of the boxes so that the numbers in the boxes are in order from least to greatest.

	51.34	62.46			84.67

For fractions, players take turns rolling all six dice and then creating two mixed numbers to add. In the example, on his fourth turn the player rolled a 1, 2, 2, 3, 4, 5 and created the problem $2\frac{1}{2}+5\frac{3}{4}$ with a sum of $8\frac{1}{4}$. The player lost his turn because there is no space to place the answer on the game board.

All Lined Up

Directions: Use digit cards to make two numbers. Find the sum or difference of the numbers. Place the sum or difference in one of the boxes so that the numbers in the boxes are in order from least to greatest.

$2\frac{7}{12}$		$7\frac{5}{6}$	$8\frac{1}{2}$		

 This resource can be downloaded at **resources.corwin.com/FOF/addsubtractdecimalfraction**.

ACTIVITY 7.13

Name: A List of Ten   **Type:** Game

About the Game: Procedural fluency means knowing how to use an algorithm *and* when to use it. Yet students don't have frequent opportunities to consider when to use an algorithm, which is the focus of *A List of Ten*. This game is a good follow-up to Activity 7.3 ("To Algorithm or Not to Algorithm").

Materials: *A List of Ten* game board; prepared set of addition or subtraction expression cards (decimals or fractions)

Directions: 1. Players shuffle the expression cards and place them face down.

2. Players take turns selecting a card and determining if the expression is best solved with or without the algorithm. If a player says "algorithm" and their opponent can tell a more efficient* method than the algorithm, the opponent steals the card.

3. Each player records their equations in the appropriate column on their recording page.

4. The first player to get a list of 10 wins.

5. After the game, both players solve the problems on their game board.

> **TEACHING TAKEAWAY**
>
> *Here is an operational definition of *efficient*: Of the available strategies, the one the student opts to use gets to a solution in about as many steps and/or in about as much time as other appropriate options.

RESOURCE(S) FOR THIS ACTIVITY

A List of Ten

Directions: Players take turns flipping over cards and deciding if the problem is best solved with or without an algorithm. Players can steal problem cards put in the algorithm list if they can solve the problem more efficiently using a different strategy.

Problems efficiently solved **WITHOUT an ALGORITHM**	Problems efficiently solved **WITH an ALGORITHM**
1.	1.
2.	2.

online resources ⌖ This resource can be downloaded at **resources.corwin.com/FOF/addsubtractdecimalfraction.**

ACTIVITY 7.14

Name: Algorithm Problem Sort   **Type:** Center

About the Center: Algorithm Problem Sort challenges students to think about how best to solve an addition or subtraction problem. You can extend the center by asking students to create their own examples of problems best solved with or without the algorithm.

Materials: addition or subtraction problem cards (using decimals or fractions), Algorithm Problem Sort recording sheet

Directions:

1. Students select a problem card.

2. Students write the problem on their recording sheet in the "Solve Without an Algorithm" or "Solve With an Algorithm" column.

3. Then students record the sum or difference (depending on the operations they are working with).

4. After solving the set of cards, students write what they look for in deciding when not to use the algorithm.

RESOURCE(S) FOR THIS ACTIVITY

Algorithm Problem Sort

Directions: Select a problem and decide if it is better solved with or without an algorithm. Record the problem in that column and solve it.

SOLVE WITHOUT an ALGORITHM	SOLVE WITH an ALGORITHM
1.	1.
2.	2.
3.	3.

online resources — This resource can be downloaded at **resources.corwin.com/FOF/addsubtractdecimalfraction**.

ACTIVITY 7.15

Name: Missing Numbers   **Type:** Center

About the Center: Missing Numbers helps students practice standard algorithms as well as reasoning. Extend this activity by including blank cards. Students can be asked to create their own Missing Number problem, using two or three question marks.

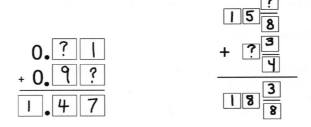

Materials: prepared *Missing Number* problem cards (see the following note)

Directions: 1. Students select a Missing Number problem card.

2. Students work to find the missing number(s) in the problem.

3. Once all missing numbers are found, students select one digit that challenged them and explain how they figured it out.

To make Missing Number problem cards, create a problem and then simply change out one or more digits with a question mark (?). The template provided is for adding decimals to hundredths. Additional templates, including decimal subtraction and addition and subtraction of mixed numbers, are available for download.

RESOURCE(S) FOR THIS ACTIVITY

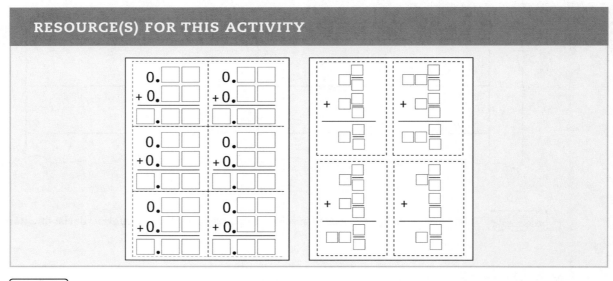

online resources This resource can be downloaded at **resources.corwin.com/FOF/addsubtractdecimalfraction.**

ACTIVITY 7.16

Name: Fraction Magic Squares   **Type:** Center

About the Center: This activity provides students a rare opportunity to add more than two numbers. Solving a Magic Square involves filling in a 3 × 3 grid with numbers such that each row, column, and diagonal adds up to the same number. In this version of magic squares, the list of numbers (fractions) is provided along with the sum. Students have to figure out where each number goes. The number in the center square is a powerful clue. To scaffold the game, you can begin with a whole number example (look online) and/or fill in one or two of the numbers in the appropriate square(s).

Materials: Magic Squares task and a 3 × 3 grid

Directions: 1. Students review the list of fractions and create any equivalencies to support their efforts.

2. Students place the fractions in the 3 × 3 grid and try to create a Magic Square—a square in which each row, column, and diagonal adds up to the same number.

3. Once the Magic Square has been solved, students record their eight equations to show the sums. Then they write a summarizing explanation of how they figured out the Magic Square. Where did they start? What did they notice?

This center can also be a partner activity within a lesson. Here are examples and discussion questions for using the center as a class activity.

Fraction Magic Square

Fill in the boxes with these fractions so that each row, column, and diagonal sums to $2\frac{1}{2}$.								
$\frac{1}{6}$	$\frac{1}{3}$	$\frac{1}{2}$	$\frac{2}{3}$	$\frac{5}{6}$	1	$1\frac{1}{6}$	$1\frac{1}{3}$	$1\frac{1}{2}$

Decimal Magic Square

Fill in the boxes with these decimals so that each row, column, and diagonal sums to **3.75.**								
0.25	0.5	0.75	1	1.25	1.5	1.75	2	2.25

Decimal and Fraction Magic Square

Fill in the boxes with these numbers so that each row, column, and diagonal sums to **1.5.**								
0.1	0.3	0.7	.9	$\frac{1}{5}$	$\frac{2}{5}$	$\frac{3}{5}$	$\frac{4}{5}$	$\frac{1}{2}$

Here are some example discussion prompts:

- If you had 1 and $1\frac{1}{3}$ in the first row, how could you find a third number that would add to $2\frac{1}{2}$? What if you had $\frac{5}{6}$ and $\frac{1}{2}$ in a column? How could you find the third number?

(Continued)

(Continued)

- If you had 0.5 and 1.75 in the first row, how could you find a third number that would equal 3.75?

- If you had 0.3 and $\frac{1}{2}$ in the middle row, how might you find a third number that adds up to 1.5?

- What values are strategic to fill in first?

- What strategies helped you to complete the Magic Square?

- How might you create your own Magic Square?

Here are some completed squares (answers):

1	$\frac{1}{6}$	$1\frac{1}{3}$
$1\frac{1}{6}$	$\frac{5}{6}$	$\frac{1}{2}$
$\frac{1}{3}$	$1\frac{1}{2}$	$\frac{2}{3}$

0.5	1.75	1.5
2.25	1.25	0.25
1	0.75	2

$\frac{2}{5}$	0.9	$\frac{1}{5}$
0.3	$\frac{1}{2}$	0.7
$\frac{4}{5}$	0.1	$\frac{3}{5}$

RESOURCE(S) FOR THIS ACTIVITY

Magic Squares Recording Sheet

online resources 🔎 This resource can be downloaded at **resources.corwin.com/FOF/addsubtractdecimalfraction.**

PUTTING IT ALL TOGETHER

Developing Fluency

FLUENCY IS . . .

How might you finish a sentence that begins "Fluency is"? . . . One way is "using procedures efficiently, flexibly, and accurately." Another option is "important." Or maybe fluency is "an equity issue." Here is another: fluency is "necessary and possible for every child." All of these are true statements. This section is the capstone of this book on fluency with addition and subtraction with fractions and decimals. If students learn a strategy in isolation and never get to practice choosing when to use it, they will not become truly fluent. Part 3 focuses on learning to *choose* strategies. The following lists reflect subsets of the significant Seven Significant Strategies.

ADDITION "MUST KNOW" STRATEGIES	SUBTRACTION "MUST KNOW" STRATEGIES
• Count On	• Count Back
• Make a Whole	• Think Addition (Count Up)
• Compensation	• Compensation
• Partial Sums	• Partial Differences

Once students know more than one strategy, they need opportunities to practice choosing strategies. In other words, you do not want to wait until they have learned four strategies and a standard algorithm before they begin choosing from among the strategies they know. For example, if you are teaching subtraction with Compensation, you have likely taught Count Back or Think Addition. So, it is time to use a Part 3 activity to help students decide *when* they will use each strategy. Then, add a new strategy to students' repertoire and return again to activities that focus on choosing a strategy. This iterative process continues through the teaching of standard algorithms, as students continue to accumulate methods for addition and subtraction with fractions and decimals. Along the way, it is important that students learn that sometimes there is more than one good way to solve a problem, and other times, one way really stands out from the others.

CHOICE

Choosing strategies is at the heart of fluency. After a strategy is learned, it should always be an option for consideration. Too often students feel like when they have moved on to a new strategy, they are supposed to use only the new one, as though it is more sophisticated or preferred by their teacher. But the strategies are additive—they form a collection from which students can select in order to solve the problem at hand.

Once students know how and why a strategy works, they need to figure out when it makes sense to use the strategy. That is when you need questions such as these:

- When do you/might you use the Count On/Count Back strategy for addition?
- When do you/might you use the Make a Whole strategy for addition?
- When do you/might you use a Think Addition strategy for subtraction?
- When do you/might you use Compensation for addition? Subtraction?
- When do you/might you use Partial Sums? Partial Differences?

- When do you/might you use a standard algorithm?
- In general, when do you/might you not use the _____ strategy/algorithm?

These prompts can be mapped directly to the Part 2 modules (and asked during instruction on those strategies, as well as during mixed practice). As students are exploring the Think Addition strategy, for example, include regular questioning about when it is a good fit and when it is not. Additionally, we help students when we ask them to think about how they will think through their options. We can ask questions like these:

- Which strategies do you think of first when you see a problem?
- Which strategies do you choose only after other options don't work?
- Which strategies do you avoid?

This latter set of questions pushes students beyond analyzing the usefulness of a particular strategy into reflecting on how they will think through their options—metacognition.

METACOGNITION

As students become more proficient with the strategies they have learned and when to use them, they benefit from reflecting on how they might solve a problem. Solving a problem mentally is quite often the most efficient option. Taking time up front to make a good choice can save time in the enactment of a not-efficient strategy. We can help students with this reasoning by sharing a metacognitive process. This could be a bulletin board or a card taped to students' desks. We can remind students that as we work, we make good choices about the methods we use. This is *flexibility* in action.

METACOGNITIVE PROCESS FOR SELECTING A STRATEGY

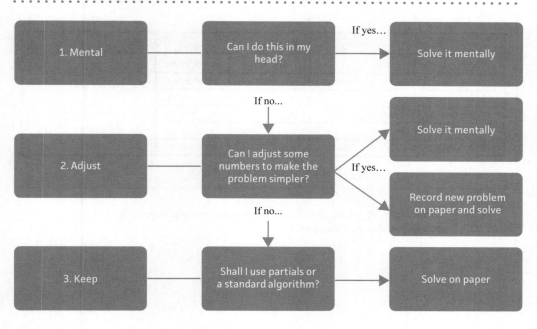

ASSESSING FLUENCY

Traditionally, fluency assessment has focused on speed and accuracy. While accuracy does matter, it is only one-third of what it means to be fluent. As you assess fluency, you want to intentionally look for each of the three fluency components and the six Fluency Actions. Flexibility and efficiency can be observed as students engage in meaningful activities.

OBSERVATION TOOLS

Observation tools can help us focus on the "neglected" components of fluency and serve as a way to communicate with students and their parents about what real fluency looks like. Three examples are shared here.

See Chapter 7 (pp. 154–175) of *Figuring Out Fluency* for more information about assessing fluency.

Student: _____   Date: _____

Problem(s): _____

Fluency Component Checklist

Procedural Fluency Components	Evident?			Instructional Next Steps
1. Efficiency	Yes	No	Not Observed	
2. Flexibility	Yes	No	Not Observed	
3. Accuracy	Yes	No	Not Observed	

Comments:

Student: _____   Date: _____

Problem(s): _____

Fluency Actions Checklist

Procedural Fluency Actions	Evident?			Comments
1. Selects appropriate strategy	Yes	No	Not Observed	
2. Solves in a reasonable amount of time	Yes	No	Not Observed	
3. Trades out or adapts a strategy	Yes	No	Not Observed	
4. Applies strategy to a new problem type	Yes	No	Not Observed	
5. Completes steps correctly	Yes	No	Not Observed	
6. Gets correct answer	Yes	No	Not Observed	

Comments:

 These resources can be downloaded at **resources.corwin.com/FOF/addsubtractdecimalfraction**.

Whole-Class Fluency Observation Tool					
Student	Date:	Date:	Date:	**Notes**	
	E F A	E F A	E F A		
	E F A	E F A	E F A		
	E F A	E F A	E F A		
	E F A	E F A	E F A		
	E F A	E F A	E F A		
	E F A	E F A	E F A		
	E F A	E F A	E F A		
	E F A	E F A	E F A		
	E F A	E F A	E F A		
	E F A	E F A	E F A		

 These resources can be downloaded at **resources.corwin.com/FOF/ addsubtractdecimalfraction**.

More specifically, observation tools can focus on strategies. The two illustrated here can be used over weeks to keep track of student strategy use. For example, you can use tallies within a box to indicate you saw/heard a student use the strategy, or you can use simple codes (dash, checkmark, dot, etc.).

Addition Strategy Observation Tool

Student Name	Addition Strategies				Algorithm
	Count On	Make Tens	Compensation	Partial Sums	

Subtraction Strategy Observation Tool

Student Name	Subtraction Strategies				Algorithm
	Count Back	Think Addition	Compensation	Partial Differences	

online resources These resources can be downloaded at **resources.corwin.com/FOF/addsubtractdec- imalfraction**

GRADING ASSIGNMENTS AND ASSESSMENTS

Efforts to teach students to use and choose efficient strategies must be assessed. Too often tests are graded for accuracy only. That sends a message that only accuracy is important. One way to focus on fluency in assessment is to use a fluency rubric, such as this one.

FOUR-POINT FLUENCY RUBRIC

BEGINNING 1	DEVELOPING 2	EMERGING 3	ACCOMPLISHED 4
Knows one algorithm or strategy but continues to get stuck or make errors.	Demonstrates efficiency and accuracy with at least one strategy/algorithm, but does not stop to think if there is a more efficient possibility.	Demonstrates efficiency and accuracy with several strategies/algorithms, and sometimes selects an efficient strategy, although still figuring out when to use and not use a strategy.	Demonstrates efficiency and accuracy with several strategies/algorithms and is adept at matching problems with efficient strategies (knowing when to use each and when not to).

With an eye on fluency and how to assess it, select fluency activities from Part 3 based on your students' needs and what type of activity you are seeking.

FLUENCY ACTIVITIES

The nine activities in this section focus on all components of fluency, providing students with the opportunity to practice choosing an appropriate strategy, enacting that strategy, and reflecting on the efficiency of the strategies selected.

ACTIVITY F.1

Name: "Strategize First Steps"   **Type:** Routine

About the Routine: This routine involves sharing how to *start* a problem. It is at this first step that students are selecting a strategy. In its quickest version, that is the only step that is ever done. Simply ask, "Which step first and why?" A second option begins the same way but after students have shared ideas for first steps, they get to choose which first step they like and finish the problem. Then, answers can be shared and students can reflect on which first step turned out to be a good one (and why).

Materials: list of three or four problems on the same topic, but that lend to different reasoning strategies

Directions: This routine involves showing a series of problems, one at a time, like a Number Talk (Parrish & Dominick, 2016). But it differs in the fact that the tasks you selected *do not* lend to the same strategy. Here is the routine process:

1. Ask students to mentally determine their first step (only) and signal when they're ready (since it is only the first step, they only need a few seconds).

2. Record first-step ideas by creating a list on the board.

3. Discuss which first steps seem reasonable (or not).

4. Repeat with two to four more problems, referring to the list created from the first problem and adding to the list if/when new strategies are shared.

5. Conclude the series with a discussion: When will you use _____ strategy?

Possible problem sets for this routine include the following.

DECIMAL ADDITION SET 1	DECIMAL SUBTRACTION SET 1	FRACTION ADDITION SET 1	FRACTION SUBTRACTION SET 1
1. $49 + 5.3 =$ 2. $1.8 + 4.1 =$ 3. $3.1 + 5.7 =$ 4. $0.20 + 4.6 =$ 5. $2.5 + 34 =$	1. $5.5 - 3.6 =$ 2. $24.6 - 6.4 =$ 3. $6.0 - 5.7 =$ 4. $9.9 - 0.15 =$ 5. $16.2 - 15.7 =$	1. $\frac{5}{8} + \frac{7}{8}$ 2. $\frac{3}{4} + \frac{3}{4}$ 3. $\frac{1}{8} + \frac{1}{2}$ 4. $\frac{5}{10} + \frac{3}{5}$ 5. $\frac{3}{8} + \frac{1}{3}$	1. $\frac{4}{3} - \frac{2}{3} =$ 2. $\frac{5}{6} - \frac{1}{3} =$ 3. $1 - \frac{6}{10} =$ 4. $\frac{11}{16} - \frac{1}{3} =$ 5. $\frac{9}{10} - \frac{1}{2} =$

DECIMAL ADDITION SET 2	DECIMAL SUBTRACTION SET 2	FRACTION ADDITION SET 2	FRACTION SUBTRACTION SET 2
1. $3.35 + 4.63 =$ 2. $0.52 + 0.42 =$ 3. $2.7 + 0.49 =$ 4. $5.7 + 5.23 =$ 5. $0.59 + 1.8$	1. $2.94 - 1.2 =$ 2. $6.8 - 5.59 =$ 3. $7.1 - 5.35 =$ 4. $28.6 - 20.57 =$ 5. $32.91 - 7.18 =$	6. $2\frac{4}{5} + 3\frac{3}{10}$ 7. $2\frac{3}{4} + \frac{3}{4}$ 8. $9\frac{1}{3} + \frac{2}{6}$ 9. $3\frac{3}{5} + 5\frac{3}{5}$ 10. $2\frac{3}{3} + 5\frac{1}{2}$	1. $4 - 2\frac{1}{3} =$ 2. $10 - 6\frac{1}{3} =$ 3. $6\frac{1}{6} - 5\frac{2}{3} =$ 4. $4\frac{6}{8} - 1\frac{1}{5} =$ 5. $6\frac{2}{5} - 5 =$

Let's say you were working with Decimal Subtraction, Set 1, Problem 1 ($5.5 - 3.6$). Here are some examples of the first steps you might hear:

"Count back 3."

"Think of 5.5 as 5.6."

"Think of 3.6 as 3.5."

"Count up 2."

You can layer in strategy names at this point. For example, write "Count Back" next to the first idea, "Compensation" by the second and third, and "Think Addition (or Count Up)" for the last idea. This list serves as a menu when students move to the next problem. They may also have a new strategy to add for problem 2 that didn't "fit" problem 1. (In this case, Partial Differences "fits" the second problem and will likely be added to the list.) With the strategies labeled, students begin to say, "I used Compensation and . . ." Some of the same strategies will be named again with different problems and students are also likely to add different ideas. If an appropriate strategy does not come up, you can ask why not or just move to the next problem. Be mindful that some problems might only lend themselves to one or two strategies and that you don't need to press for a variety of approaches. In addition, do not communicate that a certain approach is something you prefer. If students are going to solve the problem, allow them to choose from the ideas that were first stated. They can later share if they stayed with their original first step or switched out to one of the ideas from their classmates.

ACTIVITY F.2

Name: "M-A-K-E a Decision"   **Type:** Routine

About the Routine: Mental-Adjust-Keep-Expressions is a routine that, like other routines, can function for assessment purposes. Project for students an illustration of the metacognitive process, like the one discussed earlier in the Part 3 overview. If a problem can be solved mentally, there is no need to use a written method such as a standard algorithm. Students tend to dive in without stopping to think if they can solve a problem mentally. This routine focuses on getting students to pause and decide on a method. There are two ways to use the tasks in this routine. One is to show one problem at a time, each time asking, "Which way will you solve it?" Or you can show the full set and ask, "Which ones might you solve mentally? Adjust and solve? Keep as-is and solve?" The former is used below.

Materials: Prepare a set of three to six expressions.

Directions: 1. Explain that you are going to display a problem. Students are not to solve it but simply M-A-K-E a Decision: Mental, Adjust and solve, or Keep and solve on paper for the Expressions given?

2. Display the first problem and give students about 10 seconds to decide.

3. Use a cue to have students share their choice (one finger = mental, two fingers = adjust, three fingers = keep and solve on paper).

4. Ask a student who picked each decision to share why (and how).

5. Repeat step 3, giving students a chance to change their minds.

6. Repeat steps 3–5 for the next problem in the set.

7. At the end of the set, ask, "What do you 'see' in a problem that leads to you doing it mentally? Adjusting? Keep and use paper?"

Possible problem sets to use with this routine include the following:

FRACTION ADDITION SET 1		FRACTION ADDITION SET 2	
$3\frac{1}{2}+4\frac{1}{2}$	$\frac{2}{5}+\frac{1}{3}$	$\frac{4}{5}+7\frac{9}{10}$	$\frac{5}{6}+3\frac{5}{6}$
$3\frac{3}{4}+\frac{3}{4}$	$\frac{4}{8}+3\frac{1}{8}$	$6\frac{1}{3}+8\frac{1}{3}$	$12\frac{1}{5}+8\frac{7}{10}$
$\frac{7}{12}+\frac{1}{6}$	$2\frac{2}{3}+1\frac{1}{6}$	$10\frac{1}{2}+\frac{7}{8}$	$6\frac{11}{12}+5\frac{7}{8}$
FRACTION SUBTRACTION SET 1		**FRACTION SUBTRACTION SET 2**	
$1\frac{7}{8}-\frac{5}{8}$	$\frac{4}{6}-\frac{1}{3}$	$5\frac{3}{6}-1\frac{5}{6}$	$2\frac{1}{3}-\frac{2}{3}$
$3\frac{1}{2}-\frac{3}{4}$	$\frac{9}{12}-\frac{2}{6}$	$4\frac{1}{8}-\frac{7}{8}$	$3\frac{2}{5}-1\frac{2}{10}$
$\frac{11}{12}-\frac{2}{3}$	$\frac{4}{5}-\frac{1}{2}$	$6-4\frac{5}{12}$	$7\frac{2}{5}-3\frac{3}{5}$

Notice that these fraction sets mix in mixed numbers. This helps students see that their collection of strategies applies regardless of whether the number is less than 1 or greater than 1.

DECIMAL ADDITION SET 1		DECIMAL ADDITION SET 2	
30.1 + 1.8	52.9 + 46.7	29.9 + 6.72	1.35 + 4.65
64.8 + 15.5	58.1 + 90.3	25.16 + 9.013	36.9 + 4.01
47.5 + 27.6	8.1 + 84.1	1.3 + 84.13	3.88 + 7.19
DECIMAL SUBTRACTION SET 1		DECIMAL SUBTRACTION SET 2	
35.7 − 21.7	53.2 − 1.9	10.57 − 6.17	52.17 − 18.84
50.8 − 49.7	76.83 − 74.87	6.25 − 5.68	9.034 − 7.955
7.33 − 1.08	56 − 49.67	9.4 − 8.76	43.75 − 2.97

ACTIVITY F.3

Name: "Share–Share–Compare"   **Type:** Routine

About the Routine: This routine can also be a longer classroom activity, depending on how many problems students are asked to solve. Each person first solves problems independently, then has the chance to have a one-on-one with a peer to compare their thinking on the same problem.

Materials: Prepare a list of three to five problems that lend to being solved different ways.

Directions:

1. Students work independently to solve the full set.

2. Students write if they solved it mentally by naming the strategy they used. If they solved it by writing, they do not need to name a strategy.

3. Once complete, everyone stands up with their page of worked problems.

4. Students find a partner who is *not* at their table. When they find a partner, they high-five each other, and begin "Share–Share–Compare" for the first problem.

   - Share: Partner 1 **shares** their method.
   - Share: Partner 2 **shares** their method.
   - Compare: Partners discuss how their methods **compared**:
     - If their methods are different, they compare the two, discussing which one worked the best or if both worked well.
     - If their methods are the same, they think of an alternative method and again discuss which method(s) worked well.

After the exchange, partners thank each other, raise their hands to indicate they are in search of a new partner, find another partner, and repeat the process of Share–Share–Compare for problem 2 (or any problem they haven't yet discussed). In creating a problem set, make sure there are at least two strategies students have learned that "fit" the problem. While these cards separate out addition and subtraction, mixed sets are also important to include.

Possible problem sets for this routine include the following:

FRACTION ADDITION	FRACTION SUBTRACTION
1. $\frac{2}{8} + 2\frac{7}{8}$	1. $3\frac{2}{5} - 1\frac{1}{5}$
2. $5\frac{2}{5} + 4\frac{9}{10}$	2. $5\frac{3}{8} - 4\frac{1}{4}$
3. $8\frac{1}{2} + 7\frac{1}{4}$	3. $9\frac{1}{3} - 2\frac{1}{12}$
4. $3\frac{11}{12} + \frac{7}{12}$	4. $3 - 1\frac{7}{12}$
5. $6\frac{3}{4} + 6\frac{1}{2}$	5. $5\frac{3}{4} - 5\frac{1}{2}$

DECIMAL ADDITION	DECIMAL SUBTRACTION
1. $8.1 + 7.4$	1. $7.8 - 5.7$
2. $8.3 + 0.17$	2. $34.5 - 7.65$
3. $53.55 + 20.95$	3. $10.8 - 0.74$
4. $7.8 + 5.37$	4. $67.08 - 64.5$
5. $0.78 + 0.57$	5. $52.5 - 29.08$

ACTIVITY F.4

Name: Strategy Spin   **Type:** Game

About the Game: This activity can be played in many ways. You can have spinners that focus on metacognition (mental, adjust, keep; see metacognition visual), you can pick the strategies students know, or you can have the options "Standard Algorithm" and "Not Standard Algorithm." There are many online spinner tools, such as Wheel Decide (https://wheeldecide.com/), which allow you to enter the categories you want and actually spin virtually. This game can be played with two to four players.

Materials: strategy spinner (one per group) and expression cards

Directions: 1. Players take turns spinning the strategy spinner.

2. Once the spinner lands on a strategy, the player looks through the expression bank to find a problem they want to solve using that strategy.

3. The player tells how to solve the selected problem using that strategy. Opponents check solutions using a Hundred Chart, number line, or calculator. If correct, the player claims that expression card. *Note:* You might also provide an answer sheet for the cards that the opponent could check. This might be especially helpful for the fraction set(s).

4. Repeat steps 2 and 3 three times for four players, four times for three players, or five times for two players.

5. Together the group looks at the remaining expressions and labels which strategy they think is a good fit for each.

Expression Bank: Fraction Subtraction

$\frac{4}{5}-\frac{2}{8}$	$\frac{3}{6}-\frac{5}{12}$	$8\frac{3}{8}-6\frac{1}{8}$	$3-1\frac{6}{16}$
$\frac{3}{9}-\frac{1}{9}$	$\frac{4}{3}-\frac{2}{3}$	$9\frac{1}{2}-1\frac{9}{10}$	$5\frac{4}{6}-3\frac{5}{6}$
$\frac{6}{10}-\frac{2}{5}$	$\frac{2}{3}-\frac{1}{5}$	$8\frac{7}{8}-4\frac{2}{8}$	$6\frac{8}{10}-3\frac{1}{5}$
$\frac{5}{6}-\frac{5}{8}$	$1-\frac{2}{10}$	$6\frac{1}{5}-4\frac{2}{5}$	$4\frac{3}{4}-3\frac{1}{2}$

Expression Bank: Decimal Subtraction Set 1

4.8 − 2.5	9.7 − 5.3	8.8 − 0.36	6.8 − 1.3
8.9 − 3.3	8.2 − 4.3	9.9 − 0.11	55 − 4.3
5.4 − 2.7	5.3 − 2.1	7.8 − 0.28	8.9 − 3.6
6.8 − 5.5	5.9 − 0.7	6.5 − 1.2	6.4 − 0.34

Expression Bank: Decimal Subtraction Set 2

55.4 – 4.28	77.3 – 15.9	88.3 – 76.8	63.8 – 1.16
80 – 3.80	40.8 – 3.93	3.91 – 1.09	25.4 – 1.85
70.4 – 2.35	32.5 – 1.5	65.4 – 3.21	60.8 – 3.99
8.52 – 5.06	50.7 – 2.49	62.1 – 5.15	4.74 – 3.95

RESOURCE(S) FOR THIS ACTIVITY

4.8 – 2.5	9.7 – 5.3
8.9 – 3.3	8.2 – 4.3
5.4 – 2.7	5.3 – 2.1
6.8 – 5.5	5.9 – .7

$\frac{4}{5} - \frac{2}{8}$	$\frac{3}{6} - \frac{5}{12}$
$\frac{3}{9} - \frac{1}{9}$	$\frac{4}{3} - \frac{2}{3}$
$\frac{6}{10} - \frac{2}{5}$	$\frac{2}{3} - \frac{1}{5}$
$\frac{5}{6} - \frac{5}{8}$	$1 - \frac{2}{10}$

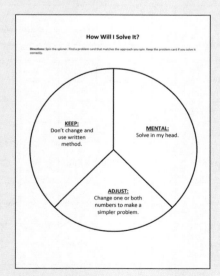

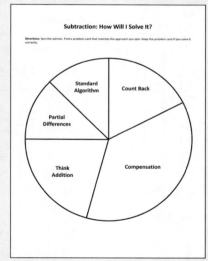

These resources can be downloaded at **resources.corwin.com/FOF/addsubtractdecimalfraction**.

ACTIVITY F.5

Name: Just Right   **Type:** Game

About the Game: This game focuses on matching a problem with a strategy. The *Just Right* game board can be adapted to incorporate the strategies students have learned. Earlier in the year, it may have three options; later in the year, it may have five options. Students may be tempted to use inefficient strategies in order to get four in a row. To counter this, require students to record the equations and the strategy they used.

Materials: expression cards (mixed strategies), *Just Right* game board, and two different colors of counters (about 15 for each player)

Directions: 1. Players take turns flipping cards.

2. Player selects a "just right" strategy, and solves it thinking aloud or on paper.

3. Opponents confirm accuracy with calculators (for decimals).

4. Having correctly solved the problem, the player places a marker on the strategy they used on the *Just Right* game board.

5. The first player to place four markers in a row on the game board wins.

For example, Sydney draws 6.8 + 2.8. She says, "My *Just Right* strategy is Compensation. I think 7 + 3 equals 10, but that is 4 tenths too many, so I subtract 0.4 to equal 9.6." Her opponent, Annie, confirms that she is correct. Sydney covers her choice of a Compensation square.

RESOURCE(S) FOR THIS ACTIVITY

Just Right: Addition Board

Directions: Flip over a problem card. Decide which strategy is "just right" for the problem. Place a marker on the strategy.
Be the first to get four markers in a row (horizontally, vertically, or diagonally).

Compensation	Count On	Make a Whole	Standard Algorithm	Partial Sums
Partial Sums	Make a Whole	Compensation	Count On	Compensation
Make a Whole	Standard Algorithm	Count On	Compensation	Partial Sums
Partial Sums	Make a Whole	Compensation	Standard Algorithm	Make a Whole
Compensation	Partial Sums	Count On	Standard Algorithm	Partial Sums

Just Right: Subtraction Board

Directions: Flip over a problem card. Decide which strategy is "just right" for the problem. Place a marker on the strategy.
Be the first to get four markers in a row (horizontally, vertically, or diagonally).

Compensation	Count Back	Think Addition	Standard Algorithm	Partial Differences
Partial Differences	Think Addition	Compensation	Count Back	Compensation
Think Addition	Standard Algorithm	Compensation	Standard Algorithm	Partial Differences
Standard Algorithm	Think Addition	Count Back	Compensation	Think Addition
Compensation	Think Addition	Count Back	Standard Algorithm	Partial Differences

online resources ✎ These resources can be downloaded at **resources.corwin.com/FOF/addsubtractdecimalfraction**.

ACTIVITY F.6

Name: Strategories   **Type:** Game

About the Game: This game is an excellent opportunity for practice or assessment once a variety of strategies are learned. Students generate three to six examples of problems that lend to using a certain strategy. For example, for Make a Whole with fractions, students might generate $\frac{3}{4}+1\frac{3}{4}$, $\frac{9}{10}+\frac{8}{10}$, or $5\frac{7}{8}+6\frac{5}{8}$. For Make a Whole with decimals, students might generate 2.9 + 0.7, 5.8 + 2.5, or 3.99 + 3.48. The directions describe this as a small group activity, but it can be modified to a center. An alternative to this game is to just focus on one strategy (e.g., Think Addition).

Materials: *Strategories* game card (one per student)

Directions:

1. Each player works independently to generate a problem for which they would use that strategy (alternatively, students can work with a partner to discuss problems that would fit in each strategory).

2. After players have completed their *Strategories* game card (i.e., they have one example expression in each strategory), place students in groups of three.

3. On a player's turn, they ask one of the other group members to share the problem on their *Strategories* card for _____ strategy. If the player explains the problem using that strategy, they score 5 points. If not, the third player gets a chance to "steal" by explaining the problem using that strategy. If the third player cannot, the author of the problem must explain using that strategy. If they cannot, they lose 10 points.

4. Play continues until all strategies have been solved, or students have played three rounds. The high score wins!

5. To facilitate discussion after play, ask questions such as these: What do you notice about the problems in _____ strategory? When is this strategy useful?

RESOURCE(S) FOR THIS ACTIVITY

Strategies: Addition	
Strategy	**My Problem**
Count On	
Make a Whole	
Compensation	
Partial Sums	

Strategies: Subtraction	
Strategy	**My Problem**
Count Back	
Think Addition	
Compensation	
Partial Differences	

online resources These resources can be downloaded at **resources.corwin.com/FOF/addsubtractdecimalfraction.**

ACTIVITY F.7

Name: Make 10 (Make 1) **Type:** Game (or Center)

About the Game: This game focuses on hitting a target (10) by creating two addends. Students will be doing a lot of adding as they try to find the best sum, which makes this a good game to use to observe what strategies students are commonly choosing (and whether they are using a variety of strategies). This game works for both addition and subtraction and you can continue to change the target. Downloadable versions include *Make 10* and *Make 1*. The latter could be adjusted to *Make 10* using mixed numbers. This game can also be played as a center in which students play to get their personal best score.

Materials: two sets of digit cards (0–9) or playing cards (queens = 0 and aces = 1; remove tens, kings, and jacks); selected *Make 10* or *Make 1* game board

Directions for *Make 10*: 1. **Decimals:** Each player is dealt six cards. Each player uses four of the six cards to make 2 two-digit decimals with a sum as close to 10 as possible.
   Fractions: Each player is dealt eight cards. Each player uses six cards to make two mixed numbers with a sum as close to 10 as possible.

2. The player records their equation and shows how they found the sum.

3. Players record how far away they are from 10. This is their score.

4. After five rounds, each player adds their scores from each round.

5. The player with the lower score wins.

For example, Amelia is playing *Make 10–Fractions*. She draws 2, 2, 0, 4, 5, 3, 8, 6, and forms this expression: $5\frac{0}{2}+4\frac{6}{8}$. She adds to get $9\frac{3}{4}$ and records her score (How far from 10?) as $\frac{1}{4}$ for the first round.

RESOURCE(S) FOR THIS ACTIVITY

Make 10 — Decimals

Directions: Deal six cards. Use four cards to make 2 two-digit decimals with a sum as close to 10 as possible. Find the sum and show how you added. Record how far from 10 you are for each round.

Round	My Cards	My Addition Problem	How Far From 10?
1			
2			
3			
4			
5			

Total Score: _____

Make 1 — Decimals

Directions: Deal six cards. Use four cards to make 2 two-digit decimals, both with hundredths, with a sum as close to 1 as possible. Find the sum and show how you added. Record how far from 1 you are for each round.

Round	My Cards	My Addition Problem	How Far From 1?
1			
2			
3			
4			
5			

Total Score: _____

online resources ▶ This resource can be downloaded at **resources.corwin.com/FOF/addsubtractdecimalfraction**.

ACTIVITY F.8

Name: A-MAZE-ing Race   **Type:** Game (or Center)

About the Game: This game is not about speed! Putting time pressure on students works against fluency, as the stress can block good reasoning. The purpose of this game is to practice selecting and using strategies that are a good fit for the numbers in the problem. It can be adapted for any addition or subtraction problem sets. You can also use it as a center in which students highlight their path, record the problems, find the solutions, and show their strategy.

Materials: *A-MAZE-ing Race* game board (one per pair), a marker or counter for each player, and calculators

Directions:

1. Players both put their marker on Start.

2. Players take turns selecting an unoccupied square that shares a border with their current position.

3. Players talk aloud to say the answer and explain how they solved the equation. An optional sentence frame to use is, "The answer is ___. I used ___ strategy to solve it. I ___, then I ___."

4. Opponents confirm accuracy with calculators. If correct, the player moves to the new square.

5. Note that the dark lines cannot be crossed.

6. The winner is the first to reach the finish.

RESOURCE(S) FOR THIS ACTIVITY

A-MAZE-ing Race

Directions: Choose an open space that touches the space you are in to move. Tell how you solve the problem. If correct, move to the new space. You cannot cross dark lines. Be the first to get to the finish.

START	1.9 + 1.2	3.9 + 1.6	7.6 + 2.4	1.6 + 1.9	2.6 + 4.9
3.7 + 6.9	1.7 + 2.9	3.9 + 3.3	4.8 + 2.3	9.9 + 2.6	1.8 + 6.3
9.7 + 0.5	4.8 + 1.7	4.7 + 5.8	5.1 + 1.8	2.5 + 3.8	8.7 + 1.4
6.8 + 3.3	5.9 + 1.3	6.8 + 2.9	7.7 + 1.7	9.9 + 5.1	6.9 + 2.7
4.8 + 5.3	2.8 + 1.7	7.3 + 0.8	1.6 + 7.9	2.4 + 6.7	9.9 + 9.7
8.8 + 0.4	6.8 + 3.9	2.7 + 0.5	8.3 + 1.8	9.9 + 9.8	FINISH

A-MAZE-ing Race

Directions: Choose an open space that touches the space you are in to move. Tell how you solve the problem. If correct, move to the new space. You cannot cross dark lines. Be the first to get to the finish.

START	$1\frac{3}{4}+1\frac{3}{4}$	$7-2\frac{1}{2}$	$9\frac{1}{3}-1\frac{2}{3}$	$3\frac{3}{4}+3\frac{7}{8}$	$5\frac{2}{3}+1\frac{2}{3}$
$2\frac{1}{2}+1\frac{3}{4}$	$\frac{3}{8}+1\frac{1}{4}$	$7\frac{1}{2}-6\frac{3}{4}$	$5\frac{5}{6}+4\frac{2}{3}$	$4-\frac{7}{8}$	$13\frac{7}{8}-5$
$5\frac{1}{2}-3\frac{5}{8}$	$6\frac{5}{6}+4\frac{5}{6}$	$4\frac{7}{10}+2\frac{3}{5}$	$\frac{3}{8}+\frac{3}{4}$	$5-1\frac{2}{3}$	$8\frac{3}{8}+1\frac{3}{4}$
$7\frac{1}{2}-6\frac{7}{8}$	$5\frac{2}{9}-3\frac{1}{9}$	$6\frac{5}{6}-3\frac{1}{6}$	$\frac{1}{3}+\frac{1}{4}$	$5\frac{2}{5}+4\frac{1}{10}$	$5\frac{1}{3}-3\frac{2}{3}$
$4\frac{7}{8}-\frac{3}{4}$	$7\frac{1}{3}+5\frac{5}{6}$	$\frac{3}{4}-\frac{1}{8}$	$6\frac{1}{2}+2\frac{7}{8}$	$\frac{7}{9}-\frac{1}{3}$	$5\frac{4}{5}+2\frac{3}{5}$
$4\frac{7}{10}-2\frac{3}{5}$	$7\frac{1}{4}-2\frac{1}{2}$	$6\frac{1}{2}-2\frac{7}{8}$	$3-1\frac{1}{6}$	$6\frac{1}{4}-2\frac{5}{8}$	FINISH

online resources These resources can be downloaded at **resources.corwin.com/FOF/addsubtractdecimalfraction**.

ACTIVITY F.9

Name: Strategy Problem Sort   **Type:** Center

About the Center: Just because a problem can be solved with a given strategy does not mean it is a good fit. This center has students sort problems based on the strategy they would use to solve them. You can conclude this activity by having students record their thinking on two problems: one from the "Fits the Strategy" column, explaining how they used that strategy, and a second from the "Does Not Fit the Strategy" column, explaining what strategy they would use to solve the problem.

Materials: set of 12 to 20 mixed problems (some that fit the intended strategy and some that do not), Strategy Problem Sort placemat (optional)

Directions: 1. Students flip over a problem card.

2. Students determine if the problem fits the strategy or doesn't fit the strategy.

3. Students then solve the problem.

To create assessment artifacts, you can take a picture of a student's completed sort. Or, you can ask students to provide written responses to questions like these:

I placed _____ in the "Fits the Strategy" side because . . .

I placed _____ in the "Does Not Fit the Strategy" side because . . .

RESOURCE(S) FOR THIS ACTIVITY

Strategy Sort Placemat

Strategy: _____

Fits the Strategy	Does Not Fit the Strategy

39.9 + 44.7	5.16 + 6.28
60.1 + 9.9	3.44 + 7.44
11.9 + 3.5	4.34 + 6.97
61 + 5.29	5.35 + 3.95
95.2 + 8.63	3.74 + 2.59

$\frac{5}{8} + \frac{7}{8}$	$\frac{2}{3} + \frac{3}{10}$
$\frac{3}{4} + \frac{3}{4}$	$\frac{1}{2} + \frac{7}{8}$
$\frac{1}{8} + \frac{1}{2}$	$\frac{4}{6} + \frac{1}{2}$
$\frac{5}{10} + \frac{3}{5}$	$\frac{1}{3} + \frac{3}{4}$
$\frac{3}{8} + \frac{1}{3}$	$\frac{9}{10} + \frac{10}{12}$

online resources ⬚ These resources can be downloaded at **resources.corwin.com/FOF/addsubtractdecimalfraction**.

Appendix
Tables of Activities

. . . .

Figuring out fluency is a journey. Fluency with fraction and decimal addition and subtraction is absolutely essential for life and for future mathematics. Each and every child must have access and ample opportunities to develop their understanding and use of reasoning strategies. It is critical to remember these points:

- Fluency needs to be a daily part of mathematics instruction.

- There are no shortcuts or quick fixes to developing fluency.

- Fluency requires instruction *and* ongoing reinforcement.

- Different students require different types and quantities of experiences to develop fluency.

- While strategy choice is about the individual student, every student must learn and practice significant strategies so that they *can* choose to use them.

- Fluency practice must not be stressful. Stress complicates thinking.

- Fluency is more than accuracy; you must assess the other components.

This book is packed with activities for instruction, practice, and assessment to support the work that you do and to supplement the resources you use. The following pages provide a listing of all the activities in this book. These tables can help you achieve the following:

- Jump between strategies, as you may not teach them sequentially.

- Locate prompts for teaching each strategy.

- Identify a specific type of activity to incorporate into your fluency instruction.

- Identify activities for specific strategies that you need to reteach, reinforce, or reassess.

- Take notes about revisiting an activity later in the year.

- Take notes about modifying an activity for use with another strategy.

- Take notes about how you might leverage the activity in future years.

- Identify an activity that is particularly useful for assessment.

MODULE 1: FOUNDATIONS FOR REASONING ACTIVITIES				NOTES
NO.	PAGE	TYPE	NAME	
1.1	26	R	"The Find"	
1.2	27	R	"Express It"	
1.3	28	G	*Math Chatter*	
1.4	29	G	*Take Ten*	
1.5	31	G	*Closer To . . . 0 or 1?*	
1.6	33	G	*High/Low*	
1.7	34	G	*Three Close Covers*	
1.8	35	R	"Guess My Point"	
1.9	36	R	"The Dynamic Number Line"	
1.10	37	R	"The Stand (Factors and Multiples)"	
1.11	38	G	*The Connects*	
1.12	39	C	Halvsies	
1.13	40	G	*The Splits*	
1.14	42	G	*Fraction Tile Take*	
1.15	43	G	*Fill the Charts*	

R (Routine) • G (Game) • C (Center/Independent)

MODULE 2: COUNT ON/COUNT BACK ACTIVITIES				
NO.	PAGE	TYPE	NAME	NOTES
2.1	47	T	Counting On: From Areas to Number Lines	
2.2	48	T	Counting Back: From Areas to Number Lines	
2.3	49	T	Beaded Decimal Number Lines	
2.4	50	T	Number Bonds for Count On/Count Back	
2.5	51	T	Prompts for Teaching Count On/Count Back	
2.6	53	W	Count On/Count Back Worked Examples	
2.7	55	R	"The Count" (skip-counting by chunks)	
2.8	56	R	"Or You Could . . . "	
2.9	57	G	*Race to Zero*	
2.10	59	G	*Count On Bingo—Decimals*	
2.11	61	G	*Make It Close*	
2.12	62	C	Find the Value of the Shape	
2.13	63	C	Logical Leaps	
2.14	64	C	Largest and Smallest Sums	

T (Teaching) • W (Worked Examples) • R (Routine) • G (Game) • C (Center/Independent)

			MODULE 3: MAKE A WHOLE ACTIVITIES	
NO.	PAGE	TYPE	NAME	NOTES
3.1	69	T	Post-Party Pizza Leftovers	
3.2	70	T	Eggs-actly How Many?	
3.3	71	T	Two-Card Equations	
3.4	72	T	Build the Fraction and Decimal Track	
3.5	73	T	Expression Match	
3.6	74	T	Prompts for Teaching Make a Whole	
3.7	76	W	Make a Whole Worked Examples	
3.8	78	R	"Paired Quick Looks"	
3.9	79	R	"Say It As a Make a Whole"	
3.10	80	R	"Same and Different"	
3.11	81	G	*Make It, Take It*	
3.12	83	G	*A Winning Streak*	
3.13	84	C/G	Fraction Track Race	
3.14	85	C	Roll to Make a Whole	
3.15	86	C	Create an Expression	

T (Teaching) • W (Worked Examples) • R (Routine) • G (Game) • C (Center/Independent)

			MODULE 4: THINK ADDITION ACTIVITIES	
NO.	**PAGE**	**TYPE**	**NAME**	**NOTES**
4.1	91	T	Start With, Get To (With Decimal Charts)	
4.2	92	T	Using Open Number Lines	
4.3	93	T	Uncovered LEGO	
4.4	94	T	What's the Change?	
4.5	95	T	Prompts for Teaching Think Addition	
4.6	97	W	Think Addition Worked Examples	
4.7	99	R	"Two Lies and a Truth"	
4.8	100	R	"Close But Not Too Much" (estimating differences)	
4.9	101	G	*The Smallest Difference*	
4.10	102	G	*Empty the Money Bag*	
4.11	103	G	*Think Addition Math Libs*	
4.12	104	C	Triangle Cards	
4.13	105	C	Make the Difference	

T (Teaching) • W (Worked Examples) • R (Routine) • G (Game) • C (Center/Independent)

MODULE 5: COMPENSATION ACTIVITIES				
NO.	**PAGE**	**TYPE**	**NAME**	**NOTES**
5.1	110	T	Quick Looks With Visual Images	
5.2	112	T	The Jumps Have It (using hundredths charts)	
5.3	113	T	Measurement Compensation (Constant Difference)	
5.4	114	T	Compensation Corners	
5.5	115	T	Prompts for Teaching Compensation	
5.6	117	W	Compensation Worked Examples	
5.7	119	R	"Or You Could . . ." (restating expressions using Compensation)	
5.8	121	R	"Same Difference"	
5.9	122	G	*Compensation Concentration*	
5.10	123	G	*Adjust and Go! Tic-Tac-Toe*	
5.11	124	C	Compensation Lane	
5.12	125	C	Prove It	
5.13	126	C	One and the Other	

T (Teaching) • W (Worked Examples) • R (Routine) • G (Game) • C (Center/Independent)

			MODULE 6: PARTIAL SUMS AND DIFFERENCES ACTIVITIES		
NO.	PAGE	TYPE	NAME		NOTES
6.1	131	T	Bags of Disks		
6.2	132	T	Partial Sums With Decimal Expander Cards		
6.3	133	T	Strategy Show and Tell		
6.4	134	T	The Missing Problem		
6.5	135	T	Prompts for Teaching Partial Sums and Differences		
6.6	138	W	Partial Sums and Differences Worked Examples		
6.7	140	R	"The Parts"		
6.8	142	R	"Decimal Number Strings"		
6.9	143	R	"Fraction Number Strings"		
6.10	144	R	"Too Much Taken"		
6.11	145	G	*For Keeps*		
6.12	146	G	*Sum Duel*		
6.13	148	G	*Decimals Target 10 or 0*		
6.14	149	G	*Decimal Partial Concentration*		
6.15	150	C	Adding With Ten-Frames and Place Value Disks		
6.16	152	C	Target 10		

T (Teaching) • W (Worked Examples) • R (Routine) • G (Game) • C (Center/Independent)

MODULE 7: STANDARD ALGORITHM ACTIVITIES				
NO.	PAGE	TYPE	NAME	NOTES
7.1	158	T	They ARE the Same! (connecting partials and algorithms)	
7.2	160	T	Connecting Partials and Algorithms (symbolically)	
7.3	161	T	To Algorithm or Not to Algorithm (deciding when to use an algorithm)	
7.4	161	T	Rethinking Subtraction With Zeros	
7.5	162	T	Mystery Solved! Making Sense of Fraction Algorithms	
7.6	163	T	"Low Stress" or Too Much Mess?	
7.7	163	T	Prompts for Teaching Standard Algorithms	
7.8	166	W	Standard Algorithms Worked Examples	
7.9	167	R	"Between and About"	
7.10	169	R	"That One"	
7.11	170	R	"Over/Under"	
7.12	171	G	*All Lined Up* (Addition or Subtraction)	
7.13	172	G	*A List of Ten*	
7.14	173	C	Algorithm Problem Sort	
7.15	174	C	Missing Numbers	
7.16	175	C	Fraction Magic Squares	

T (Teaching) • W (Worked Examples) • R (Routine) • G (Game) • C (Center/Independent)

PART 3: CHOOSING AND USING STRATEGIES				
NO.	PAGE	TYPE	NAME	NOTES
F.1	182	R	"Strategize First Steps"	
F.2	184	R	"M-A-K-E a Decision"	
F.3	186	R	"Share–Share–Compare"	
F.4	188	G	*Strategy Spin*	
F.5	190	G	*Just Right*	
F.6	191	G	*Strategies*	
F.7	192	G/C	*Make 10 (Make 1)*	
F.8	193	G/C	*A-MAZE-ing Race*	
F.9	194	C	Strategy Problem Sort	

R (Routine) • G (Game) • C (Center/Independent)

References

Baroody, A. J., & Dowker, A. (Eds.). (2003). *Studies in mathematical thinking and learning. The development of arithmetic concepts and skills: Constructing adaptive expertise.* Lawrence Erlbaum Associates.

Bay-Williams, J., & Kling, G. (2019). *Math fact fluency: 60+ games and assessment tools to support learning and retention.* ASCD.

Bay-Williams, J. M., & San Giovanni, J. J. (2021). *Figuring out fluency in mathematics teaching and learning, Grades K–8: Moving beyond basic facts and memorization.* Corwin.

Carpenter, T. P., Corbitt, M. K., Kepner, H. S., Lindquist, M. M., & Reys, R. (1980). Results of the Second NAEP Mathematics Assessment: Secondary school. *The Mathematics Teacher, 73*(5), 329–338. https://www.jstor.org/stable/27962023

Chein, J. M., & Schneider, W. (2012). The brain's learning and control architecture. *Current Directions in Psychological Science, 21*(2), 78–84. https://www.jstor.org/stable/23213097?seq=1

Cramer, K., & Whitney, S. (2010). Learning rational number concepts and skills in elementary school classrooms. In D. V. Lambdin & F. K. Lester, Jr. (Eds.), *Teaching and learning mathematics: Translating research for elementary school teachers* (pp. 15–22). NCTM.

Cramer, K., Wyberg, T., & Leavitt, S. (2008). The role of representations in fraction addition and subtraction. *Mathematics Teaching in the Middle School, 13*(8), 490–496. https://doi.org/10.5951/MTMS.13.8.0490

Cramer, K. A., Post, T. R., & del Mas, R. C. (2002). Initial fraction learning by fourth- and fifth-grade students: A comparison of the effects of using commercial curricula with the effects of using the rational number project curriculum. *Journal for Research in Mathematics Education, 33*(2), 111–144. https://doi.org/10.2307/749646

Curcio, F. R., & Schwartz, S. L. (1998). There are no algorithms for teaching algorithms. *Teaching Children Mathematics, 5*(1), 26–30.

Deliyianni, E., Gagatsis, A., Elia, I, & Panaoura, A. (2016). Representational flexibility and problem-solving ability in fraction and decimal number addition: A structural model. *International Journal of Science and Mathematics Education, 14*(2), S397–S417. https://doi.org/10.1007/s10763-015-9625-6

Empson, S. B., & Levi, L. (2011). *Extending children's mathematics: Fractions and decimals.* Heinemann.

Explicit. (2021). *Merriam-Webster.com.* https://www.merriam-webster.com/dictionary/explicit

Fuchs, L.S., Newman-Gonchar, R., Schumacher, R., Dougherty, B., Bucka, N., Karp, K. S., Woodward, J., Clarke, B., Jordan, N. C., Gersten, R., Jayanthi, M., Keating, B., & Morgan, S. (2021). *Assisting students struggling with mathematics: Intervention in the elementary grades* (WWC 2021006). National Center for Education Evaluation and Regional Assistance, Institute of Education Sciences, U.S. Department of Education. http://whatworks.ed.gov/

Fuson, K. C., & Beckmann, S. (2012–2013, Fall/Winter). Standard algorithms in the Common Core State Standards. *NCSM Journal,* 14–30.

Hurst, M. A., & Cordes, S. (2018). Children's understanding of fraction and decimal symbols and the notation-specific relation to pre-algebra ability. *Journal of Experimental Child Psychology, 168,* 32–48. https://doi.org/10.1016/j.jecp.2017.12.003

Johanning, D. J. (2011). Estimation's role in calculations with fractions. *Mathematics Teaching in the Middle School, 17*(2), 96–102.

Kilpatrick, J., Swafford, J., & Findell, B. (Eds.) (2001). *Adding it up: Helping children learn mathematics.* National Academy Press.

Lamon, S. (2020). *Teaching fractions and ratios for understanding: Essential content knowledge and instructional strategies* (4th ed.). Taylor & Francis Group.

Locuniak, M. N., & Jordan, N. C. (2008). Using kindergarten number sense to predict calculation fluency in second grade. *Journal of Learning Disabilities, 41*(5), 451–459.

Lortie-Forgues, H., Tian, J., & Siegler, R. S. (2015). Why is learning fraction and decimal arithmetic so difficult? *Developmental Review, 38,* 201–221.

Martinie, S. L. (2014). Decimal fractions: An important point. *Mathematics Teaching in the Middle School, 19*(7), 420–429.

Monson, D., Cramer, K., & Ahrendt, S. (2020). Using models to build fraction understanding. *Mathematics Teacher: Learning & Teaching PreK–12, 113*(2), 117–123. https://doi.org/10.5951/MTLT.2019.0105

National Center for Education Statistics. (2019). *NAEP Report Card: 2019 NAEP Mathematics Assessment.* https://www.nationsreportcard.gov/mathematics/nation/achievement/?grade=4

National Council of Teachers of Mathematics (NCTM). (2014). *Principles to actions: Ensuring mathematical success for all.* NCTM.

O'Connell, S., & SanGiovanni, J. (2015). *Mastering the basic math facts in addition and subtraction: Strategies, activities, and interventions to move students beyond memorization.* Heinemann.

Parrish, S., & Dominick, A. (2016). *Number talks: Fractions, decimals and percentages.* Math Solutions.

Ruais, R. (1978). A low stress algorithm for fractions. *Mathematics Teacher, 71*(4), 258–260.

SanGiovanni, J. J. (2019). *Daily routines to jump-start math class: Elementary school.* Corwin.

Siegler, R. S., Carpenter, T., Fennell, F., Geary, D., Lewis, J., Okamoto, Y., Thompson, L., & Wray, J. (2010). *Developing effective fractions instruction for kindergarten through 8th grade: A practice guide* (NCEE 2010–4039). https://ies.ed.gov/ncee/wwc/practiceguide/15

Star, J. R. (2005). Reconceptualizing conceptual knowledge. *Journal for Research in Mathematics Education, 36*(5), 404–411. https://doi.org/10.2307/30034943

Van de Walle, J. A., Karp, K. S., & Bay-Williams, J. M. (2019). *Elementary and middle school mathematics: Teaching developmentally* (10th ed.). Pearson Education.

Index

A SAGE Publishing Company

CORWIN HAS ONE MISSION: to enhance education through intentional professional learning.

We build long-term relationships with our authors, educators, clients, and associations who partner with us to develop and continuously improve the best evidence-based practices that establish and support lifelong learning.

CORWIN Mathematics

Supporting TEACHERS | Empowering STUDENTS

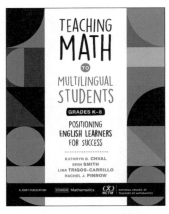
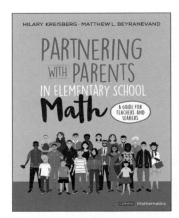
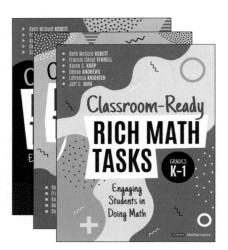

**JENNIFER M. BAY-WILLIAMS,
JOHN J. SANGIOVANNI, ROSALBA SERRANO,
SHERRI MARTINIE, JENNIFER SUH**

Because fluency is so much more
than basic facts and algorithms

Grades K–8

**KAREN S. KARP,
BARBARA J. DOUGHERTY,
SARAH B. BUSH**

A schoolwide solution for students'
mathematics success

Elementary, Middle School, High School

**JOHN J. SANGIOVANNI, SUSIE KATT,
LATRENDA D. KNIGHTEN, GEORGINA RIVERA,
FREDERICK L. DILLON, AYANNA D. PERRY,
ANDREA CHENG, JENNIFER OUTZS**

Actionable answers to your most pressing questions
about teaching elementary and secondary math

Elementary, Secondary

**SARA DELANO MOORE,
KIMBERLY RIMBEY**

A journey toward making
manipulatives meaningful

Grades K–3, 4–8